The Private Provision of
Public Welfare

List of previous books:

Dr Elim Papadakis
    The Green Movement in West Germany, Croom Helm, London, 1984.

Dr Peter Taylor-Gooby
    Public Opinion, Ideology and State Welfare, Routledge & Kegan Paul, London, 1985.
  (with Dr J. Dale)
    Social Theory and Social Welfare, Edward Arnold, London, 1981.

  (with Prof. R. Plant and Dr H. Lesser)
    Political Philosophy and Social Welfare, Routledge & Kegan Paul, London, 1980.

The Private Provision of Public Welfare

State, Market and Community

Elim Papadakis
Lecturer in Sociology
University of New England, Armidale

Peter Taylor-Gooby
Reader in Social Policy and Administration
University of Kent, Canterbury

WHEATSHEAF BOOKS · SUSSEX

ST. MARTIN'S PRESS · NEW YORK

First published in Great Britain in 1987 by
WHEATSHEAF BOOKS LTD
A MEMBER OF THE HARVESTER PRESS PUBLISHING GROUP
Publisher: John Spiers
16 Ship Street, Brighton, Sussex
and in the USA by
ST. MARTIN'S PRESS, INC.
175 Fifth Avenue, New York, NY 10010

British Library Cataloguing in Publication Data
Papadakis, Elim
    The private provision of public welfare:
    state, market and community.
    1. Privatization—Great Britain
    I. Title II. Taylor-Gooby, Peter
    363′.0941   HD4148

    ISBN 0-7450-0172-6
    ISBN 0-7450-0244-7 Pbk

Library of Congress Cataloging-in-Publication Data
Papadakis, Elim.
    The private provision of public welfare.

    Bibliography: p.
    Includes index.
    1. Great Britain-Social policy. 2. Privatization—
    Great Britain. 3. Welfare state. I. Taylor-Gooby,
    Peter. II. Title.

    HV248.P26 1987   361.7′0941   87-9425
    ISBN 0-312-00950-X

Typeset in Times 11 on 12 point by
Witwell Ltd, Liverpool

Printed in Great Britain by
Mackays of Chatham Ltd, Kent

List of Contents

List of Tables

Preface

To a casual observer, the health of the welfare state in the late 1980s might not appear too sound. Public welfare policy has been buffeted by three developments: the slow-down in state welfare spending in most advanced countries from the mid-1970s, often associated with the 1974–6 oil price rise; the election of governments of the right in Britain, the USA and elsewhere, committed to 'rolling back the frontiers of the state'; and the disquiet felt by academics, professionals and the public about the post-war record of the welfare state. One symptom of the indifferent health of state welfare is the entry onto the political agenda of radical proposals to effect a fundamental shift in the boundary between public and private provision.

This book considers recent debates about the privatization of state welfare provisions. The focus is on the boundary between state and market. Many writers have pointed to alternative approaches, stressing family and community provision against the state (Lait 1986: 291). We deal primarily with market issues for two reasons: first, it is state–market transfers that form the nub of recent policy debates in this country, and which offer plausible directions for feasible policy change. Second, the main sociological traditions which have nourished analysis of social policy have stressed categories of class, production relations, exchange and consumption levels based on the market system. These traditions influence our approach.

First, we consider the development of the current pattern of state and private-market provision; the current politics of private welfare and its impact on arguments in political sociology and on new theoretical accounts of social policy; and the redirection of state involvement in welfare. Rather than contrasting a monolithic welfare state with an untrammelled market, we adopt a framework (developed by recent approaches to social policy analysis) which examines the expansion of private provision mainly in terms of a reduction of state activity (in service provision, in subsidy or in regulation). This provides a basis for analysing changes in four major areas of social policy: health and education, where the state is and remains heavily involved in the provision of mass services; pensions and housing, where private provision is not confined to a small minority. The detailed analysis in these four chapters serves both as an introduction to recent changes and an exploration of the limitations of social policy analysis. Part of the 'problem' is the absence of any general pattern to the process of expansion of the private sector. The process contains contradictions. It is shaped by old conflicts and engenders new struggles creating many changes in the provision and the experience of consuming services.

The final chapter focuses on these processes by contrasting the limits to and contradictory nature of Conservative policies with their impact on alternative strategies (emerging in social policy analysis) for coping with the problems of the welfare state. The radical proposals by the Conservatives for a fundamental shift in the boundary between public and private provision are seen more as a symptom than a cause of the problems confronting the welfare state. The problems reflect long-term changes in the social structure which preceded the attempts to alter the direction of the welfare state; the proposals are both contradictory and subject to a wide range of constraints.

In practice the expansion of the private sector corresponds neither to the theory of the free market nor to the burgeoning of freedom of choice. In addition, the impact of recent changes is not as straightforwardly inegalitarian or oppressive as some critics tend to suggest. None the less, the rhetoric has channelled the debate over the welfare state in new directions. In some respects the effect has been to reinforce the contrast between public welfare and privatization and, as a consequence, to draw attention away from the most likely alternatives available to policy-makers. In other respects it has stimulated new proposals for a redirection of policies, particularly towards decentralization, 'mixed' economic enterprises and far-sighted planning. However, these alternative strategies tend to underrate the contradictory nature of recent changes in the private provision of public welfare. This reflects their inadequate evaluation of the social and political context which will determine whether the prescribed remedies to the problems of the welfare state are likely to succeed or not.

Many people contributed to this book. We should like particularly to record our thanks to the Economic and Social Research Council as well as the Internal Research Grants Committee and the Department of Sociology at the University of New England for supporting our interest in the area; Stewart Clegg, Bleddyn Davies, Vic George, Barry Hindess, Ray Pahl, Chris Pickvance and Peter Townsend, who helped with ideas; Joe, Gabriel, Alice, Elizabeth, Sue and Anya, who provided distractions; Noelene Kachel and Janet Batchelor, who efficiently typed drafts of the manuscript; Social and Community Planning Research, and particularly Gillian Courtenay and Sharon Witherspoon, who carried out the survey; the 2,000 citizens who sat through interviews in an act of collective and practical altruism; and Margaret Thatcher, who, in her own way, made it all possible.

List of Abbreviations

BUPA   British United Provident Association
CSO   Central Statistical Office
DES   Department of Education and Science
DHSS   Department of Health and Social Security
DoE   Department of the Environment
HMC   Head Masters' Conference
ISIS   Independent Schools Information Service
LEA   Local Education Authority
NHS   National Health Service
OPCS   Office of Population Census and Surveys
PPP   Private Patients Plan
RHA   Regional Health Authority
SERPS   State Earnings Related Pension Scheme
WPA   Western Provident Association

1 Introduction

THE RETREAT OF THE WELFARE STATE

Many commentators agree that the 'privatization' of state welfare is an idea whose time has come. From the assertion in the manifesto of the winning party in 1979: 'the balance of our society has been increasingly tilted in favour of the state ... this ... may be the last chance we have to reverse that process' (Conservative Party 1979: 5) to the claim in the Treasury's public spending White Paper of that year that 'public expenditure is at the heart of Britain's present economic difficulties' (Treasury 1979: 1), through to the recognition in the main Opposition party's current 'Freedom and Fairness' campaign, that private home ownership is an aspiration of the majority, that private pensions are here to stay and that the abolition of private health care and education is politically impossible (Labour Party 1986), the shift from state toward private welfare seems resistless.

The spread of support for privatization and the growth of disquiet with state welfare is not confined to one country (Mishra 1984; Eisenstadt and Ahimeir 1985; Seldon 1981; Cameron 1985: 9; George and Wilding 1984: 256; Marshall, Rose, Vogler and Newby 1985: 279; Plant 1985: 3; and so on). Policies of privatization have been pursued with notable success in other areas of state economic intervention: Cable & Wireless, Associated British Parts, Britoil, British Aerospace, British Telecom, British Shipbuilders, Jaguar Cars, the National Freight Corporation, British Airports, British Shipbuilders, parts of British Leyland, the National Bus

Company, the Royal Ordnance Factories, British Gas and British Airways have been denationalized, yielding some £12.5 billion at 1985-6 prices. In addition, government share holdings in BP, ICL, Ferranti and British Sugar have been sold. Future sales are expected to realize some £5 billion each year between 1986 and 1990 (Treasury 1987: 6, 18). Evidence that state welfare provides benefits that are much appreciated by social groups who can afford to pay gives good reason to think that expanded private pensions, housing, health care, education and social care might find a ready demand. Why should state welfare not be privatized, as well?

THE DEVELOPMENT OF PRIVATE WELFARE

If privatization is an idea whose time has come, it might also be pointed out that, from some perspectives, private welfare is a reality whose time is past. Different writers have seen the welfare state as fulfilling a variety of roles in society. At the most basic level state welfare is an organized system for meeting minimal needs (Beveridge 1942); in relation to the economic system, welfare assists the regeneration and maintenance (housing, health care, education) of necessary workers (Gough 1979: 44); at the political level welfare provision has been seen as an essential part of government policies designed to gain popular support (George and Wilding 1984: 187; Offe 1984: 65); and at the most general level, welfare has been seen as providing the glue of legitimation to bind society together whether this is understood as 'compulsory altruism' (Titmuss 1970) or as the 'management of motivation', designed to ensure the intermeshing of individual incentives (Habermas 1976: 380; 1975, part 1).

In addition to its systemic roles, welfare fulfills functions for other groups within society: it buttresses male advantage so that it can be described as 'created by men to shape the lives of women' (Wilson 1983: 33). It enables dominant ethnic, religious and communitarian groups to express their distinctive values and to marginalize weaker groups. This reinforces their hegemony in social life (Higgins 1981: 48). It is also concerned to separate social classes, to police the lower and to nurture the privilege of the upper (Ginsburg 1979: 2; Le Grand 1982: 3).

Before the development of the modern web of state interventionism, these roles were filled (more or less successfully) by other social institutions. Charity and private insurance enabled social groups to defend their privilege and define roles for each other. From this perspective the development of the welfare state is partially a story of official colonization of friendly society and trade-union self-insurance for the different fractions of the working class (Yeo 1979: 69; Disney 1982: 49), of the absorption of working-class education and child care (Johnson 1976: 48), of the co-ordination and extension of the private, voluntary and municipal health-care system (Thane 1982: 217, 294). The extension of state power also enabled powerful groups to increase their control of the weaker by the use of law and superior resources to assimilate and mould the institutions set up by those groups for themselves—for example in the definition of women's education (David 1980, ch. 6); in mass working-class housing programmes (Ginsburg 1979: 141); in the imposition of strict work-conditions in social insurance and assistance tests (Thane 1977; Disney 1982).

The approach that emphasizes the role of private and public welfare in the separation of social groups enables us to examine the balance between the two forms of provision in the development of the welfare state. Many writers tell the story of state welfare in terms of the demands of working- and middle-class groups and the requirements of the capitalist economy (Marshall 1963; see Gough 1979 for a Marxist version). A simple periodization divides the tale into five sections.

The stance of government for the greater part of the nineteenth century could be summed up under the slogan of *laissez-faire*. Policy was characterized by a concern to facilitate the operation of competitive markets whenever possible (as in the 1838 Recovery of Possession of Tenements Act, designed to speed evictions, or the 1834 Poor Law Relief Act, designed to hold poor relief below wage levels); to pursue a minimalist provision of public goods (as in the Public Health Acts from 1848 onwards or the Factory Acts from the early years of the century) when political pressures made this necessary; and to attempt to support and co-ordinate the private provision of welfare services (as in the growing subventions to the religious societies for working-class education from the late 1830s, or the attempts of the Poor Law Board to persuade Charity Organisation Society voluntary relief agencies to follow policies that supported the Poor Law from the 1850s). The volume of welfare relief channelled though private and charitable agencies was far greater than that directly provided by government. In addition, informal and neighbourly help outside the structure of charitable agencies was the first resort for most of the poor (Thane 1982: 19).

The second phase, from the 1870s to the early years of the twentieth century marks an interregnum. State policy expands in many areas of provision. The most obvious is the development of state-provided elementary education from 1870 onwards supervised by directly elected school boards, first to 'fill the gaps' in provision by charitable, religious bodies, but later to supplant and incorporate much of it. Legislation in the late 1880s and 1890s gave judges powers to remove children from families in cases of ill-treatment. At the same time local authority borrowing for house building for the working class was eased by housing Acts. The move towards greater interventionism was signalled by a spate of official investigations into labour, the housing of the working classes, the aged poor, sanitary laws, the factory Acts, distress from want of employment, national provident insurance, old-age pensions and poor relief culminating in the influential Inter-Departmental Committee on Physical Deterioration and the Royal Commission on the Poor Law in the early 1900s. Central control of administration was facilitated by local government reform. Self-help through friendly societies, savings clubs and trade-union insurance as the trade-union movement expanded from the 1880s onwards, became a major source of support in sickness, unemployment and old age for the upper working class.

The third stage of welfare state development covers the period up to the Second World War. Government provision expanded steadily. Much of the upper-working-class system of private and friendly society insurance was assimilated and state welfare was extended to cover lower working needs. A national system of regulation of private renting and of council house construction was established. Local government support for hospitals and health care increased. Legislation to enable state regulation of adoption and child-care agencies was passed in the 1930s. Education authorities increased the length of elementary schooling and expanded secondary education through the assimilation of subsidized grammar schools and the founding of new institutions. At the same time, private provision expanded, for some groups, especially in the growth of private home ownership and private and occupational pension schemes for the middle class.

These developments set the scene for the fourth stage of state welfare—the fully fledged provision of a guaranteed national minimum in social security, secondary education for all and health care through the NHS at the close of the Second World War. This was reinforced by government commitment to the maintenance of high levels of employment and the continued expansion of council housing. The continued development of the welfare state involved the assimilation of much private provision: most of the remaining friendly society insurance schemes for unemployment insurance and retirement pensions were amalgamated into national insurance; the National Health Service (NHS) included voluntary and local government hospitals and clinics and most general practitioners transferred to the nationally financed system from the patchwork of private, voluntary, insurance, occupational and trade-union finance; the commitment to council housing reinforced the tendency of private landlordism to decline. Yet private welfare has continued to expand in defined areas, particularly in home ownership (assisted by a favourable tax regime since the 1960s) and in pensions (especially in the 1950s: reforms in state pensions appear to have limited the growth of private pensions through the 1960s and 1970s). The mass welfare state restricts itself to particular fields of operation, and even in those fields permits the retention of private provision for some groups.

Welfare provision in Britain may now be moving into a fifth phase characterized by the retreat of government from the national minimum (in policies of targeting social security on defined groups of the poor and real cuts in many welfare benefits), curtailment of mass provision on a social-need basis (in the policy of selling off local authority housing stock and restrictions in social services provision and residential accommodation) and an expansion of support for private and occupational provision in the areas of pensions, sick pay, owner-occupied housing, assistance with private school fees and the encouragement of private medical practice.

The significance of the changes of the 1980s is a matter of controversy. Studies of state expenditure and of benefit levels show that, with the exception of certain provisions for poor minorities—most notably council housing, and un-employment, housing, supplementary and single parents' benefits—standards have not fallen. The level of welfare spending continues to rise and the value of provision in the mass services has not declined (Robinson 1986). This is only half the picture. Studies of class structure and life-chances show a growing polarization between the better-off mass and the social minority—in work (Pahl 1984); in income, health, opportunities for social mobility and employment (Halsey 1987: 18); in health and sickness (Whitehead 1987); and in housing, poverty and life-chances in general (Archbishop of Canterbury's Working Party 1985; Walker and Walker 1987). The living standards of the majority have risen while the minority has been largely left behind.

The division between the comfortable mass and the weak, excluded from social progress, is partly due to changes in household structure, a decline in employment which is not entirely the result of government inaction, and the structural inability of the welfare system to cope with the pressure placed upon it. Government economic policies in refusing to promote employment against the control of inflation as a goal, have certainly created much more severe problems for poor minorities than would otherwise exist. At the same time, social policies which protect mass services, such as the NHS, while imposing stringent controls on the services most necessary for the victims of economic change, have increased the miseries of the poor.

Current developments indicate that the impact of new policies on welfare may be less far-reaching than this argument suggests: demographic pressures on the labour market reached a peak in 1986 and the number of elderly people (who require pensions and the most costly health care) seems set to decline in the last decade of the century (O'Higgins 1986). Thus the welfare of the poor may tend to improve (for reasons entirely outside the control of the government). It is at present unclear whether the changes of the 1980s add up to a radical new departure in the fortunes of the welfare state.

THE PATTERN OF PUBLIC AND PRIVATE WELFARE

The past century has witnessed a massive expansion of state involvement in welfare, mainly as a result of demands by both working- and upper-class groups. Within the sum total of welfare provision, the division between private and public services corresponds to the success of different social interests in maintaining privilege through social services. The balance between public and private has varied in different areas of provision. Over the period of the fully fledged welfare state in the UK, since the Second World War, private welfare has continued to flourish and to jostle state provision. It is possible to distinguish three main patterns: first, areas in which the state provides mass services. In the field of education, state provision has assimilated almost all education between the ages of 5 to 16 and most sixth-form and further education: much pre-schooling and post-school vocational training, and by far the greater part of child care takes place outside direct state provision, in institutions regulated more or less by law and inspection; similarly, professionally accredited curative health care is almost entirely the preserve of the state, while alternative, preventive and occupational medicine are to a great extent private, although state law regulates conditions of work and of environmental hazard. In these two areas there is strong evidence of class and to some extent gender demarcation. Private services corresponding to the core areas assimilated by the state are almost entirely the domain of upper-class and mainly male groups; the specific needs of women (well-women clinics, control over childbirth practices; treatment for depressive illnesses—Brown and Harris 1978; Doyal and Elston 1986—or arguably, separate schooling in

maths and science, assertiveness and civil-rights training—
Whyte 1986: 11; Arnot 1986: 156–68) are not well served.

The second pattern concerns areas where private provision
is not confined to a small minority. In both housing and
pension provision, the private sector has been radically
changed by state policies. At the same time sharp divisions
between class and gender groups persist within both public and
private services. In housing, the dominant form of tenure up to
the 1930s was private renting. Both owner occupation and
council building programmes expanded rapidly in the inter-
war period. By 1951 about a third of all housing was owner-
occupied. The expansion of the building society movement,
the growing importance of mortgage interest relief and the
abolition of tax on the annual value of owner-occupied
housing in 1963, together with other state subsidies, has taken
the proportion from two-fifths in that year to about two-thirds
at the time of writing. Private renting (controlled and
regulated by the state) has fallen from about half to about a
tenth of all households, and subsidized council renting has
risen from a sixth to under a third over the past four decades.
State policy has heavily influenced the pattern of tenure.

The pattern of tenure by gender shows graphically the
predominance of men in the most heavily subsidized areas of
private provision. In the General Household Survey sample
for 1983, male heads of household outnumber women by three
to one: two-thirds of men are house owners, two-fifths
receiving morgage subsidies, and just under a third are council
tenants. For women, two-fifths are owners, a tenth receive
mortgage subsidy and nearly half are council tenants (Office of
Population Census and Surveys (OPCS) 1985: 73; see Dale
and Foster 1986: 114). Mortgage finance means that those
higher up the class ladder can use the value of owner-occupied
housing transmitted by parents to 'gear up' their house
purchase and create a gap between the more and less privileged
beneficiaries of state subsidy within the dominant tenure group
(Murie 1983; Donnison 1979: 156).

In social security, the state benefits for the contingencies of
working-class life (principally unemployment, housing and supplementary benefit) are inadequate, stigmatic and involve unpleasant application (Deacon and Bradshaw 1983, chs 5 and 6).

As the number of long-term unemployed grows and more school leavers go straight on to the unemployment register, National Insurance benefits have declined in importance as a source of support for those out of work. In 1971 over two-thirds of the unemployed who got benefits received some National Insurance benefit; by 1987 the proportion had fallen to just over a quarter (Central Statistical Office 1987: 90; Treasury 1987 vol. II: 243). Child Benefit, which has become more important for claimers as child additions have been withdrawn from National Insurance benefits, has received lukewarm political support ever since it was introduced in 1946 at about half the level recommended by Beveridge. Over the 1980s increases for all other benefits have at least kept pace with inflation, whereas child benefit has lost about 15 per cent of its value in real terms (Treasury 1987: vol. II: 245). The Fowler review discusses selective benefits for low-income families at some length but has nothing to say about future plans for uprating child benefit.

The main benefit for the better-off is the retirement pension. The value of this is reinforced by the greater life expectancy of upper social groups. The Registrar General commented in a review of the early 1970s: 'out of every 100 aged 15 . . . 77 could be expected to survive to retirement in Social Class 1 compared with 64 in Social Class 5' (OPCS 1978: 196). The gulf in life-expectation after retirement increases the class division in pension benefit according to evidence from a longitudinal study carried out by OPCS (Whitehead 1987: 13). Preliminary reports on the early 1980s indicate that the class gap has widened further. This is widely attributed to the rise in numbers in poverty (Hart 1986; OPCS 1986, part 1; Townsend 1986: 20; Whitehead 1987: ch. 3). Legislation in the 1950s led to a rapid expansion of tax subsidies to occupational pensions. Coverage increased from about a third to about half the labour force over the decade (Government Actuary 1981: 6). Governments have been concerned since the early 1960s to develop an earnings-related supplement to basic state pensions alongside occupational provision. The final agreement negotiated with the private pension industry (embodied in legislation in 1976) allowed those in approved occupational schemes to contract out of state earnings-related pensions

(SERPS). However, when set against economic changes, these concessions failed to give the private sector any great stimulus. While the proportion of full-time employees covered continued to rise to about two-thirds by 1983 (CSO 1986: 68), the proportion of the total workforce covered (including part-timers, the self-employed and unemployed) actually fell slightly from 54 per cent in 1967 to 51 per cent in 1983 (Department of Health and Social Security [DHSS] 1986: 21). The differences are due to the increased participation of married women in paid work and their greater likelihood of working in part-time, non-pensionable jobs, and the sharp rise in unemployment. The use of workforce rather than employee based figures in the government's social security review uses changes in employment structure to emphasize the limitations of the state scheme.

There is a large variation in coverage between men and women and social-class groups. Although the proportion of women workers included has risen from about a fifth in 1963 to slightly less than half by the mid-1970s (CSO 1979: 94), it has since remained constant. Coverage for men has stabilised at nearly two-thirds of all employees (full and part-time).

The class differential in provision is highlighted in the most sophisticated study of income distribution to date: whereas only 5 per cent of retired people fell into the top 20 per cent of the income distribution in 1982, this income group received just over one-quarter of the occupational pension income (O'Higgins 1985, Table 8.2; see Creedy 1982, ch. 6). Standards within the schemes vary sharply, the most striking divisions lying between benefits for non-manual and manual workers.

The third category of private welfare concerns areas such as personal social services and the employment service. Here the state has never attempted to assimilate more than a small proportion of private or charitable effort. It has taken on the role of regulation, inspection and to some extent the subsidy and co-ordination of private provision, through, for example, partnership with the National Council of Voluntary Organisations, Help the Aged or the employment aspects of the Youth Service.

State social-work intervention has often been seen as principally concerned to monitor the care behaviour of the lower working class in child-rearing (Handler 1973; Donzelot 1980, chs 2 and 3) or in looking after dependants (Dale and Foster 1986: 101). Since women are the principal carers, such intervention necessarily involves surveillance over their lives (Beresford and Croft 1986: 115–19). However, state social services are only able to offer small amounts of help on a piecemeal basis through imperfect mechanisms of allocation (Equal Opportunities Commission 1980: 7; Baldock 1985; Audit Commission, 1986: 4). It is important not to exaggerate their capacity to have a material effect on the conditions of private social care (Ungerson 1987).

How are we to explain the different patterns of private provision? The development of the welfare state itself may be explained in terms of pressures from the principal political actors: the needs of capital, the demands of the organized working class and the demands of middle- and upper-class groups.

The functional utility of mass health care, education and social security in advanced capitalist society is not in question: the demands by upper social groups to limit the extent and cost of provision and the demands by lower ones to expand it are also unsurprising. These demands played out on the parliamentary stage explain the fitful and incomplete pattern of state encroachment on private welfare. At the same time, the retention by socially powerful groups of small enclaves of private provision, both to differentiate their own privileged status from that of the mass and to assure superior service is easily explained. What is less easy to understand is the difference between those areas where private provision has been retained at a level beyond minority provision (e.g. pensions and housing, where state policy is responsible for the expansion of home ownership and occupational pensions) and those where it has not (e.g. health care and education).

Interests created by the involvement of state-sector workers in the welfare system have played an important role (Parry 1985: 54). The division between the three categories of interventionism corresponds roughly to the involvement of professional workers in the service areas. In health care and education, access to the service is access to the time of relatively well-paid professionals. Acceptable standards in the supply of medical care and education (the definitions themselves are influenced by professional interests—Wilding 1981; Illich 1971) require expensive provision; in these areas it is easy to see how a combination of working-class demands and professional self-interest arose. State intervention could conveniently provide a stable system of mutual access, for consumers to professional workers, and for the workers to new consumers.

Pensions and housing require finance but relatively few workers. Working-class demands for high levels of provision had no obvious ally within the service and were challenged by the vested interests of middle- and upper-class groups who had acquired rights to property in private pensions and housing. The outcome is a compromise between state fiscal subsidy of private provision within a framework of law to guarantee its market area, and direct state provision for the core working class. Divisions between social groups now have to be maintained both within the private sector, as its zone of operation extends down the class ladder under the new subsidy regime, and between private and state welfare consumers.

The third category of minimal state involvement covers areas where professionals are involved, but in small numbers, and where relatively small proportions of the population are served. Professional social work remains as a residual service and residential provision and home-care support are tiny outposts in a hinterland of private caring.

The development of state intervention had taken place against a backdrop of the absorption or destruction of some facets of private provision. As the result of the combination of working-class demands and the needs of capital, state services have taken on social roles played previously by private welfare, yet in the heyday of the welfare state private welfare has continued to flourish. In some fields only the most powerful groups have been able to call a halt to state encroachment, and private provision has become limited to upper-class, predominantly male minorities, while the state provides mass services. The failure of state attempts to erode these islands of privilege will be charted in the chapters on education and health care. In other fields, the demarcation lines have been more widely drawn. State policy has operated to subsidize and underwrite the private welfare market for upper-class and male groups, while at the same time showing a different face in its provisions for lower classes and for women. In these areas market provision had been more widespread and more concerned to control the cost of maintaining the mass. The social division of private welfare will be apparent in chapters on pensions and housing. In yet other areas state involvement has been more hesitant. The regulation and management of people's own provision to meet their needs has been the dominant theme.

THE APPEAL OF PRIVATE WELFARE

Private welfare has always formed the arena in which the manoeuvres of state social policy may be traced out. If the return of the private is an idea whose time has been and gone and come again, why the current interest? One factor has already been mentioned: the 1979 and 1983 governments have carried out a large number of denationalization exercises and the 1987 government plans to expand the programme. These have yielded considerable savings under the conventions of state accounting which do not set capital losses against current account gains. State windfalls may help to finance tax reductions which are politically profitable under the accounting conventions of democratic electioneering. The expansion of the private sphere involves real short-term political gains (Le Grand 1985: 309; Heath, Jowell and Curtice 1985: ch. 7; Steel and Heald 1984: 21).

Welfare policies constitute a major divide between the political parties. The 1987 Labour manifesto identified the 'essential tasks' as 'combating unemployment and poverty'. (Labour Party 1987: 4). The Liberal/SDP Alliance highlighted unemployment and industrial relations but also stressed the contribution of social services—especially health care, pensions and education—to its principal objective of 'creating one community'. The Conservative Party is concerned to defend its record in government—again on the key issues of the NHS, education and pensions—and to advance the moral case for spreading the 'ownership of homes, shares, pensions and savings' (Conservative Party 1987: 9).

While state spending on the mass services of the NHS, education and pensions is clearly seen as popular by all parties, there has traditionally been a division in approaches to private welfare: the Conservative Party stresses the role of occupational and private pensions alongside the state scheme, argues that private health insurance and education 'lift a burden' from the state sector, and points to the 'right to buy' scheme for council tenants as the 'foundation-stone of a capital-owning democracy' and the assisted places subsidy to private schooling as allowing 'the privileges of a few' to 'become the birthright of all'. Labour says nothing on private pensions, promises an end to subsidies to private education and health care, but plans to continue the popular 'right to buy' scheme. Alliance policies on the private sector are more ambivalent: the rights to private education and health care are upheld but all state subsidies are to be withdrawn. In subsequent political debate, conflict on the issue of private provision has been more muted than conflict over state-sector cuts and standards of service. Michael Meacher (Labour DHSS spokesperson) insists that private health care is 'well down my list of priorities' (Laurence 1987), and Labour's housing policy includes the sale of council housing. There remains a gap between Conservative plans to expand private pensions and the Labour policy of maintaining the current balance between state and private provision. The Alliance's latest policy statement has little to say on the role of the private sector despite an extended discussion of improvements in the NHS, and personal social services, although the abolition of assisted places and 'greater co-operation between state and independent schools' is proposed (Owen and Steel 1987, ch. 4).

Conflicts over welfare denationalization have become less marked than those over the privatization of state-owned industries. The place of private services in welfare is not seriously challenged by any of the main parties. Two developments may explain the move towards acceptance of a substantial private sector. These factors are, first, the long-term shift in social ethos away from the collectivism which nourished the welfare state and towards greater valuation of the private in all spheres of social life (leisure, family, work and politics); second, the development of a new consensus in social policy theory which centres on a radical disenchantment with state welfare. Both these developments are arguably of more significance than a prudential psephology driven by shrewd assessment of the current balance between desire for tax cuts and the valuation of the social wage. Both imply that the long march of the welfare state has now crossed a watershed and will require the development of a new range of social policy theories to command its new environment. Social policy debate increasingly accepts the 'crisis in the welfare state' as an unargued postulate of analysis (Mishra 1984; Bean, Ferris and Whynes 1985; Klein and O'Higgins 1985; Dunleavy and Husbands 1985; Berthoud 1985).

PRODUCTION, CONSUMPTION AND POLITICAL CONSCIOUSNESS

The claim that the dominant current in the political culture of contemporary Britain runs from collectivism to individualism and thence to privatism is sustained by two lines of thought. Sociologists of class have become dissatisfied with traditional frameworks based on occupational location as a basis for people's political ideas. Allied to this, political sociologists have emphasized the growing importance of consumption, and particularly of private-market consumption, as an explanation of current patterns of political support.

PRIVATISM AND SOCIAL CLASS

The traditional concept of class based on the division of labour in formal work, and centring on the cleavage between manual and non-manual occupations, has become unsatisfactory for three reasons. First, feminists have pointed out that classification by formal work ignores much of the experience of women within the home. Women's informal work of care is essential for the daily and inter-generational existence of the workforce. In addition, the manual–non-manual distinction has little to say about women's formal work, which often combines non-manual status with the lack of autonomy and prestige associated with manual labour, for example in the role of copy-typist (Dale, Gilbert and Arber 1985: 385; Britten and Heath 1983). Second, new developments within work involving the growth of the informal economy, the widening gap between the stable core workforce and the intermittently unemployed marginal workers, and the structural decline of traditional industries providing a male family wage (Pahl 1984), have directed attention to the household as the basic unit by which work of all sorts is done. The overall 'work strategy' of this unit becomes the central issue, rather than the formal occupation of an assumed (male) 'head' (Pahl 1984).

Third, the new economic conditions of Britain in the 1970s and 1980s (short-run stagflation set against long-run decline), coupled with the resurgence of nationalism and of individualistic social orientation, lead Newby and his colleagues to postulate that the basis of political consciousness has changed. Britain has collapsed as a world power. None of the political parties seems able to reverse economic decline. People turn away from civic or political collectivism to the consolations of a 'retreat into the privatized world within home and family' (Marshall *et al.* 1985: 274; see also Newby *et al.* 1986). Just as Goldthorpe and his colleagues argued that stability and security engendered a mood of privatization among affluent workers (Goldthorpe *et al.* 1969, Introduction), so current analysis locates the genesis of the same ideology in experience of the failure of collectivism (Rose *et al.* 1984: 157; see also Alt 1979: 272; Seabroook 1984; Pahl and Wallace 1986).

The conception of class is the storm-centre of much current debate (e.g. Roberts, Finnegann and Gallie 1985 or the ESRC symposium recorded in Crompton and Mann 1986). Each of the currents in thought listed above throws a renewed emphasis on the private sphere, whether as the complement to formal work, as the domestic nexus within which the household negotiates work strategy, or as the arena of satisfactions to which the casualties of a failed collectivism retreat. In so far as political consciousness goes, the current is set firmly towards privatization, and the creation of a climate in which private-sector welfare is nurtured.

Interest in the private–public divide among political sociologists stems from two sources. First, many writers have found traditional notions of class inadequate as an explanation of the tediously practical but significant fact of how people vote. Second, a new theoretical framework based on the conception of consumption-sector divisions has been formulated. This stresses access to private or public housing, transport and other services as a major political cleavage. In recent empirical work it has proved of little importance as an explanation. None the less, the approach has commanded a great deal of interest and assisted in focusing attention on the privatization of welfare.

POLITICS AND CLASS

Sarlvik and Crewe argue that 'class' has been the 'primary, almost exclusive, social basis of party choice' in Britain since the first war (Sarlvik and Crewe 1983: 74). The general thrust of their work is to demonstrate the additional importance of other factors: particularly 'voters' opinions on policies and on the parties' performances' (p. 113). This has led a number of writers to analyse current political trends as reflecting a decline in solidaristic class cleavages and a shift towards a new and free democracy: voters actively choose for themselves, untrammelled by the ideological baggage of the division of labour. Space is now cleared for centrist political groupings. 'The decline in the class basis of voting amounts to a weakening of constraints on volatility and self-expression and ... open[s] the way to choice between parties on the basis of issue preferences' (Franklin 1985: 176; see also Rose and McAllister's aptly titled *Voters Begin to Choose* 1986). This approach suggests that although welfare may not be the most significant policy issue, the mass of the electorate support current shifts to the private sector (Rose *et al.* 1986: 162).

An alternative approach which also undermines emphasis on class as the basis of political behaviour is provided in consumption-sector theory. The point (e.g. see Dunleavy 1979b: 425; 1980: 78) is that divisions in the population between consumers of goods which are allocated predominantly through the private market and consumers of services which appear to be directly state provided, can cut across traditional class allegiances. The cleavage between home-owners and private tenants on the one hand, and council tenants on the other, or between those with private cars and those dependent on public transport, divides the traditional category of the manual working class. People define their own. interests in relation to their perception of shared of consumption patterns *vis-à-vis* the other consumption groups they perceive in society. The bus queue glares at the limousine owner and the home-owner bemoans the public burden of the council house building scheme. Thus the underlying pattern of state subsidies to private services through tax relief is irrelevant: it is the social construction of public–private divisions, 'the basically inaccurate picture of home owners paying their own way and of council tenants as heavily subsidized' (Dunleavy 1979b: 430) that counts.

The attraction of the consumption-sector thesis derives from its assonance with recent developments in policy both at local government and national level: to oversimplify, Conservatives identify with home ownership and private transport. Thus they sell council houses and cut public transport subsidies and council building programmes. Labour traditionally embraces converse policies, although recent campaign statements indicate an attempt to poach some of the private sector's support (Dunleavy and Husbands 1985: 143; see also Duke and Edgell 1984).

The significance of consumption sector is challenged by Heath and his colleagues. They use a revised conception of class that pays more attention to authority in work and self-employment than the definition used by Sarlvik and Crewe (1983). Their analysis focuses on the most significant consumption cleavage, home ownership, over the period from 1964–83. They point out that tenure

has little importance, net of class, in explaining changes over time. ... The paradox arises because ... housing cross-cuts class; there are many working-class owners ... (although rather fewer salaried council tenants). ... Their proportions within each class stay roughly constant ... and therefore cannot be a major source of change.

(Heath, Jowell and Curtice 1985: 52)

This throws the emphasis back onto changes in class structure (see Franklin and Page 1984: 536).

The outcome of this debate is to undermine the role of traditional notions of class in political sociology and to throw attention onto the new approaches that have developed within sociology. The methodological claims of consumption-sector theory may prove misleading. However, the approach has had widespread influence because it coincides so neatly with developments in the practical politics of welfare—the pork-barrelling of consumption-sector interests. Thus approaches to political consciousness that emphasize the importance of private-sector interests have gained widespread attention. The contribution of political sociology and the sociology of class is to reinforce the claim that the privatization of welfare is an idea whose time has come, or rather is returning. The dominant current in theory among writers on social policy is set in the same direction, for complementary reasons.

THE NEW CONSENSUS: THE DISENCHANTMENT OF THE INTELLECTUALS

Since the early 1970s, popular and political confidence in state welfare has withered. At the same time, academics have developed new theoretical accounts of social policy. The dominant approach of the 1950s and 1960s, empiricist reformism—an approach often unfairly stigmatized as mere 'social bookkeeping'—has been succeeded by two separate waves of theoretical sophistication. First, the major traditions nurtured in the metropolitan disciplines of economics, politics and sociology and transmitted through the applied outposts of urban sociology, economics of welfare and political sociology, have colonized the subject (e.g. George and Wilding 1976; Gough 1979; Ginsburg 1979; Room 1979; Taylor-Gooby and Dale 1981; Mishra 1981, 1984; Pinker 1971, 1979). The common core is a categorization of approaches to welfare into the threefold schema of Marxist, centrist (Fabian; reformist) and new right (anti-collectivist, liberal) corresponding crudely to a three-step along a left–right political spectrum.

This is worked out at the level of political economy in

judgements about the extent to which market systems can be seen as self-stabilizing without welfare state intervention. At the level of political philosophy, normative theory ranges from the celebration of the value of individual liberty to the argument that people's lives can only be understood in terms dictated by the conflict of social class. Anti-collectivist individualism links freedom to the free market, centrism points to the problems of economic depression and the political machinations of vested interests against the spread of effective access to citizenship rights; Marxist materialism argues that the economic relations that lead capitalism to crisis also generates a political dialectic of class conflict.

In the 1980s such approaches have been washed over by fresh waves of theory, casting doubt on the utility of the left–right dimension. The new theories have three things in common: a closer attention to the detailed analysis of empirical evidence and a suspicion of official data; the fact that they are not housed conveniently in any of the pre-existing approaches but are concerned to modify all of them; and the scepticism which they bring to judgements about the present and potential performance of welfare states. It is these new theories that are most valuable in shaping our understanding of private welfare.

FEMINISM

The most important new perspective in undoubtedly feminism, engendered by the realization that social policy 'is a set of structures created by men to shape the lives of women' (Wilson 1983: 33). As Pascall writes: 'feminist analysis is most obviously about putting women in where they have been left out ... but to do this suggests questions about the structures that have left women out; about the way academic disciplines work; about language, concepts, methods, approaches and subject areas' (Pascall 1986: 1). While debates about the structural priority of class and gender have not been resolved (Hartmann 1979; Barrett 1980: 9–41; Cockburn 1986), feminism has developed closer links with Marxist and socialist critiques of welfare policies than with centrist and anti-collectivist approaches. However, there are important resonances between feminist analysis and new right and centrist frameworks. The main influence has been a reappraisal of methodological assumptions (Charvet 1982).

The fundamental feature of Marxism is an emphasis on an objective notion of class as relation to means of production, and on ideology as the product of social relations rather than free reflection. These become the major analytic categories of social science. Centrism conceives class inequalities in terms of consumption, and the distribution of power as the reflection of organized group interest. Thus the possibility of progressive social change is brought closer than it is if change is conceived as dependent on a revolution in production relations. Anti-collectivism conceives individuals as social atoms and society as their interaction: injustices can be eradicated by the abolition of monopoly and the conspiracy of vested interests. Feminism has reintroduced to radical socialist approaches an emphasis on the importance of individuals both as the ends of social policy and as the means of social oppression. It has also thrown the emphasis back on to the empirical charting of women's needs. As Rose puts it:

> until we have a transformative theory of a social formation that is both patriarchal and capitalist it is too soon to abandon the painstaking documentation of inequalities in the relations of redistribution. We might be in danger of throwing out the materialist baby along with the idealist bathwater.
>
> (Rose 1981: 501)

The invitation that feminism offers to the empirical tradition in social policy is to re-enter the world of 'social bookkeeping' with eyes that are not gender-blind. The focus is cast back onto the systematic disadvantaging of women in housing (Auster-berry and Watson 1983); in education (Arnot 1986); in health (Doyal 1983), in social security (Bennett 1983); and onto the concrete organization of male power against women's interests, in political parties (Siltanen and Stanworth 1984, part 2) in trade unions (Rowbotham, Segal and Wainwright 1979) in welfare (Wilson 1983) and in work (Beechey 1977; Cockburn 1986). Women as individuals experience oppression:

It has been the development of an autonomous feminist movement which has insisted that the experience of shared, lived oppression must be an integral—and not denied—part of how we understand the world. ... Only then is it possible to see how the form and content of welfare services have so often shored up the hierarchical racist and patriarchal relations of the social formation itself.

(Rose and Rose 1982: 15–16)

Feminism has reintroduced an emphasis on the reality of individualism and the operation of social groups to the left.

Four other aspects of new theory cut across previous analytics. These may be termed accumulation crisis, legitimation crisis, redistribution failure and paternalism. They refer to the view that state welfare spending damages economic growth, that it leads to a decline in popular support for government, that it fails in its goal of redistribution from better to worst off and that the system is intrinsically oppressive because policy-makers assume that they know people's needs better than people do themselves. These theoretical propositions have cut across the grand tradition. All four have found acceptance among prominent representatives of the tradition schools of Marxists, centrists and New Right thinkers. After the intellectual schisms of the 1970s, a new orthodoxy has emerged—that neither structural theory nor the welfare state is entirely successful in delivering the goods.

ACCUMULATION CRISIS

The thesis that state welfare impedes growth has been echoed by Marxists debating whether the labour of welfare sector workers is productive or non-productive (Gough 1979; Fine and Harris 1979; O'Connor 1973); by centrists concerned with relative price effects and the pre-emption of factors of production (especially workers) by the state (Bacon and Eltis 1976; Hague 1980; O'Higgins and Patterson 1985; Pliatsky 1985); and by New Right theorists who claim that state spending undermines 'wealth creation' (Minford 1984; see Holmes 1985, ch. 5). While theoretical underpinning is at variance, the conclusions betray remarkable similarity: for

Gough, state welfare is 'indirectly productive'. However, concern at state spending is what fuels pressure for a reduction in the state sector; and it is in the areas where there is most potential for private profit (housebuilding and NHS capital programmes) that the state has drawn back most sharply (Gough 1979, ch. 7). O'Higgins and Patterson's analysis throws emphasis on the issue of 'efficiency gains': 'the efficiency issue deserves urgent attention in social policy analysis' (O'Higgins and Patterson 1985: 128). Efficiency is of central importance because it is only through achieving efficiency gains corresponding to those in the market that the welfare state can avoid pre-empting more resources each year. Advocates of the mixed economy of welfare argue that 'there is some evidence to suggest that private enterprises can be more efficient than public organizations' (Judge and Knapp 1985: 149). Friedman writes, 'sooner or later ... an even bigger government would destroy both the prosperity that we owe to the free market, and ... human freedom' (Friedman and Friedman 1981: 25). In the welfare state, 'the bureaucrats spend someone else's money on someone else. Only human kindness, not the much stronger and more dependable spur of self-interest, assures that they will spend money in the way most beneficial to the recipients. Hence the wastefulness and ineffectiveness of the spending' (Friedman and Friedman 1981: 147).

All three approaches point to concern about economic growth as a reason for transferring welfare to the private sector, a view summarized by government more succinctly in the claim that lower taxes lead to higher growth in a 'virtuous circle' (Treasury 1984: 20), or the repeated reference to social spending as simply a 'burden' on economic growth (DHSS 1986: 2). A similar link between analysis and pressure for the private is to be found in legitimation crisis theory.

LEGITIMATION CRISIS

The problems of legitimation crisis are discussed in detail by Marxists such as Offe (1984) and Habermas (1975), centrists such as Brittan (1975) and Douglas (1976), and anti-collectivists such as Seldon (1981) and Friedman (1981). The theoretical arguments differ. Marxists see the roots of legitimation crisis in the conflict between the ideologies fostered by the market and by state interventionism. The former determines allocation simply by the pattern of supply and effective demand, whereas the latter offers the hope of a rationally justified system of distribution according to the outcome of reasoned debate. However, the government must always bow to the demands of the capitalist economy; welfare must not evade work incentives and must maintain the workforce. In addition, the requirements of powerful groups in the market must be met: 'if the capitalist system is not able to survive *without* bourgeois-democratic forms of political power, the contradiction between economic and legitimation functions of the capitalist state points ... to the fact that it cannot live with them' (Offe 1974: 54).

Centrists also see the expansion of government as inversely proportional to popular satisfaction. However, here the mechanism is more to do with the way in which vested interests conspire to direct policy away from the limited sphere of what government should do and does well:

Government has become more and more diversified in its functions and this is weakening its ability to carry out its core functions ... the power of producer groups and bureaucracies and the extent of fiscal illusion all tend to reduce the inhibitions to adding functions.

(Bosanquet 1983: 200)

Anti-collectivists see legitimation problems in two factors: the 'tyranny of momentary majorities' (Friedman 1962: 15) and the inevitable slide on the road to serfdom that the extension of state interventionism into the freedom of market economies produces. In addition, the unresponsiveness of big government to individual need leads to frustration, apathy, a decline in participation and, where people can get away with it, tax revolt. Hayek has developed a theory of ideology to account for the glamour of statism: this stems from the misplaced appeal of just allocation in advanced societies. In principle, the political system of a small-scale tribal society could centralize enough information on needs, wants and abilities to make justice possible. In mass society, a fair allocation cannot be achieved, simply because there is too much information about peoples' separate wants and capacities to synthesize. Even the simplified model of economic planning in the USSR postulates some 12,000 plan-positions which would require evaluation before the fairest balance of work and want could be determined (Nove 1983, part 2). Hayek claims that in a world as complex as this the summons to follow the dictates of social justice is simply meaningless. The failure to achieve the mirage of fairness offered in democratic political debate must lead ultimately to the collapse of support for the system (Hayek 1979).

All these approaches suggest that government promises more than it can provide. The result is a disenchantment with state policy. In the welfare area, the apparent advantages of responsiveness and brisk adaptation to need expressed as effective demand, give private service an edge. From this perspective the call for privatization is an attempt to staunch the flow of disquiet, by imposing a return to a 'take it or leave it' allocation, not subject to distinctions of fairness, because markets are driven by supply and demand not moral principles; it has also led Offe and others to suggest that the way forward lies in 'decommodified' exchange outside state and market systems, prefigured by co-operatives, voluntarism, self-help and the informal economy (Offe 1984: 297).

THE FAILURE OF REDISRIBUTION

Titmuss (1955), Sinfield (1978), Field (1981), Walker (1984: 28) and many others have pointed out that in addition to direct state welfare in cash and kind there exist systems of private, occupational and charitable welfare within the general structure of state subsidy and regulation. The net effect of redistribution within these systems is towards the better-off and most powerful groups, because the structure of reward follows labour market pressures, accounting skills and the vested interests of upper-class groups. In a seminal work, Le Grand (1982) has drawn together evidence on a wide range of services to show that much state welfare (especially education, housing and transport subsidy) redistributes resources in the same direction. This point must be qualified in two ways. First, as O'Higgins points out, at any one point in time, many social security transfers go to the less well off because low income or exclusion from the labour market is a condition of receipt. However, middle-class groups tend to live longer than lower-class groups and therefore receive a sufficient slice of pensions payout to wipe out all other redistribution. Second, rising unemployment and demographic change have operated to increase inequalities: state policies have mitigated this effect (O'Higgins 1983: 181). The issue of redistribution failure has contributed powerfully to generalized concern with the capacity of state welfare to deliver the goods. On the left, George and Wilding conclude from an extensive review of evidence about the impact of the welfare state: 'What clearly is an unrealistic expectation is that there will be a direct and serious assault on inequalities of outcomes' (George and Wilding 1984: 154). From a centrist perspective Hadley and Hatch argue for decentralised participatory policies, (Hadley and Hatch 1981, ch. 9) and Glennerster for a 'larger concept of citizenship': 'where services disproportionately benefit the higher income groups, subsidies can be withdrawn and the proceeds used to expand the services that reach the poorest' (Glennerster 1983: 225). Le Grand himself concludes that 'the strategy of equality through public provision has failed ... primarily because it implicitly accepted the ideology of inequality' (Le Grand 1982: 151). This is an acceptance that current distributions are fair, or at least that egalitarianism would involve prohibitive economic penalties (Le Grand 1982: 142).

Anti-collectivists have drawn substantially on Le Grand's work, taking up the 'ammunition' offered 'to those who wish to suggest that the welfare state is failing' as two prominent Fabians have put it (Davies and Piachaud 1983: 44). The remedy is the extension of the private sector.

THE CRITIQUE OF PATERNALISM

The fourth area of agreement cutting across previous theoretical divides concerns state paternalism. Traditional welfare state structures are criticized as centralized, bureaucratic and unresponsive from many viewpoints (Rose and Rose 1982; London to Edinburgh Weekend Return Group [LEWRG] 1982; Hadley and Hatch 1981; Williams 1985: 83; Friedman and Friedman 1981: 53; Harris and Seldon 1979: 84). Proposed solutions fall into two main groups. On the one hand, many writers, predominantly on the left, call for more use of small-scale participatory systems (Deacon 1985; Rose and Rose 1982; Offe 1984; and so on), although some are concerned to argue for the development of state planning to enable locally based committees to represent the needs of their area to the central machine (Walker 1984a: 221). On the other hand, writers of the right and centre argue for a greater role for the market to enable people to express their preferences directly and allocate resources through the price mechanism (Minford 1984; but see also advocates of the 'mixed economy of welfare': Judge in Judge, Smith and Taylor-Gooby 1983: 486; Bosanquet 1983, ch. 14; Weale 1983: 111–20).

STATE WELFARE ON THE DEFENSIVE

This brief review of the development of welfare state theory enables us to draw some general conclusions about the state of play in arguments for private welfare. The Fabian tradition of the 1950s and the 1960s argued for state interventionism against the market as the expression of a policy of allocation according to criteria of need against the barbarities of effective demand. This debate is graphically summarized in Titmuss's analysis of the market in blood (Titmuss 1970). Developments in the 1970s reformulated the conceptual division between market and state welfare. The Marxist left added a thoroughgoing critique of market ideology and capitalist class structure to Fabian concern about class as vested interest group. The New Right reinforced anti-collectivist arguments about the inefficiency and subversion of freedom inherent in state systems with a vigorous analysis of the civic status of the private individual. Against this background of struggle, the keynote of the 1980s has been a new consensus. Feminism, accumulation and legitimation crisis theory, critiques of the failure of redistribution and concern at state paternalism all lead to the linking of recurrent themes across disparate theories. One outcome has been a growing sobriety and disillusion with state welfare. The left has focused on non-state decommodified solutions but many writers are prepared to see a role for market provision as an antidote to the development of monolithic state power (Nove 1983; LEWRG 1982). Market privatization has made considerable headway into the centre, in the idea of a mixed economy of welfare. The terms of debate have shifted to put state interventionism on the defensive.

The new debates in social policy have had considerable impact on thinking in the subject. Two important results are that discussion of new theoretical approaches outside the left–right political spectrum is more widespread, and that there is far greater readiness to test theoretical assumptions against empirical evidence. This is not to say that the arguments against state provision are compelling.

The most significant theoretical developments concern feminism, as has been already noted. However, other approaches such as public-choice theory (Goodin and Le Grand 1986; Taylor-Gooby 1985: 122), comparative analysis (Higgins 1981; Jones 1985) political economy (Robinson 1986; Glennerster 1985) and social philosophy (Weale 1983) are playing a greater role. Complex empirical debates play about all the four themes reviewed in the preceding pages, which have directed attention towards private provision of welfare. The balance of evidence in these debates appears to tell against the view that large-scale welfare privatization is necessary or desirable. In relation to accumulation crisis, the argument that current levels of welfare expenditure will not inevitably lead to economic instability have been reworked a sufficient number of times from different starting points to be convincing (Davies and Piachaud 1985; O'Higgins and Patterson 1985, Glennerster 1985: 235). The plausibility of the 'legitimation crisis' thesis has taken a substantial knock from the fact that major changes in official ideology appear to have taken place in the UK and the USA without disturbing the equanimity of the polity. The case that 'big government' produces allegiance deficit is unproven (Taylor-Gooby 1985, ch. 1). The failure of redistribution is only unsettling to those who see the original objective of state welfare as the pursuit of a strategy of equality. The view that the most widely accepted goal was a national minimum — 'a floor beneath which no-one may fall', rather than 'a ceiling above which no-one may rise', as Beveridge puts it—is more plausible. This strengthens the credibility of state welfare because the case against the welfare state on the grounds that it fails to achieve minimum living standards is far less convincing than the case that redistribution has failed. Finally, the significance of arguments about paternalism depends on the degree of importance attached to choice and control. The evidence of opinion surveys (for what it is worth) indicates that people are much more exercised about level of service than about consumer sovereignty (Taylor-Gooby 1987).

Taken individually, the various arguments about the weakness of state welfare do not add up to a knock-down case. They have, however, combined to create a climate in which privatization has arisen as a major issue on the agenda of the subject. The principal reason for this is an abrupt change in the context of the study of state welfare—the retreat from confidence in the welfare state at the political level. The fact that a party which emphasizes welfare constraint can gain mass support, puts a practical edge to all four arguments: as Davies and Piachaud point out, the real impetus behind public spending cuts 'is not based on economic constraints but rather on a political desire to give absolute priority to tax cuts' (Davies and Piachaud 1985: 110). Issues of legitimation crisis do not arise from an inevitable conflict between capitalist and democratic values, but from decisions to curb resources going to weaker groups. The obvious solution to the failure of redistribution—the expansion of state programmes that do benefit the poor—is not considered, because it is assumed that the market-based ideology of inequality is too powerful. This derives from the example of tax cuts for better-off groups, coupled with cuts in welfare services for the poor. The problem of paternalism becomes an argument for privatization because the development of consumer control is not a major issue.

The intellectual case for privatization is lent impetus by the practical politics of privatization. The arguments about the development of private welfare earlier in the chapter claimed that the balance of private and public provision is the outcome primarily of class and gender pressures for service provision and of similar pressures within services once they were set up. These forces have created different structures in different areas. This raises the question of how privatization policies have worked out in practice. To consider this we must first delineate the notion of privatization and then review current developments.

THE DEFINITION OF PRIVATE WELFARE

The term 'privatization' is applied to a diverse range of policies, from the reduction of spending targets for future welfare state programmes (Heald 1983: 299) to the deregulation of bus transport (Le Grand and Robinson 1984: 6). The starting point for most discussion is the direct state provision of welfare services. The welfare state is the insertion of social services designed to meet need into a more or less capitalist market economy and a party-mediated democratic political system: it involves a whole complex of private market interactions often mediated by political pressures. These may be considered from two viewpoints: service consumer and service producer. On the consumption side, welfare services may be state subsidized up to the level where they are free at the point of demand; or the service may be allocated by market forces but regulated by state law or state inspection. From the producer's viewpoint, the services may be produced directly by the state (usually involving basic materials purchased from the market) or by private enterprise. Putting these two frameworks together produces a model that distinguishes between the state provision and the state subsidy of services (Klein 1984: 14; Rose 1985: 7; Glennerster 1985: 6; Judge, Smith and Taylor-Gooby 1983: 486). The effect has been to widen the debate in social policy studies by drawing people's attention to the level and variety of state involvement in welfare services. The distinction between monolithic state welfare and the untrammelled market (cherished in the Institute of Economic Affairs debates with Titmuss in the 1960s—Lees 1964; Titmuss 1967; Cooper and Culyer 1968) becomes untenable. The crucial policy questions concern what combination of state and private services and what regulatory framework provide the best outcomes for whom.

This kind of analytic structure is most clearly developed by Le Grand and Robinson. They start from the proposition that 'the state can involve itself in an area of social and economic activity in any of three ways: provision, subsidy or regulation' (Le Grand and Robinson 1984: 3). Of course, the actual practice of state welfare in Britain involves all three activities. In council housing, social work, state education, health care and social security, services, staff and benefits are directly provided. In rent benefit and mortgage interest relief, in the provision of support for home care and residential personal services, in most schooling, in the supply of health care 'free at the point of demand' and in the use of tax revenues to fund social security and of tax remissions to encourage some private pension and sick-pay insurance, services are state subsidized. Finally, a complex web of regulation controls access: law specifies housing standards and fitness, aspects of child care and the minimum length of education (for most people in state schools). State employed professionals determine access and compulsion while standards in housing, education, residential and nursing homes both in private and state sectors are subject to the scrutiny of state inspectors.

The process of expansion of private provision can be understood as the reduction in state activity in the three areas: cuts in service provision, in subsidy or in regulation. For example, the decline in council house building since the late 1970s, the contracting-out of hospital cleaning and the flirtation with education vouchers all involve a reduction in state provision; the rapid council rent increases, the introduction or increase of charges for NHS dental, optical or prescription services, the removal of earnings-related supplements from short-term social security benefits and the reduction in support for school meals all involve a cut in subsidy; and the creation of shorthold private tenure with little security from eviction or rent control, the effective simplifying of arrangements by which workers contract out of the State Earnings Related Pension Scheme (SERPS) and the derestriction of competition between public and private transport undertakings are all examples of deregulation.

These changes in state policy can be seen as privatization from two standpoints. First, reduction in state involvement in any service to meet need involves the expansion of the private sector, because people are compelled to meet their needs privately, if they can. Second, many of the policies described are part of a package designed to encourage private-sector expansion. For example, the well-publicized combination of rent increases, housing-benefit cuts, guaranteed mortgage payments and price reductions at up to 60 per cent of valuation formed part of a policy of encouraging the expansion of home ownership described as 'the greatest success story of housing policy' in the 1987 Conservative election manifesto (Conservative Party 1987: 11); the erosion of state pension commitments together with the substantial deregulation of private alternatives are concerned to 'keep the costs of the state scheme within limits which future generations can afford and to increase the number of people getting their own pension with their job', in short, to shift a burden (Treasury 1986: 228).

Both these policies are influenced by short-term electoral considerations: we have already noted the link between home ownership and Conservative Party support. The fact that the revenues from council house sales exceed projections in all public expenditure White Papers since 1981 indicates that the popularity of this policy was not anticipated: the haste with which the government added a clause to increase discounts to Section 3 of the Housing and Building Control Bill at the time of the 1983 election shows that the point was soon grasped. Several commentators have pointed out that the full impact of pension policy changes in the 1986 Social Security Act will not be felt for some two decades whereas the revenue effects, enabling tax cuts, will come into operation before the next general election (*Economist* 1985: 23; Piachaud 1985: 408).

The approach that starts out from the threefold categorization of state activity has considerable merits: it enables us to apply the same term to a number of apparently disparate policies, which have been initiated at the same time with common goals by a government keen on radical change. However, policies do not operate independently of each other.

The expansion of the private sector in one area may involve an increase in state activity in another. 'Privatization' in this sense is not equivalent to 'rolling back the state'. In recent policy developments attempts to restrict state involvement in welfare have only succeeded in redirecting it.

We now consider some prominent examples of the way in which expanding the private involves redirecting rather than diminishing state power.

PRIVATIZATION AND STATE RESTRUCTURING

The most significant privatization programme is the sale of council housing. Over a million sales took place in Great Britain between 1979 and 1987. The fall in council provision from 31.5 to 27.3 per cent of all dwellings over the period (DoE 1986: 26; Treasury 1987 vol II: 154) has been associated with a current account cut in Exchequer subsidy to local authority Housing Investment Plans of nearly 80 per cent between 1979 and 1986, and a fall in total local spending of over 50 per cent (Robinson 1986: 5). About half the reduction may be offset against increases in rent benefits, which are paid out of the social security budget. The local housing cuts thus represent something like £1 billion a year at 1985 prices.

Against this must be set the net outflow from the state. Right-to-buy discounts represent an average capital loss to councils of nearly £1 billion a year at 1985 prices from 1979 to 1987—a large subsidy to this form of home ownership and roughly equivalent to the net saving to central government in direct subsidies to local authority housing. To this must be added a proportion of mortgage interest relief (totalling some £4,750 billion in that year—Treasury 1986: 30) plus capital gains tax exemption (totalling some £3,000 billion—ibid.) and other benefits. There is no precise calculus for trading off state sales against subsidies. The reduction in direct council-housing provision is partially balanced by an expansion of indirect state subsidy. State support is being redirected from council tenants in general to the very poor (on benefits) and to the better-off young or middle-aged (who can command mortgages).

The competitive tendering system for NHS ancillary services has attracted considerable attention. Here the impact of the use of a market system on the balance of direct provision and subsidy has been the converse of that in housing. The decline in direct state provision is limited. The NHS has won some 63 per cent of the 226 contracts let so far and is currently winning over 90 per cent of the 2,000 odd remaining, as the stock of obviously profitable areas for private enterprise runs low (*Economist* 1986: 24). Over half the £23 million saved so far has been produced by driving down the conditions of work of NHS direct labour. The subsidy cut is more significant than the cut in provision, at the cost of an expansion of regulatory activity (Mohan 1986). The Social Services Select Committee concluded that competitive tendering 'has failed to bring home the bacon after four years' despite the waste of much management time and the engendering of industrial conflict (Social Services Select Committee 1985).

The proposals for the restructuring of pensions involve a substantial reduction both in direct state provision and in state subsidy. The earnings-related component will no longer be based on an individual's best twenty years' earnings, the pension will be calculated on 20 per cent, not 25 per cent, of earnings, widow's entitlements to inherit their spouse's pension rights will be cut in half and state obligations to inflation-proof occupational schemes will be subject to an annual ceiling of 3 per cent. Taken together, these changes will cut state pension spending by £13.5 billion (at 1985 prices) by the year 2033 (Government actuary's estimate, DHSS 1985a: 52). State regulatory activity through the Occupational Pensions Board quango is likely to increase. Policy-makers assume a substantial expansion in private occupational and 'personal' pensions, attracting support from employers at a minimum rate of 2 per cent of wages. This is to be encouraged by an additional subsidy through National Insurance rebate. Other tax reliefs broadly similar to current arrangements will involve state subsidy. The extent of tax subsidy to occupational pensions under current arrangements is a matter of accounting convention—different methods produce a figure varying between £3.5 billion and £9.6 billion, in 1985 (Inland Revenue 1983; Treasury 1987 vol II: 37).

The total Exchequer subsidy to the National Insurance fund currently runs at some £4 billion. The balance in subsidy under new arrangements is hard to predict. It is likely that new arrangements will involve a much smaller cut in state support for pension schemes than official pronouncements imply, in the swings and roundabouts transfer from direct to tax-relief subsidy.

The best-known example of the confusion which often surrounds the transfer of welfare responsibilities to non-state agencies is Statutory Sick Pay. This scheme was finally introduced in 1983 after being twice deferred on the parliamentary timetable and after four different schemes had been rejected by the employers, who were to take over the running of sickness benefits. National Insurance sickness benefit is now paid to about a fifth of the number who received it in 1979. Direct state social security spending in this area has fallen by a corresponding amount (Treasury 1986: 224). The money saved (about £435 million in 1983/4) is more than offset by the agreed compensation to employers of £615 million. It is only by including in the equation the £215 millions proceeds of the coincidental introduction of taxation on sick pay, that DHSS officials are able to claim that subsidy has been reduced (Social Services Select Committee 1983: 95). As with the right-to-buy scheme and the excoriation of SERPS, Treasury accounting conventions confuse the issue by failing to associate the concomitant fall in tax revenue with a cut in direct spending. Whereas the National Insurance Scheme redistributed from the tax-payer at large to the sick employee and (usually) his or her dependants, statutory sick pay transfers from everyone, including the sick, to employees with no families and to employers who previously ran voluntary schemes. It is also accompanied by an increase in state regulation.

The Assisted Places Scheme in education, designed to sponsor bright children from poor backgrounds in private schools, involves a decline in direct provision in state schools. However, the subsidy to the private sector of £22.15 million in 1984/5 provided bursaries for 17,386 pupils—an average of over £1,200 each (Hansard Written Answers, vol. 84, col. 259, 1984/5). This was about one and a quarter times the average spending per head in state secondary education in that year (CIPFA 1985: 11). The marginal cost of including the small number of pupils involved in the state system would be much lower. Even allowing for the disproportionate number of sixth-formers covered by the scheme, the state subsidy to the education of this group has been increased by the shift to the private sector. There has also been an increase in state regulatory activities, although this is less marked since selection of beneficiaries and the administration of means tests are carried out by the schools themselves.

In the area of social services, the direct provision of residential accommodation for the elderly is now beginning to decline after reaching a peak of over 122,000 places in 1983 (CSO 1986: 128; 1987: 133). It now stands at less than 120,000. This decline forms part of the major policy shift toward community care.

Whether it involves a fall in subsidy is debatable. The cost of provision of community care services varies from area to area and in some areas is equivalent to the cost of residential accommodation. Indeed, in one study the cost for each elderly person was greater in community care, because under this system, people tended to live longer (Davies and Challis 1985). The second point is that private residential accommodation has been expanded rapidly, from 51,000 places in 1979 to over 100,000 by 1986 (CSO 1987: 133). One supporting factor has been the DHSS decision to subsidize places up to a ceiling of £120 (1986 figures), through Supplementary Benefits. These benefits supported substantially more than half the residents in private homes in that year (Audit Commission 1986: 2). The subsidy to private provision is closely comparable to the cost of provision of a local authority place, (currently £120 in Kent, for example—Kent Social Services Department (SSD) 1986: 9), although both DHSS and SSD real costs are less due to the operation of means tests. The increased demand for residential care by the frail elderly is being met by a shift to the private sector. It is unclear whether state subsidy has fallen. There is an accompanying expansion of state regulatory activity through the 1984 Registered Homes Act which requires periodic inspection, and the laying down of guidelines on standards and staff training by the Avebury Committee

(Avebury Report 1984).

The point of this review of some prominent examples of policy changes drawn from the five main areas of welfare provision is not that the situation is hopelessly confused. In all the cases discussed changes have resulted in a decline in direct state provision and thus merit the term privatization. This has been accompanied by an increase in subsidy in half the cases (statutory sick pay, the Assisted Places Scheme, council house sales) and an increase in regulation in five out of six (the exception being the right to buy). The pattern could be repeated in other areas of social policy, for example the introduction of shorthold tenure with its increases in rent benefit subsidy to tenants paying higher rents alongside the removal of regulation. Counter-examples of a simultaneous reduction in all three areas are the 1985 Transport Act, which ends subsidy to public road transport undertakings with a consequent decline in state provision and also removes the state regulation of competition between public and private enterprises; and the reductions in school-meal subsidies, which have led to a fall in use of the service from 62 to 48 per cent of pupils between 1979 and 1984. These were accompanied by the abolition of regulation of nutritional standards in 1980 (CSO 1986: 49). The ending of free meals in the 1986 Social Security Act, to be replaced by an income subsidy rather less than the cost of an average school meal will take the process further. In some areas the school-meal service has been withdrawn. A further example concerns opticians' services. Free NHS lenses have been restricted to the poor (a simultaneous cut in subsidy and provision) and restrictions on the supply of glasses by people who are not opticians has been lifted. There is no general pattern to the process of expansion of the private sector. In many areas, state policy is shuffling interventionism along the path from direct provision through subsidy towards regulation of private provision. Government intervenes in different directions with different effects for different social groups.

The net impact of the expansion of the private sector so far seems to have been to redistribute from the lowest social groups to higher social groups and to damage services for women. In order to avail themselves of 'right to buy' windfalls, council tenants must be able to command capital or a mortgage. Those who cannot, face large rent increases and housing benefit cuts. The net effect of the subsidies to occupational pensions since 1976 has been to benefit the better-off, and the scheme laid down in the 1986 Social Security Act will increase class differentials. The expansion of private health and welfare will not transmit benefits to less well-off groups. Just as changes in tax rates since 1979 have benefited small minorities of the rich (who have always had access to high-quality private welfare), shifts in welfare policy direct more of the gravy towards the middle of the class structure.

Women are less likely than men to be able to become home-owners; they are likely to lose out in the reduction in widows' rights to inherit the SERPS entitlements of spouse, and are more likely to be among the group of workers dependent on the curtailed SERPS scheme in any case; as the majority of lower-grade workers in the welfare sector, they have borne the brunt of job cuts (Webster 1985: 19).

There is no intrinsic reason why the development of private welfare should have any preordained distributional effect (O'Higgins 1984: 130; Blaug 1984: 161). However, the experience of recent measures taken together with the pattern of state interventions into and delineations of the market sphere over the post-war period indicates the direction of probable changes. The core functions of welfare will be sustained while the structure of class and gender advantage will continue.

CONCLUSION

The politics of the recent past have brought private welfare to the fore. This process has been underpinned by the widening of divisions of class interest that have increased the influence of the groups who gain most through state-subsidized private welfare. The theory of social policy has reflected this process in the new consensus of radical disenchantment with state welfare. Current shifts in welfare policy are not towards root-and-branch privatization, any more than developments since the mid-1970s have constituted wholesale cuts. Behind the banner of privatization, state involvement in welfare for the middle and to some extent the upper working class is undergoing a restructuring that increases the state subsidy to, and the relative privilege of, these groups.

The private provision of public welfare represents an adjustment in the impact of social policy to parallel the contours of changes in social structure over the past two decades. The gap between the middle mass and the marginal groups at the bottom of the pile has widened. The structure of poverty in richer societies is coming more closely to resemble the 'pedestal inequality' of poorer ones (Townsend 1986: 9). In some areas the interests of state professionals have combined with popular demands to severely limit the growth of private provision. In others, mass public welfare is less securely defended. The following chapters analyse changes in more detail.

2 Private Health

BACKGROUND

In terms of its size the private health-care sector appears to be of marginal significance. Yet, in the context of recent challenges to the NHS, the debate over the private provision of health care suggests that significant changes may have taken place in the complex boundaries between public and private welfare. To test this hypothesis, we need to examine not only the expansion of the private sector but the multifarious pressures on the public sector: the policies of a government that linked constraint in public expenditure to notions of freedom of choice and competition; demographic change which has placed an increasing burden on services to the elderly; the absorption of increased expenditure by the cost of new technologies; wage rises and the conflict between government and unions; shifts in popular attitudes, perceptions and expectations along with a greater preparedness to contemplate the 'private option'; and the new forms of co-operation that have emerged between the two sectors. Although these pressures have not brought about as radical a shift in practice as the creation of the NHS in 1948, they may have established the preconditions for a profound questioning of the service. The NHS remains the most popular component of the welfare state. The search, however, for a new mixture of public, private and voluntary initiatives would appear to be well underway.

PRIVATE PRACTICE AND THE NHS:
FROM CONSENSUS TO CONFLICT

Before the creation of the NHS in 1948, about half of the
population was covered by the National Insurance Scheme
established in 1912. Thus about 24 million employees were
able without charge to receive care from a general practitioner
(GP), as well as drugs and a limited amount of surgical and
medical appliances. For those not covered by the 1912 scheme,
particularly women, children and other dependants, protection
was offered by hospital contributory schemes organized by
voluntary societies. By 1947 the British Hospitals Contributory Schemes Association had about 10.5 million
members and benefits were extended to dependants. Higher-
income groups were able to contribute to schemes like the one
organized by the Hospital Savings Association of London and
to 'provident societies'. Only the poorest sections of the
population received free treatment. This mixed system of
health care created precedents for the interaction of public and
private care which were not entirely overcome by the creation
of the NHS.

For instance, the costs of hospital treatment varied for
different income groups and the well-off had to come to an
arrangement with hospitals on the level of their contribution.
As charitable institutions, the hospitals did not charge for
medical services, but there was 'a gradual development of pay
beds in the twentieth century, and this trend became greatly
accelerated during the 1930s (Mencher 1967: 13). In addition,
the fees charged by consultants became an important part of
their income, making up, according to them, some of the losses
they had incurred when free hospital services had replaced
what they had provided privately. The expansion of general
hospital facilities by local authorities and the difficulties encountered in recruiting salaried staff reinforced, from the 1930s onwards, the trend of employing part-time consultants who could
supplement their salary with income from fee-paying patients
using private beds. Other forms of interaction between public
and private practice were developed by general practitioners who
received income from capitation payments for 'public' patients
and continued to serve 'private' fee-paying patients.

The creation of the NHS did not necessarily contradict these tendencies. Neither of the major political parties sought actively to restrict the choice of doctors or patients to remain outside the NHS. Although some doctors and consultants gained a private income from private nursing homes, clinics and hospitals that had remained outside direct state control, their most significant source of private income was from pay beds (permitted under Section 5 of the Health Services Act). Bevan, in response to the critics of pay beds, argued that, if they were not provided, it would stimulate the growth of private nursing homes and specialist practice outside the NHS. Another argument in favour of employing part-time consultants was that it would attract the most talented ones to the public sector and encourage their distribution throughout the country. The most significant consideration, however, was the requirement by Bevan to make a concession to a powerful occupational group 'in return for their support of the principle of the NHS' (Klein 1983: 118).

Until the mid-1970s the major focus of government policy was on the continued development of the state sector. Few conflicts arose over the relative roles of state and private provision. Whilst some pointed to the (inevitable) conflict that would arise from leaving the door open to the private sector and others stressed the symbiotic relationship between the two, politically it was a dormant issue. Both major political parties achieved consensus in opposing the supply of drugs from the NHS to private patients and (throughout the 1960s) in not reducing the cost of private beds. The conflicts were confined to the arena of the health-care professionals who failed to gain public support on either of the above issues or on preventing the reduction in the number of pay beds. At any rate, the medical profession was also aware of its material stake in the NHS.

The apparent stability of the post-war legacy was disrupted during the 1970s. The causes were both economic and political-ideological: a vigorous campaign within the Labour Party to phase out pay beds coincided with the worsening economic situation and decline in economic growth, prompting a reassessment of public spending on health care. Although the Labour Party had opposed pay beds on the grounds of under-utilization, it now criticized them as symbols of privilege and inequality—as a means for some patients to 'jump queues' and gain unfair access to facilities. The 1974 Labour Party manifesto declared that pay beds would be phased out, even though only 4,500 of all NHS Beds were used for private patients. The ideological motivation had further practical implications when the Party proposed to load the consultant contract in favour of those who were engaged full-time in the NHS and to abolish entirely private medicine. The Labour government used the notions of efficiency and rationalization to justify the proposed changes in consultants' contracts. By loading the contracts in favour of full-time doctors, it wanted to discourage doctors from moving easily into specialized fields of practice and working in the more lucrative South East region. The medical profession wished to afford individual consultants greater freedom of choice between prevailing options and offered stiff resistance.

The government was finally compelled to appoint a mediator, Lord Goodman, to arrive at a compromise (incorporated in the 1976 legislation): private beds and facilities should be separated from the NHS; the government formally recognized the right to existence of private practice and of doctors to work in both public and private spheres; only 1,000 pay beds would be phased out immediately and decisions about further reductions would be taken by an independent Health Services Board, not by the secretary of state. On the Board would sit four medical professionals, four trade unionists and an independent chairman with a casting vote. No firm commitment was made for bringing to an end private practice within the NHS and, in a compromise over consultants' contracts, the latter were to receive payment for overtime whilst full-time consultants were to benefit more than part-time staff.

However, in 1980 the Conservative government abolished the Health Services Board. Whilst the latter had supervised the reduction of pay beds from 3,444 to 2,533, the former reversed the process: by the end of 1982 the number of pay beds in the NHS had risen to 3,220—an increase of about 27 per cent. Since then the figure has remained fairly static because of the expansion of the private hospital sector. Plans to phase out pay beds were abandoned and a new contract drawn up with consultants.

The dispute between the medical profession and the Labour government had undoubtedly strained the previous consensus over the boundaries of private health care. The victory of the Conservative Party in 1979 signalled a further stage in the boundary shift between private and public health care. In their manifesto the Conservatives had promised to end the 'vendetta' by Labour against the private health sector, and to 'simplify and decentralise the service and cut back bureaucracy'. Once again, but in a different form, notions of efficiency and rationalization were used to justify significant changes in policy. Social justice appeared to play an altogether subordinate role.

ECONOMIC CONSTRAINT ON THE NHS: A STIMULUS TO PRIVATE EXPANSION?

In the debate over constraint on public expenditure on health and over the expansion of the private sector, the framework of inequality that existed prior to the election of a Conservative government in 1979 is frequently overlooked; in fact, the government refused to make available for public purchase a report commissioned by its predecessor on the nature of such inequalities (Townsend and Davidson 1982). The framework of inequality is only partially determined by health-care policies and any retrenchment in a re-allocation of expenditure must be placed in the context of an overall questioning, including at the international level, of a commitment to the public sector. In the UK this coincided with a government which, on ideological grounds, was vigorously opposed to the public sector in general. The links between this and the expansion of private health care are not, in, practice, particularly obvious; direct support for the private sector has been limited (and has not even included wide-ranging tax relief on insurance premiums), and campaigns have been launched to 'prove' that public expenditure on the NHS has increased in real terms (DHSS 1985b) and that the government has no intention of 'dismantling' the service. Certain policy changes since 1979 have none the less contributed to the privatization of services: the new consultants' contract which made it easier for them to work part-time in the private sector; the termination of free NHS opticians' services; the increase in dental and prescription charges; the subsidy to and expansion of private residential accommodation; and the contracting-out to private contractors of some NHS ancillary services.

There has also occurred a significant restructuring of and attempt to rationalize state expenditure in this area, for which the preconditions had been created before the advent of the Conservatives in 1979: the reduced rate of economic growth in the 1970s came at the tail-end of an era (1951–75) in which expenditure on the NHS rose from 4.1 to 6.0 per cent of GNP; the number of staff doubled to over a million; and there was an increase in annual expenditure of 3.0 to 3.5 per cent in real terms. From 1975 to 1982 this rate was restricted to 1.5 per cent. However, recent government statistics present the figure of a real rise of 24 per cent over the period 1979–86, and point to the increase in in-patient cases treated per available bed in acute and geriatric services; in staff numbers; in new facilities; and in special initiatives to provide community care (DHSS 1985b).

These 'statistically correct' assertions give a misleading gloss on the nature, direction and impact of increased expenditure; long-term trends; and significant measures of constraint and restructuring in certain areas. Increases in numbers of nurses and midwives are not adjusted to take into account their reduction in working hours and the 5 per cent increase in the birth rate (Radical Statistics Group 1986: 304); and no adjustments are made for increases in need and demand among particular population groups.

Vast increases in the number of patients treated per available bed have been significantly influenced by two factors: first, the decrease in the average daily number of occupied in-patient beds from 75,000 in 1980 to 69,000 in 1983; and second, the fall in the average length of stay. For instance, in the acute hospital sector the number of in-patient cases per available bed rose from 28.0 in 1978 to 33.2 in 1983, whilst the average length of stay dropped from 9.4 to 8.1 days. Over this period, the fall in the average length of stay in the acute hospital sector was 2.9

per cent per annum; in obstetrics and GP maternity services, 4.4 per cent per annum; and in geriatric and younger disabled cases, 6.5 per cent per annum (Treasury 1985: 161). There may of course be professional reasons for these practices, but they are not mentioned in attempts by the government to create the impression of real increases in health provision.

To gauge the precise nature of changes in the health sector, adjustments need to be made to the aggregate expenditure figures provided by the government and a more careful analysis of its targeting is required. Robinson, for instance, arrives at a figure of growth in expenditure considerably at variance with that issued by the government by making adjustments which give special consideration to the specific programmes in question. Thus the cost of health services is likely to increase more rapidly than in the economy as a whole because they are more labour intensive, have a slower rate of productivity and consequently imply 'greater than average rates of growth of input prices' (Robinson 1986: 3). By taking into account increases in pay in a labour-intensive health industry, the real increase in expenditure between 1979/80 to 1984/5 is reduced from 17 per cent to 8 per cent. Even if one were to accept the figure of a 24 per cent increase in real terms between 1978 and 1986, one would have to consider how the money was spent. Most of it, 70 per cent, went on wages and salaries—with nurses receiving a 33 per cent increase and doctors around 40 per cent over that period—and was mainly the outcome of an award made under the Labour government (Clegg Commission 1978/9). In addition, a proportion of recent pay rises was overtly being funded by resources previously allocated to services for patients.

Of particular relevance to the funding of health services are increases in needs and demands as a result of demographic change; the failure of government employment policies; and the high cost of new medical techniques (such as heart transplants and joint replacements). The latter alone accounted for 2.3 per cent of the increased expenditure between 1978/9 and 1983/4 (Robinson 1986: 13). Account also has to be taken of sections of the population that have increased in numbers and are disproportionate users of the service—especially the unemployed and the aged. According to one estimate, the NHS required an annual increase of 0.8 per cent 'to compensate for the ageing of the population' (Forsyth 1982: 61–2). Attempts to rationalize the regional distribution of funds in accordance with the Resource Allocation Working Party (RAWP) Scheme (introduced in 1976 and which considers demographic variables and standardized mortality ratios among other factors) has exacerbated some problems in trying to solve others. Initiatives towards equalization in the context of real reductions in expenditure to 'overfunded' regions has led to severe constraint. This is especially true of the four London regions where large expenses are incurred in running teaching hospitals and where the drain in population from the poor inner-city districts have placed them in the overfunded category. Initiatives towards equalization have none the less been slow and may only contribute partially to the general burden on services. General practitioner services in the poorer inner-city districts need to be included in the equation since pressure on this part of the service has led many people to use hospital casualty departments as an alternative.

Yet, here too the pressures have mounted not only through the closure of many hospitals but through a deliberate policy of rationing existing facilities by reducing surgeons' working hours. According to the Royal College of Surgeons, 500,000 people were waiting for surgery, while out-patients generally had to wait between eleven weeks (in better-provided districts) and seventeen weeks (in the worst districts) for an appointment with a consultant (*Times*, 20 June 1986). The British Medical Association, on the basis of a study of 130 hospitals revealed that in 70 per cent of them beds were either temporarily 'closed' or consultants complained they were forced to discharge patients too early in order to make room for those on waiting lists (*Times*, 24 June 1986). These developments reflect the immense pressure on the general acute sector of the service, which has been exacerbated by the apparent priority accorded by the government (within the context of a constrained budget) for those suffering from the effects of old age, chronic illness and mental and physical handicap.

The response also reflects the capacity of powerful lobbies within the service to voice their concern. Although resistance has also emerged from less powerful groups, it has been far less effective. Pressures on administrative staff have led to limited promotion opportunities, non-replacement and greater work-loads. Ancillary staff have been under the greatest threat. Many have lost their jobs and have only been able to recover them under worse conditions, that is as employees of private contractors in the areas of cleaning, catering and laundry services who often pay lower wages and ignore previous conditions of employment. The number of ancillary workers has been reduced from 172,000 to 150,000 (Treasury 1985). Although other occupational groups did not experience any overall losses, nurses in particular have been placed under much greater pressure as they are often compelled to carry out tasks formerly carried out by ancillary staff. In some hospitals the practice has evolved of employing nurses from agencies on a limited contract basis. This came in the wake of the employment from the private sector of general managers on three-year contracts. Their introduction into the highest levels of the administrative structure, and on very high salaries, was foreshadowed by the Griffiths Report (1983) as part of a new efficiency drive within the parameters of limited expenditure.

Part of this exercise would, in the spirit evoked by the Griffiths Report, entail collaboration between state and private sectors. The most publicized form of collaboration has been the contracting-out of services to the private sector. Between 1980/1 and 1981/2 NHS spending on some contracted-out services rose by substantial proportions: engineering and maintenance, 15 per cent; building main-tenance, 28 per cent; maintenance of medical and surgical equipment, 28 per cent; maintenance of laboratory equipment, 23 per cent; and gardening or farming, 18 per cent. In 1981/2, between 24 per cent and 46 per cent (according to different regions) of building and maintenance service costs were contracted out. The greatest resistance to contracting out arose where only a relatively small proportion was affected: catering (usually 0.1 per cent); domestic and cleaning (between 1 per cent and 6 per cent) and laundry (between 1 per cent and 21 per cent). Regionally, contracting out has been concentrated in the Thames, South Western, East Anglian and Oxford authorities (Harrison and Gretton 1984: 52–3). Yet, one of the overriding motives for the efficiency drive in provision of ancillary services may have been political rather than economic. This is partly revealed by the resistance from the unions in areas where only a small proportion of services was being contracted out. The determination of the government to undermine union power has been most apparent in situations where it has opted for private services despite clear evidence that the public sector could have done the job at lower cost. The 'demonstration effect' of such decisions in which 'ideology may override the results of investment appraisal' (Maynard 1984: 109) is directed at unions (hence, the 'threat' of privatization) and management (as part of the efficiency drive).

Echoing the message of the Griffiths Report (DHSS 1983), the private sector is now also involved in building hospitals for the NHS and in taking on some patients. In order to reduce NHS waiting lists the King Edward VII Hospital in Midhurst has provided hip replacements for NHS patients from Portsmouth, Bath and Chichester at 'competitive prices'. However, when the Canterbury and Thanet District Health Authority investigated contracting out these operations to the Chaucer private hospital, it discovered that they could be done both cheaper and better at Guy's public hospital in London. The pressure on general managers (and from them) to pursue collaboration between the two sectors is likely to increase despite resistance. However, it is not, as with most of these developments, entirely obvious that the government is simply applying pressure on the public sector in order to compel consumers to use the private option if they can afford it. Certainly, a number of services have effectively been privatized without any apparent lobbying or resistance, for instance in optical and dental services (and even in the cost of prescriptions) through high charges that now have to be met directly by consumers. On the other hand, the NHS is not only moving towards greater collaboration with the private sector, it is also competing with it (much to the chargin of the latter) for instance by 'undercharging' private patients in NHS hospital beds (National Audit Office 1986).

Another area in which links can be established between state policy and support for privatization is in the reduction of public-sector residential care. The shift in policy has been encouraged by economic pressures (the increasing cost of care for the elderly) and widespread criticism of the effectiveness and viability of residential care. Between 1979 and 1983 the number of places in residential care declined at an annual rate of 8.5 per cent for children, 2.5 per cent for the younger physically handicapped and 0.5 per cent for the elderly (Robinson 1986: 16). In the long-term substantial reductions are planned in residential care for the mentally ill and handicapped (Henwood and Wicks 1985: 358). The alternative offered by the state is an increase in day-care and support services such as home helps, and in a range of 'special initiatives' to provide community care. Government figures which indicate an increase in the number of people in residential homes, for instance from 152,000 in 1978 to 172,000 in 1983 (DHSS 1985b) may give the impression that facilities have actually increased. In fact, they simply reflect greater turnover in the use of facilities since there were, in 1983, only 122,000 places for the elderly in residential accommodation. Another explanation for the increase in 'throughput' is that care of the elderly formerly provided in hospitals has been imposed on local authorities—that is, care of those people requiring medical care for incontinence and so on, who are more frail and consequently die sooner. The crucial point, however, is that the increase in demand for residential accommodation has been catered for privately.

If the public sector was becoming more efficient (even with limited resources) at coping with demand and was successful in promoting community care, there would be little scope for the expansion of the private sector. In reality, the boost given to the private sector by state policy has nowhere been clearer than in the provision of residential care. This will be explored in the next two sections on the ideology of privatization and on the development of the private sector. What needs to be emphasized is the immense cost to the public sector implied by demographic and social changes. From 1901 to 1981 there has been an increase as a proportion of the total population of those aged 65 and over from 5 per cent to 15 per cent, that is from about 2 million to 8 million (Henwood and Wicks 1985: 359). The number of people in the particularly vulnerable 75-

and-over group increased from 1,987,000 in 1961 to 3,084,000 in 1983. The projected increase of those over 75 is 25 per cent by the year 2000, at an estimated cost of between six times (West 1984: 113) and ten times (N. Fowler, *Times*, 10 July 1986) the amount required for those aged 18 to 64. Henwood and Wicks project increases of 122,000 (1981 to 1991) in the number of elderly requiring help to wash themselves all over; 270,000 (1981 to 2001) in the number of people over 65 living alone; and 64,000 (1981 to 2011) in the elderly unable to get in and out of bed without help (Henwood and Wicks 1985: 365–6). Long-term trends in employment suggest that women are less likely to provide as much unpaid 'community care' as they did in the past. This of course does not accord easily with the ideology of women remaining in the home.

THE IDEOLOGY OF PRIVATIZATION

Although the measures adopted by the Conservative government do not amount to a 'dismantling' of the welfare state, they have fuelled a controversial debate over issues such as community care, competition in health-care markets, choice for the consumer, the bureaucratic control of services, and economic efficiency. Perhaps the Conservatives are merely articulating the disquiet voiced across the political spectrum over the decline of the welfare state, be it a legitimation crisis, or the failure to achieve greater equality, or a stifling paternalism, or gross inefficiency. The distance taken by Margaret Thatcher from the more radical aims of the New Right may only be for short-term, tactical purposes. However 'unrealistic' some of the aims may appear, they have influenced the current debate and contributed to a reassessment of the boundaries between private and public welfare.

This is reflected in the issue of community care and the potential expansion of the private sector in providing services for the elderly. The issue of community care, frequently regarded as the 'central guiding principle' (Walker 1982: 1) in the development of health and personal social services, allows us to examine the capacity of a government motivated by both ideological and economic considerations, to influence the scale and nature of the private sector. In a 1981 White Paper the government set out its interpretation of this concept:

Whatever level of public expenditure proves practicable, and however it is distributed, the primary sources of support and care are informal and voluntary. These spring from the personal ties of kinship, friendship and neighbourhood. They are irreplaceable. It is the role of public authorities to sustain and, where necessary, develop—but never to displace—such support and care. Care *in* the community must increasingly mean care *by* the community.

(DHSS 1981: 3; quoted in Henwood and Wicks 1985: 358)

Clearly, Conservative ideology favours care by the community, a view echoed by Norman Fowler, who stressed that progress could only be made if state, private and voluntary organizations worked to provide a 'partnership' in care. He argued that the elderly should not have to leave their homes and families when they needed care; that provision of services in the home would preserve their quality of life; and that such an approach would be both more economical and effective, especially if it involved the support of relatives and neighbours (*Times*, 10 July 1986).

The difficulties of transforming ideology into efficient practice are particularly acute in this sphere. The work of Abrams and, more recently Bulmer, illustrates how difficult it will be for the government to achieve a workable relationship between statutory, private commercial, voluntary and informal sectors. The most common outcomes are 'co-existence' (with each side playing a major role) or 'confusion' where 'both sides of the divide are unsure whether to retain an element of informality even at the expense of upsetting the rules, or to accept formal support and run the risk of professionalizing the informal ties', for instance over the issue of payment of certain volunteers (Bulmer 1986a: 19; Bulmer 1986b; Abrams 1984; Froland 1980). Other outcomes include 'colonization' (by statutory over informal provision) and 'competition or conflict' (between informal practices and formal rules and regulations). As Bulmer (1986a) suggests, attempts by the government to produce a coherent strategy have not yet surfaced partly because of the intractable difficulties in interweaving varying structures of accountability and responsibility between the two sectors; variations in the time commitment of carers; and the boundaries between and within services. Further deliberation is also required over the ethical implications of providing a licence to 'strangers, even volunteers, to look into the personal circumstances of citizens who have neither asked for help nor committed any offence' (Bulmer 1986a: 20).

Critics of the new emphasis on community care also argue that this simply means care by women, the traditional bearers of such activity (Finch and Groves 1980); there has not occurred a shift in resources from residential to community care, particularly because of the resistance by professional and trade-union interests; the family 'is the main source of social care, personal aid and support for dependents; and the amount of care provided by families far exceeds that provided by the state' (Walker 1982b: 23). The lack of support for carers, who carry out difficult and often unpleasant tasks at home, is reinforced by the social security system: 'attendance allowance is restricted to nursing and not domestic tasks' (Walker 1982b: 34) and, until a recent ruling (1986) by the European Court, the invalid care allowance could not be claimed by married women living with or being maintained by their husband or another man. As Rimmer points out, community care policies often cost the state less than other options, mainly because community care is inadequate and many extra costs are not included: not only the everyday expenses for food, heating and equipment but the loss of earnings, skills and occupational benefits by the carer (Rimmer 1983: 134).

Finch and Groves adopt a pessimistic view of the prospects for women: their marginal position in the labour force along with the pressure of mass unemployment will force them (especially if they are working class) to return to their traditional role. This in turn may conflict with the preference of many women to remain in employment rather than having to care for the sick and elderly in their families. Graham argues persuasively that caring is often associated with women and with certain professions. Hence 'women are accepted into and feel they belong in the social world' (Graham 1983: 30), both at home and in the labour market, through the experience of caring. In the labour market the prejudices of male employers and the gap in earnings between male and female employees who are performing similar tasks acts as a further inducement for women to act as the main carriers of community care. Clearly, women from certain occupational groups will be under more pressure than others to care for the sick and elderly, although changes in the occupational structure place many in a stronger position to resist this. Thus some will use the option of private health care and only reinforce the dual structure of care available to different occupational groups, contributing, perhaps inadvertently, to a further shift in the public–private boundary.

Evidence from a recent survey on the relationship between gender, age and the supply of informal care revealed that 13 per cent of women were involved in caring for sick or elderly dependants, with around two-thirds caring for aged parents or parents-in-law. Most of the carers were married women in the 40–59 age groups. The impact on employment aspirations was fairly significant for 29 per cent of carers who were not in employment and 12 per cent of those who were (Henwood and Wicks 1985: 366–7; Martin and Roberts 1984). Although long-term trends suggest a move away from the traditional role of women as carers, the pattern remains encouraging for Conservative ideologists. Studies have estimated that there are at least 1.3 million people (mostly women) who provide informal care for an average range of 24.5 to 35.0 hours per week, representing an immense contribution to the welfare of society (Henwood and Wicks 1985). The policy of encouraging community care is often cheaper either because it is underfunded in the public sector or as a reflection of foregone earnings and career opportunities for many women.

Government policies over these issues are far from consistent, although one of the unintended consequences may be the reinforcement of variations in access to and quality of services. We refer later to the contradictory effects of policy on the allocation of hospitals between Northern and Southern Regional Health Authorities (RHAs) and how this policy has been subverted by the expansion of the private sector in the south. Similarly, whilst many Conservatives may hope that more women can be pressurized into relieving the state from looking after their elderly relatives, economic rationality has led to the incorporation of many women into the labour force and changed their expectations. Conservative ideology may often clash with Conservative practice.

THE DEBATE OVER EFFICIENCY

In some instances, the ideology of privatization threatens to override the pursuit of efficiency. It is therefore hardly surprising to discover a 'somewhat schizophrenic ideological attitude to health care' (Maynard 1984: 100) in the attempts to stress the importance of the private sector as a genuine alternative to state monopoly, whilst frequently defending the universalistic aspects of the NHS and publicizing the massive increase in real expenditure on it. Attempts by the New Right to redefine the concept of a public health service by regarding it as an 'ordinary service industry' comprising a plurality of doctors' partnerships, hospitals, ambulance services and 'nursing firms' in competition with each other (Minford 1984: viii) have made some impact on government policy, particularly in the debate over efficiency and performance. However, critics of state expenditure on health are not only concerned with the 'essential' inefficiency of anything controlled by the state, they also seek to break its monopoly power, particularly in the form of producer pressure groups who oppose the privatization of services. The critique of the power of pressure groups has become a cornerstone of recent work which challenges the concept of a pluralist society from a New Right perspective (as discussed in Crouch 1983); and is also a recurring theme in approaches from the Left (LEWRG 1982; Ginsburg 1979; Cawson 1982) and Centre (Bosanquet 1983). The New Right, however, is particularly concerned with the power of trade unions (rather than business groups) and with the expansion of the commercial private sector.

The New Right also ignores the fact that resources can be used more effectively without increasing the proportion of private production or finance. One way of improving the service would be through specific campaigns and measures aimed at preventing illness (Henderson and Cohen 1984: 63–8). Consultants and doctors could also be made much more aware of the financial costs of certain types of treatment (Stillwell 1984: 101) and be given more information on how to manage their health-care systems (Maynard 1983: 34). Conservative practice, as opposed to New Right ideology, has attempted—through new efficiency drives and management systems—to implement some of these measures in the public sector. These issues have been highlighted by recent attempts to compel doctors to prescribe the cheapest available form of a drug rather than well-known and expensive brand names. However, attempts to evaluate more accurately levels of efficiency would require an increase in administrative costs; whilst the liberalization of the state monopoly would, paradoxically, necessitate even more intervention in order to issue standardized guidelines. There is no guarantee that the private sector will operate more efficiently or that it will contribute to a strategy of prevention instead of purely commercial exploitation of needs and expectations. As Maynard points out, patients in both state and private sectors have had little incentive to minimize costs since the third party (either the NHS or an insurance company) usually pays the bill.

These arguments suggest that the controversy over health care is directed towards strengthening the political-electoral power of certain groups rather than improving health and welfare on the basis of economic rationality. Whilst expenditure on a service is not necessarily the best indicator of quality, it is worth noting that the amount spent in Britain has been much less than in most other Western countries both in terms of health staffing and hospital activity levels and as a proportion of GNP over the last three decades (Maxwell 1984). In 1982, for instance, the UK spent 5.3 per cent of GNP on health care in comparison to 9.9 per cent by the USA, 8.1 per cent by France and 8.8 per cent by West Germany (Mohan and Woods 1985: 200). Similarly, criticisms of the bureaucratization of the NHS do not appear to take into consideration its lower-than-average expenditure on administration in comparison with most other health-care systems (Maynard 1983: 33; OECD 1978). Even if we focus exclusively on the UK, we may question the extent to which the private provision of health care improves efficiency, let alone reduces inequalities, especially in the light of criticisms, on the one hand, of the NHS as failing to achieve egalitarian goals (Le Grand 1982) and, on the other, of the private sector accentuating these inequalities (O'Higgins 1985: 174–8). The development of the private sector is now considered in more detail.

THE DEVELOPMENT OF PRIVATE HEALTH CARE

Massive state intervention in the provision of health care has, until recently, left little room for the expansion of private health schemes. The largest private health insurance company, the British United Provident Association (BUPA) was formed in 1947 and expanded mainly on the basis of mergers with the other provident societies (e.g. the Oxford and District Provident Association). In 1949 BUPA, the London Provident Association for Hospital Services and the Western Provident Association (WPA) had 49,000 subscribers out of an overall total of only 65,000 subscribers to provident societies. Over the next fifteen years there was a gradual though unspectacular expansion: in 1964, BUPA had 510,000 subscribers, the London Provident Association, 81,000 subscribers and the WPA, 25,000 subscribers. This pattern of growth continued for another decade and was followed by a drop in subscribers (Table 2.1). However, from 1977 the number of subscribers has increased rapidly from 1 million to 1.6 million (1980) and 1.9 million (1982). The number of people covered by these subscriptions has risen accordingly from 120,000 (1950), to 995,000 (1960), to 1.9 million (1970) and 4.5 million (1985). The latter figure represents 8 per cent of the population.

Rising incomes, particularly for certain occupational groups, have contributed to the recent expansion in 'occupational' and 'group' subscriptions rather than 'individual' subscriptions (Table 2.2). In fact, the latter have dropped significantly over the past four years. Group schemes are organized by an employer or trade union or professional body and enable the group to obtain a discount. Occupational schemes are run by employers for their staff, often as part of the terms of employment; and the subscriptions are paid either entirely or

Table 2.1   Private health coverage and subscribers, 1950–85

Year	Person insured (000s)	Subscribers (000s)	Annual net change (000s)
1950	120	56	7
1955	585	247	52
1960	995	467	48
1965	1,445	680	48
1970	1,982	930	44
1975	2,315	1,087	–9
1976	2,251	1,057	–30
1977	2,254	1,057	0
1978	2,388	1,118	61
1979	2,765	1,292	174
1980	3,577	1,647	355
1981	4,116	1,863	216
1982	4,200	1,916	53
1985	4,500	2,100	61

Sources: BUPA 1983; Maynard 1982: 139; CSO 1987: 132.

partly by the employer. As West points out, group schemes have increasingly become a standard fringe benefit, partly as a result of wage restraint exercised in the 1970s (West 1984: 113). The schemes usually cover in-patient and out-patient treatment and nursing at home including payment towards the cost of accommodation in a hospital or nursing home; the fees of physicians, anaesthetists, specialists and surgeons; and the cost of tests, treatment and consultations. They provide a service mainly in the area of elective surgery rather than emergency care or treatment for long-term chronic illnesses. The main problem for the societies has been to market insurance premiums at a sufficiently low price to be competitive with a free health service. Adjustment and innovation have been key factors in ensuring their survival.

The growth of the private sector should also be seen in the context of a general rise in expenditure on health. Firstly, the amount spent on private health services constitutes only a very small fraction (between 3 per cent and 5 per cent) of the total health budget (Klein 1983: 154). In 1980 expenditure on health care by the provident associations was 1.09 per cent of the

Table 2.2   Changes in type of subscriber, 1976–80

		No. (000s)	Change (%)
(a)	Individual subscribers		
	1976	275	–6.5
	1977	257	–6.5
	1978	249	–3.1
	1979	260	+4.4
	1980	270	+3.8
(b)	Occupational subscribers		
	1976	335	–7.2
	1977	320	–4.5
	1978	333	+4.0
	1979	368	+10.5
	1980	497	+35.0
(c)	Group subscribers		
	1976	447	+3.5
	1977	480	+7.4
	1978	536	+11.7
	1979	671	+25.2
	1980	869	+29.5

Sources: BUPA 1983; Maynard 1982: 138

amount spent on the NHS and 0.06 per cent of GNP (Maynard 1982: 141). However, the private sector is expanding rapidly—total private spending on health care grew at an annual rate more than four times that of the NHS to exceed £1 billion or about 5 per cent of NHS spending in 1986 (Office of Health Economics 1987 quoted in the *Guardian* Newspaper 15th June 1987).

The market leaders in providing private insurance are BUPA (62 per cent), Private Patients Plan (PPP) (20 per cent) and WPA (7 per cent). As shown in Table 2.3, they are all non-profit organizations, although in future there is likely to be an increasing challenge from the commercial private sector, particularly the new 'for profit' organizations such as the American company 'Health First'.

The private sector is important both in symbolic and material terms. Even in the 1950s and 1960s the provident societies were used by critics of the NHS as a sign of its

Table 2.3   Private health-care coverage and benefits, 1983

	Numbers covered (1000s) & percentage share		Benefits paid (£000s) & percentage share	
Non-profit				
BUPA	3,015	62.1	191,261	59.9
PPP	950	19.6	79,637	25.0
Western Provident	350	7.2	20,495	6.4
Bristol Contributory	75	1.5	4,618	1.4
Exeter Hospital Aid	50	1.0	604	0.2
Civil Service Medical Aid	36	0.7	1,489	0.5
Provincial Hospital Services	10	0.2	270	0.1
Private Patients Anglia	3	0.1	25	—
Total non-profit	4,498	92.4	298,399	93.5
For profit				
Crusader	156	3.2	7,700	2.4
Mutual of Omaha	60	1.2	3,400	1.1
Orion	60	1.2	5,100	1.6
Allied Medical	50	1.0	2,000	0.6
Iron Trades	40	0.8	2,600	0.8
Crown	2	—	6	—
Total for profit	368	7.6	20,806	6.5
Overall totals	4,857	100.0	319,205	100.0

Source: BUPA 1983.

limitations and the desire by many people for an alternative to it. The provident societies became a 'rallying point for critics of the welfare state' (Mencher 1967: 30–1). On the other hand, there has always been a more obvious material basis for the survival of the societies. In the late 1960s and 1970s they managed to capture the occupational sector, whilst in the 1980s the prospects for expansion are most evident in the construction of new hospitals and nursing homes, a trend undoubtedly encouraged by the shortcomings of the state sector under both Labour and, especially, Conservative policy. American Medical International has been a forerunner in the construction of private hospitals: sixteen had been completed by 1986 and several more were under construction. Their location close to NHS hospitals may serve several strategic purposes: to shift emergency cases back to the NHS and to gain access to expensive equipment; to attract patients and staff to the private sector; and to make it easy for part-time consultants to move swiftly from one place of work to the other. 'For profit' organizations have begun to outpace charitable and religious institutions as providers of hospital beds: their proportionate share of private-sector hospital beds rose from 29 per cent in 1979 to nearly 50 per cent in 1986; and within the 'for profit' sector, 'American chains have increased their market share from 2 per cent to 22 per cent' (Jenkins 1986: 6).

Amendments in supplementary benefit regulations (1980 and 1983) have also had a direct impact on private provision by extending such benefits to cover the cost of residential accommodation in the private sector for those who needed it but could not find it in the state sector. Payments by the Department of Health and Social Security for such privately run accommodation rose from £6 million in 1978 to £280 million in 1985, with the latter figure representing around 10 per cent of state expenditure on the personal social services (Loney 1986: 11). These changes have provided managers in the public sector with 'an incentive to transfer those elderly in need of long-term care, and eligible for assistance via supplementary benefit payments, to the private residential sector' (Robinson 1986: 16).

Stimuli to the expansion of private hospitals have been provided by the government-sponsored Business Expansion Scheme, which granted tax-payers in the highest bands generous tax relief if they invested in the development of British businesses for a maximum of five years; and by certain organizational changes—for instance, the abolition of the Health Services Board and the requirement that private developers refer instead to the secretary of state; and the relaxation of town and country planning legislation implicit in the request to local authorities to 'avoid placing unjustified obstacles in the way of development' (Mohan and Woods 1985: 206–7).

The practical outcome of these determinants of private expansion is uneven. There has been a rapid increase in the number of beds available in private hospitals and nursing homes from 32,900 in 1980 to 51,000 in 1985 (Table 2.4). This may reflect the impact of the above factors. However, the provision of hospital beds (Table 2.5) is in danger of exceeding current demand (partly because of the fall in length of hospital stays), is concentrated in particular regions (Table 2.6) and is thus likely to contradict government policies which favour a transfer of resources from the London RHAs to the relatively deprived North and the Midlands (Mohan and Woods 1985: 211). By comparison, there is still considerable scope for the expansion of private nursing homes and of sheltered accommodation for long-term residents. In 1985 there were about 30,000 beds in the private sector for geriatric and terminal care and 125,000 places for long-term residents in rest homes. According to one recent study there is a need for between a quarter and half a million units of sheltered accommodation, although they are only being developed at the rate of about 8,000 units per year (*Times*, 7 June 1985). The link between public expenditure constraint and private expansion (and *vice versa*) is direct. With the public sector also providing a subsidy to private access, the following trends are hardly surprising: a 60 per cent increase between 1979 and 1983 in the number of private registered places for the elderly and disabled (Robinson 1986: 16); and an increase between 1982 and 1984 in private and voluntary nursing homes offering long-term care (from 1,085 with 27,039 beds to 1,259 with 32,713 beds) and in residential care homes (from 3,949 with 81,089 beds to 5,222 with 101,314 beds) (Day 1985: 282).

Politically, the various forms of private sector expansion since 1979 may have weakened resistance to the notion of private provision of health services, particularly when this has been related to direct state intervention, for instance in the

Table 2.4 Nursing homes and private hospitals, England and Wales (beds available) (000s), 1971–85

Registered nursing homes and private hospitals (beds available)	1971	1976	1980	1981	1982	1983	1984	1985
	25.3	30.6	32.9	33.5	36.0	39.5	44.5	51.0

Source: CSO; 1987: 132.

Table 2.5   Private surgical beds and hospitals, UK, 1975–80

Year	Hospitals	Beds
1975	105	2,279
1976	128	2,802
1977	130	3,305
1978	141	2,971
1979	142	3,033
1980	153	3,150
1984	172	8,241

Note: All the figures except those for 1984 include the Republic of Ireland

Source: BUPA (personal communication); Maynard 1982: 151.

Table 2.6   Regional distribution of private beds and institutions

Region	Private hospital (acute) beds (1984)	Registered private nursing homes & clinics (1983)	Total beds available (1983)
Northern	98	22	794
Yorkshire	557	80	2,508
Trent	475	82	2,377
East Anglia	254	40	956
North West Thames	834	58	2,504
North East Thames	1,537	76	2,988
South East Thames	632	212	5,601
South West Thames	847	161	4,454
Wessex	508	142	3,146
Oxford	425	57	2,048
South West	329	144	3,478
West Midlands	384	90	2,531
Mersey	235	83	2,135
North West	446	69	2,534
Total	7,561	1,316	38,054

Source: BUPA (personal communication); CSO 1985: 70.

loosening up of statutory monoplies, finance of private services and regulatory legislation. Thus recent legislation (Health and Social Services and Social Security Adjudications Act 1983, and Registered Homes Act 1984), aimed at preventing unscrupulous practices and raising standards in private residential accommodation, may have enhanced its appeal. The 1983 Act made it illegal for an unregistered nursing home to advertise or imply that it offered nursing care. More stringent controls have been applied on the staffing of nursing homes; and guidelines have been introduced for homes to provide information about the cost of the service and of the facilities available. These and other requirements have been incorporated in documents produced by the Avebury Report (1984) and by the National Association of Health Authorities (1985). The most important control on private residential homes is the requirement for annual inspection. However, it is very difficult for a local authority to close a home if it is starved of funds and has no residential places for the displaced occupants. Private provision of care for the elderly has surpassed the voluntary sector; in turn, the two combined offer as many, if not more, facilities than local authorities. The proportionate role of the private health sector has increased most of all in the development of hospitals and nursing homes. It has not generated the same degree of resistance and controversy from public health employees as the competitive tendering of some services, since there have been very few closures and job losses in state residential care.

Social changes have not produced uniform effects in acceptance of and access to private health care. Regional differences in the provision of private health care are particularly striking with 39.8 acute beds per 100,000 people in the North East Thames RHA and 2.1 per 100,000 people in the Northern RHA (Mohan and Woods 1986: 207). The proportion of people privately insured ranges from 13 per cent in the outer metropolitan area in the South East to between 7 and 10 per cent in all other areas with the exception of the North, Wales and Scotland with only 3 per cent. (see Table 2.6). Future plans for the expansion of private hospitals indicate a similar bias. This is hardly surprising, particularly if one considers income and employment patterns across the nation.

Within the occupational structure, status, income and gender are important determinants of access to private health care. Twenty-three per cent of professionals and 19 per cent of employers and managers were covered by schemes. This is particularly true of the 45–64 age group. Among semi-skilled and unskilled manual workers coverage, at around 2 per cent, was minimal. Among professionals, men outnumbered women by a ratio of 7:1; and among employers and managers the ratio was 5:1. Women in paid employment were much more likely to be covered by the policy of a spouse than one of their own. Men who worked part-time were almost as likely as those in full-time employment to hold a policy whereas among women, full-time workers enjoyed a 5:1 advantage over part-time workers. Part of the difference may be accounted for by the fact that women who work part-time are more likely to be married than those who work full-time.

Apart from location in terms of region, class, income and gender, action by employers was also a crucial determinant of membership: 52 per cent had been enrolled onto a scheme by their employer and in over half of these cases the employer paid the entire subscription. The remainder had either joined an individual scheme or a group scheme not run by the employer. Among those who were in employment, 55 per cent were in group schemes run by an employer or a company scheme. Membership of individual schemes varied from 19 per cent of those who were in employment to 50 per cent of those who were not. Although similar proportions of men and women were covered by policies, among policy-holders men predominated by 3:1. However, single women were more likely than single men to hold their own policy, for example by about 2:1 among those over 45 years of age (OPCS 1985: 169–72).

Although in the 1984 survey on Attitudes to Welfare (University of Kent) we found that social location was usually a weak indicator of overall satisfaction with the NHS, it is undoubtedly a strong indicator of access to private health care. This may conflict with the assumption by critics of state services that people are opting for private care simply because they are dissatisfied with the public sector; the more plausible explanation is that those with better incomes, occupations and levels of education have greater choice. This corresponds with the findings from the 100 in-depth interviews which followed the above survey: certain groups expressed much greater interest in the notion of freedom of choice (even if only within the NHS) rather than in voice and control of services (Papadakis and Taylor-Gooby 1987). This applied particularly to people with university qualifications who were much more likely than those with fewer formal qualifications to emphasize choice. A similar division emerged in relation to income, class and occupational group. An interest in freedom of choice was more closely related to a desire to maintain rather than increase levels of state expenditure. Emphasis on freedom of choice related strongly to a desire for exit from the NHS.

Private health care is clearly more acceptable to certain social groups. Socio-economic location also influences perceptions of redistribution in health and other services: people on high incomes see the state sector as giving the best value for money to those on low incomes, whilst those on low incomes adopt the opposite view. The critique of welfare spending is supported by the most vocal and influential groups, although this might wane if they perceive a threat to the benefits they derive from the welfare state (Taylor-Gooby and Papadakis 1985). Although not as strongly favoured as the NHS, private health care was regarded as very important by 33 per cent of the national survey sample, and as fairly important by 41 per cent. In the in-depth interviews, Conservative Party supporters expressed the greatest interest in freedom of choice. If the Conservatives continue to pursue a policy of retrenchment, leading to a decline in standards, many people might be compelled to opt for 'freedom of choice'. This is not, however, likely to relate in a straightforward manner to social location.

Whilst the existence of the private sector may be less a reflection of the shortcomings of the NHS and more a result of private affluence linked to an ideology of choice, events over the past decade have begun to provide a material basis for the critique of and exit from the NHS. To this extent, the private sector does become a reflection of the shortcomings of the NHS. In the 1984 survey, the most frequent complaints about the service were about the length of waiting lists and the inadequate numbers of doctors and nurses. People also complained about the impersonal attitude of doctors and their own experiences of remoteness, lack of communication and inflexibility on the part of specialists and administrators.

Not surprisingly, some of these complaints form the basis of advertising campaigns by the private health sector: flexibility and choice in admission to hospital; choice of doctors and specialists; privacy and flexible visiting hours; almost instant attention; and, in an appeal to occupational groups, the value in terms of business efficiency and productivity. Choice, consumer control and company efficiency are three important selling points for the schemes. However, to ensure their expansion and survival, both the provident societies and commercial health companies need to pursue a strategy on three fronts: remain competitive despite spiralling costs; introduce innovations and adapt schemes to changing needs or preferences; and sustain an atmosphere of discussion over public and private welfare with a view both to co-operation with the NHS and to redrawing or blurring the boundaries between the two.

In considering the private sector independently of political pressures one is struck by its tiny size, the pressures it faces in terms of costs, and the incentive to market itself effectively. An important consideration, particular to health care, is that the cost of medical care has always risen faster than the average rate of inflation. Between 1979 and 1984 hospital charges for private patients doubled; in 1981, for the first time ever, the provident societies suffered losses; and the rate of growth of private medical insurance dropped from a peak of 27 per cent in 1980 to 9 per cent in 1983. To counter these difficulties a number of innovations have been introduced: in April 1984 BUPA arrived at an agreement with 140 private hospitals for inclusive charges covering accommodation, meals, theatre fees, nursing care, dressing and drugs, but excluding doctors' fees; the trend towards building luxury-style hospitals has been reversed and some even offer patients shared accommodation; and the ocupational sector has assumed prime importance, accounting for 75 per cent of new business and covering two-thirds of everyone with private medical insurance. Some of the smaller companies have begun to experiment with new cost-cutting schemes: PPP have a plan which provides cover if the NHS waiting list stretches out to more than six weeks—if not, the subscriber uses the NHS and receives a cash benefit; Crown Life offer 'no claim' bonuses and discounts; and in some schemes one can receive cover only for serious medical conditions. The arrival of commercial private health companies into a sector so far dominated by non-profit making provident associations has intensified competition and the effort to contain costs. It is also leading to greater co-operation between the state and private sectors.

The financial viability of the private sector will largely depend on how quickly it can continue to introduce innovative practices. The interest, particularly among women, in preventive medicine has led to a growth in private screening clinics: in 1983 BUPA screened over 10,000 women at its London centre compared to 2,600 women in 1971. This form of welfare reflects both new forms of economic rationality and the involvement of women in the labour force since employers pay for about half of these screenings. In 1983 BUPA screened 40,000 people. Many day-surgery units provide quick and effective treatment and undoubtedly help to relieve the pressure on the NHS. The costs of and pressures on the public GP service may give rise to further initiatives, like the Harrow Centre, which offered a private GP service to around 3,000 patients. However, even this initiative was short-lived and has since been taken over by an American firm concentrating on 'occupational medicine' such as the screening of potential employees.

CONCLUSION

Public dissatisfaction over certain aspects of the NHS was accompanied by governmental emphasis on the importance of individual, family and community provision of welfare. The 1985 Green Paper on social security reform set out to implement change on the 'twin pillars of provision—individual and state—with stronger emphasis on individual provision than hitherto' (DHSS 1985a: 45). However, government strategies are not unambiguously poised to support the private sector: they do not include tax relief on private health insurance premiums and they often encourage competition between the two sectors. The private sector does not represent a coherent, united alternative. It is characterized by heterogeneity particularly in the contrasting approaches of non-profit and profit-making institutions in competition with each other (Maynard 1984: 107). Financial losses linked to spiralling costs are likely to limit its potential for further expansion. Despite the greater willingness among sections of the population to contemplate exit from the state sector, most cannot afford it. Ironically, the choice of private health care is one taken up not so much by individuals or families (who comprise a diminishing proportion of subscribers) but by companies and other employment-based organizations, thus running 'counter to the argument that individuals should be left to make their own purchasing decisions' (West 1984: 113).

A number of perspectives emerge from the preceding discussion. The deterioration of public services linked to increasing availability of private services could mean that 'many of the articulate professional and middle-income groups who frequently spearhead the defence of the welfare state will find it more feasible to strive for improved access to private benefits than to campaign for public services' (Crouch 1985a: 11). While the pessimistic perspective adopted by Crouch is based on the work of Olson (1965) and the notion of a 'collective goods handicap' that would inhibit such campaigns, Hirschman points to the mechanisms that might facilitate the emergence of collective action (Hirschman 1982). (This is discussed further in the final chapter.)

Despite the widespread support for the NHS, there has been little resistance to the changes that have occurred over the two terms of Conservative government. The government has no doubt adopted a more cautious approach than it originally intended because of the massive support in favour of the NHS. However, the lack of resistance may also reflect the increasing preparedness of the public to contemplate the private option, and the manner in which economic pressures have effectively privatized part of a service which had set as its goal the universal provision of services. The state, however, still remains heavily involved in the process of regulation and subsidization of the private sector, and the boundaries between public and private provision remain highly complex and enmeshed.

3 Private Education

BACKGROUND

If education is the organized acquisition of knowledge and 'private' is enterpreted to mean 'outside the state-maintained sector', the scope of private education is vast. Much of people's lives is concerned with learning in informal conversation, access to social networks, use of mass media and specialist journals, books and information technology, attendance at commercial and voluntary courses and training sessions, use of state and private higher and further education facilities, private or state schooling or tutoring at primary and secondary stages in accordance with the parental duties laid down in the Education Acts, and the use of various forms of pre-school education, shading off into child care. In addition, there are a wide range of systems of supplementary schooling, including private tutoring for examinations, compensatory schooling to counter racist bias in the state system (Stone 1981) and tuition in athletic and cultural pursuits not fully covered in the state curriculum.

Here our focus is on formal school systems for three reasons: these form the central issue in political and social policy debate about public and private education; the public–private division has been seen as underlying important aspects of the system of class inequalities with which much of public policy has been concerned since the Second World War; and the structure and influence of private education has been seen as amenable to influence by public policy though social engineering.

STATE INTERVENTION IN SCHOOLING

The first formal involvement of the state in education was in the requirement that instruction be provided in the Factory Acts of the early nineteenth century. These were tentative interventions into a field in which working-, middle-, and upper-class groups made their own arrangements to meet needs for child care, instruction and the demarcation of privilege. The development of state education can be seen as the incursion of official policy into a highly developed and differentiated sphere of activity, with different effects for each social class.

For the various fractions of the working class, dame schools, the Sunday schooling movement, and the voluntary and fee-paying schools of the religious societies, often organized on a monitorial basis, provided a system of child care and education, partially supported by government grants to the voluntary societies from 1833 onwards. Writers such as Johnson argue that state involvement was primarily motivated by 'a Tory–Anglican coalition' anxious to inculcate the values of 'work and loyal citizenship' (Johnson 1976: 51). The 1870 Foster Act supplemented this system by 'filling the gaps' (MacLure 1974: 100). The progressive extension of state grants and the creation of county Local Education Authorities (LEAs) in 1902 gave the state effective control over working-class elementary education. In the first quarter of the twentieth century, the development of Board of Education grants, the large-scale extension of a range of state secondary schools and the creation of an expanding national system of scholarships culminated in the provision of secondary education for all in the 1944 Act.

The Newcastle Commission had estimated that some 95 per cent of the children of the poorer classes received between four and six years of schooling in the late 1850s (Newcastle Report 1861, ch. 6). The Clarendon Commission of 1864 investigated the nine great all-male 'public' schools, 'the chief nurseries of our statesmen', and the Taunton Commission of 1868 the endowed and profit-making privately owned schools provided for other members of the middle and upper classes—mostly for boys. This was an expanding market: the Commission identified over 3,000 endowed and 10,000 privately owned schools. The principal results of these investigations were a series of recommendations to modernize curriculum, increased support for the extension of the middle-class schooling, especially for women, and the reorganization of endowments to enable schools to apply resources to meet the effective demands of the middle class rather than the objectives identified by benefactors. While the working-class educational tradition investigated by Newcastle had passed almost entirely into the state sector by the end of the century, the upper-class system studied by Clarendon has remained formally independent, and the middle-class tradition studied by Taunton has become divided. Those schools which accepted state grants and scholarship pupils were assimilated as state grammar schools in the early twentieth century, while those which were able to command sufficient fees and endowments maintained an independent private status.

Of these, virtually all have become educational charities. Less than 10 per cent of the private schools listed in the Independent Schools Information Service Census are run as limited companies, and less than 15 per cent are owned by individuals. These are almost all preparatory (Independent Schools Information Service [ISIS] 1986a: 6). To these must be added a small number of quasi-private schools which received direct grants from the Board of Education in return for a commitment to provide at least a quarter of their places free under regulations set out in 1926. Our interest in private schooling is focused on these schools which have preserved a complete separation from the development of the state education service over the past century—from one perspective, the last vestiges of private education for all, from another an extraordinarily resilient phenomenon in the face of the hurricane of state intervention which has swept through many aspects of social life.

Private schools in the UK may be divided into four categories: the pre-eminent 'inner nine' investigated by Clarendon (Charterhouse, Eton, Harrow, Merchant Taylor's, Rugby, Shrewsbury, St Paul's, Westminster and Winchester), the remaining 217 Head Master's Conference (HMC) schools (membership depends upon selection by existing members using criteria of academic freedom, educational policy and academic standards, and confers considerable prestige—Burnet 1986, Introduction), the 1,127 schools which are members of the less prestigious associations (the Society of Headmasters of Independent Schools, the Girls' Boarding School Association, the Governing Bodies' Association, etc.) and the rump of 1,488 schools whose academic standards and social prestige do not enable them to join the more favoured group. Over the period since the Second War, changes have occurred which are explicable to a considerable extent in terms of development of state schooling and the labour market. These constitute an indirect state challenge to the private sector by undermining its market position. The most prestigious private schools have resisted this attempt to encroach on their preserve as successfully as they resisted earlier interventions.

The numbers of private schools has declined absolutely, the decrease being concentrated among the weaker schools not recognized as efficient and particularly in the primary age-range (Table 3.1). This is probably partly the result of the expansion of state secondary education and of the shift to comprehensive schools (which has destroyed two markets: that for schools geared to coaching for state selection tests and that for those who regard state secondary modern education as inferior or stigmatic). In addition improvements in primary education, given official approval in the Plowden Report (1967), have further undermined private preparatory schooling.

The 'tightening bond' between schooling and work, linked by the conduits of certification at O level and A level and at university (entrance to which is typically dependent on A level qualifications) has been reflected in an increasing exam orientation and in the expansion of sixth-forms in both state and private sector. Pass rates at A level in private schools have improved at a rate sufficient to ensure that pupils have an even greater relative chance of gaining university matriculation. The market challenge of state sixth-form colleges in some areas has recently attracted pupils from some weaker private schools (Walford 1986).

Third, opportunities for women's education have expanded,

Table 3.1   Schools and pupils, England and Wales, 1963, 1973, 1983

1963	Private schools		Direct grant	Maintained		
	Recognized efficient	Not recognized		Primary	Non-selective secondary	Selective secondary
Schools	1,509	2,111	179	23,083	4,392	1,499
Male pupils Primary	72,100	52,300	6,200	2,124,000		
Secondary to school-leaving age	41,800	19,400	27,800		913,000	241,000
Secondary above-school-leaving age	42,400	9,200	21,600		110,000	174,000
Female pupils Primary	52,300	49,400	10,100	2,021,000		
Secondary to school-leaving age	44,900	20,200	28,200		861,000	241,000
Secondary above school-leaving age	32,700	9,800	18,300		92,000	148,000

1973	Private schools		Direct grant	Maintained		
	Recognized efficient	Not recognized		Primary	Non-selective secondary	Selective secondary
Schools	1,382	1,027	176	23,148	4,297	862
Male pupils Primary	78,500	33,700	6,500	2,484,000		
Secondary to school-leaving age	53,400	7,100	31,800		1,237,000	163,500
Secondary above school-leaving age	37,300	2,300	19,900		223,900	93,300
Female pupils Primary	51,500	30,600	9,300	2,374,000		
Secondary to school-leaving age	44,700	8,200	32,900		1,174,000	173,400
Secondary above school-leaving age	26,600	2,400	19,500		205,400	91,500

Table 3.1   continued

1983	Private schools	Direct grant	Primary	Maintained Non-selective secondary	Selective secondary
Schools	2,342	—	20,361	3,717	188
Male pupils Primary	88,800	—	1,673,000		
Secondary to school-leaving age	132,300	—		1,666,000	61,400
Secondary above school-leaving age	39,100	—		149,700	16,700
Female Primary	79,300	—	1,787,000		
Secondary to school-leaving age	111,900	—		1,605,000	62,300
Secondary above school leaving age	27,500	—		166,200	16,300

Notes:
— Direct grant excludes special, hospital, institutional and technical schools.
— The distinction between recognized and unrecognized schools was terminated in 1978.
— Nursery schools are excluded from all categories.
— State selective refers to grammar and technical schools.
— The minimum school-leaving age was raised to 15 in 1963–4 and to 16 in 1972–3.
— The direct grant was phased out in 1976; about two-thirds of direct-grant schools became private, and most of the rest joined the state sector.

Sources: DES Statistics of Education 1963, part 1, Tables 4 and 6; 1973, part 1, Tables 1 and 5; 1983, Schools section, Tables A2/83c and A4/83.

particularly in the development of mixed schooling in previously all-male schools. This is partly a result of pressures for women to gain credentials, and of the expansion of girls' education in state schools expressed in the Equal Opportunities and Sex Discrimination legislation of the 1970s, partly the outcome of cultural changes which have enabled women to enter arenas of male privilege. The proportion of girl boarders in HMC schools has risen from 2.5 per cent to 12.5 per cent between 1974 and 1986 and the proportion of girl day-pupils from 3.5 per cent to 15 per cent (Walford 1986: 142; ISIS 1986a: 6). John Rae, Head of Westminster, writes that 'in the early sixties no public [HMC] school was co-educational. ... In 1979, sixty out of 210 schools in the HMC admitted girls' (quoted in Walford, 1986: 140). Most HMC schools now have girls, although some only admit at sixth-form level. The increase in the proportion of girls in the high-status schools has been balanced to some extent by a decrease in the numbers attending single-sex Girls' Boarding School Association schools.

The proportion of school children in England and Wales in private schools fluctuated within a narrow band of 6–8 per cent over the post-war period. Recent interest in private education stemming from a generalized concern about state standards expressed in 'Black Papers' from 1969 onwards and Callaghan's 1976 Great Debate, and lent added impetus by the effect of spending constraint and industrial action by state school teachers between 1985 and 1987 has produced an increase of less than 1 per cent in numbers at schools covered by the ISIS census. The operation of changes in demand and in the character of state schooling thus have a considerable effect. Many commentators suggest that there has been a major shift in school ethos reflected in curriculum and a revaluing of academic achievement.

Simon and Bradley chart the shift in public school educational values in the nineteenth century from 'muscular Christianity' to Matthew Arnold's ideal of 'godliness and good learning' (Simon and Bradley 1975, ch. 1). More recently, the revolution in academic emphasis in private schools had been charted by Walford, who stresses the new professionalism among teachers (Walford 1984b: 111); by Rae, who emphasizes the contribution to curriculum development (Rae 1981); and by Halsey, Heath and Ridge who analyse the increases in A level pass grades (1984: 23). The claim that private schools overemphasize sport or classical as against modern studies is hard to substantiate. One example of public school involvement in teaching development is provided by the Association for Science Education, the largest and most influential subject-orientated teachers' association in the UK, with some 17,000 members. It has strong links with the Institute of Physics, the Royal Society of Chemistry and the British Association for the Advancement of Science. Its historical roots lie in the Association of Public School Science Masters (founded in 1902) and it is still heavily influenced by private schools, who provide some 30 per cent of its committee members and the editor of its journal. The association is highly influential in curriculum development in science. An illustration of the level of private-school involvement is provided by the fact that about a third of the schools chosen for the trials of Nuffield A level physics were private. The proportion of university entrants from private schools reading science is still rather lower than that for state schools, but proportions for medicine and technology are now closely comparable (ISIS 1986a: 12).

The distinctive school ethos has also shifted. Many schools have moved away from the traditional emphasis on chapel, sport, house spirit and hierarchy:

In its place has grown a revised version of the traditional doctrine of the whole man, which includes an almost Maoist devotion to the idea that academic studies should be tempered with both culture and practical skills ... art, music, drama and handicraft have started flourishing as never before.
(Venning 1973: 174)

THE INFLUENCE OF THE PRIVATE SECTOR

Private schooling for the upper class unlike private schooling for the lower classes has shown itself resilient and adaptable— virtually uninfluenced directly by state intervention, and well able to protect its market in response to the indirect challenges of changes in state provision. However, private schools provide education for a small proportion of the total number of those in school. They have declined in the long term and seem unlikely to expand on a mass scale, although they are well able to hold their own. Indeed, Halsey's work showed that only a third of members of his top social class (higher-grade professionals, administrators, managers and proprietors; Halsey, Heath and Ridge 1980, Table 4.3) were schooled in the private sector. It might reasonably be asked: why is private education a matter of interest?

The extent of the sector's influence in both educational and social terms belies its size. It contains about a twentieth of all pupils, but about a sixth of all sixth-formers. Of these over 60 per cent leave with A levels as against 14 per cent for the state sector (Halsey, Heath and Ridge 1984: 25). It produces a quarter of entrants to higher education and a half of entrants to 'Oxbridge'—Oxford and Cambridge universities.

The second factor concerns social influence. Entrance to private schooling is effectively restricted by selection and fee-paying. Private school pupils have a greater probability of occupying prestigious social positions. These two features— the educational and the social significance of private schooling—have underlain policy debates in this area. Both come together in assertions about privilege and social division—as Kinnock puts it: 'private schools are not "incidental" to the class system. They are the very cement in the wall that divides British society' (1981, quoted in Walford 1984a: 1). This is the central claim that Dennison in a recent Hobart paperback is concerned to deny as 'meaningless' (Dennison 1984: 29) and Salter and Tapper describe as uninformed 'by a clear understanding of educational realities' (Salter and Tapper 1984: 200).

PRIVILEGE AND PRIVATE SCHOOLING

The issue of privilege is perhaps the most widely discussed aspect of private schooling. The claim that the schools both cater to a class and gender élite and serve to perpetuate the influence of that élite is widespread (Halsey, Heath and Ridge 1984; Rubinstein 1979; Delamont 1984; Arnot 1986: 144–5). In one sense the argument is simple. Very few people attend private schools. They are mainly upper class and (in the most prestigious schools) male. They get schooling that is in many ways better in quality than that provided by the state. This gives them access to élite positions. In any case, their access is improved by personal contact beyond that commmanded by ability.

However, the analytic implications of this empirical linking of class, gender, private schooling and privilege may be questioned. Just because many people who occupy high-status positions have attended private schools, this does not imply that attendance at the school is a causal factor in the production of élite status. The rich might be wasting their money!

Evidence for the simple version of the argument is available, but imperfect. We have seen already that just under 5 per cent of all pupils and some 8.5 per cent of secondary pupils are in private schools, the majority of these being male (see Table 3.1).

Quality of education is a contested issue. There is simply no agreement on what features of schools produce desired educational outcomes (Lawton 1980, ch. 7; Rutter *et al.* 1980, ch. 1). Private schools certainly have lower pupil–teacher ratios—11.9:1 in 1984 as against 16:1 in state secondaries, and 17.6:1 in all state schools [DES] (Department of Education and Science 1985, Table 1). However, as Walford points out, the difference may not be so striking when the larger proportion of private pupils demanding sixth form teaching is taken into account (Walford 1986: 230). They also offer a wider range of courses. The attractions of small-group teaching are commonly seen as an advantage of private schooling (Taylor-Gooby 1986: 238) and figure prominently in lists of the benefits of private schooling (Rae 1981; Gilkes 1957: 32; Walford 1986: 229). Teachers at private schools are more likely to be qualified and of graduate status—68 per cent were graduates in 1984 as against 43 per cent in state schools (DES 1985, Table 8). The fact that private schools appear willing to offer higher salaries may also be reflected in teaching quality. Information on salary levels is not conveniently available. However, the chair of the HMC has implied salaries are substantially higher (*Times Educational Supplement* 1986). In addition, Halsey and his colleagues in their study of educational experience (restriced to men) found that children at private schools were more likely to gain A levels whatever their class background (Halsey, Heath and Ridge 1980, ch. 8). All these factors point to, but do not demonstrate, a superior quality of schooling in the private sector.

Sixth-form education, A level qualifications and university entrance (in particular, Oxbridge entrance) are all strongly correlated with high earnings and social status (OPCS 1985, ch. 7; Reid 1979: 179–85; Halsey, Heath and Ridge 1980: 115).

Private schools account for 17 per cent of those over 16 years old in school (DES 1985, Table 12). The proportion increases with age (15 per cent of 16 year olds; 19 per cent of 17 year olds; 22 per cent of 18 year olds and 34 per cent of 19 year olds) and is about a third again as high for boys than girls. The schools also account for 23 per cent of those on A level courses (28 per cent for boys and 19 per cent for girls—as against the state sector which has roughly equal numbers of each sex) but only 7 per cent of those on non-A level courses over 15 (DES 1983: Table A/14). Over 60 per cent of private school leavers have at least one A level, as against 13 per cent for all state schools. Private schools produce about a quarter of all university entrants and about half of Oxbridge entrants.

The argument that private schooling improves life-chances through providing access to an 'old boy network' in addition to specifically educational resources is more difficult to substantiate. Rhetorical evidence of the small number of high-status social positions occupied by the male products of private schools (especially major private schools) is presented by many writers, mainly but not exclusively critical of private schooling (Newsom 1968, vol. 2: 236; Field 1981: 171; Miliband 1973: 57; Reid 1979, Table 6.13; Boyd 1973; ISIS 1986b: 12). Sampson traces some of the individual links between groups of pupils of particular schools whose interest is mutually advantageous in later life (Sampson 1983: 138–44). Perhaps the most arresting expression of the disproportionate influence wielded by the minorities educated in specific institutions is Newsom's histogram, in which the proportion of 14 year olds at six major HMC schools in 1963 is too small to show in the printer's ink, but the schools had none the less supplied two-thirds of the Cabinet at that time (Halsey, Heath and Ridge 1984: 18).

The application of this evidence can be criticized in a number of ways. First, as Dennison (1984, ch. 5) and ISIS (1986b: 13) point out, contemporary élites were educated some forty years ago, in the context of a somewhat different system.

Also, the list of groups ignores some of the most powerful individuals in modern society—such as trade-union leaders and pension-fund managers. A further line of criticism points out that the majority of private school products do not attain these élite positions.

The review of empirical evidence on the link between class, gender, private education and social status is an incomplete basis for argument. The social group that attended private schools might have got where they did anyway, either through individual ability or because class privilege operates in a manner to which schooling is incidental. Those who wish to describe the educational or social opportunities of private schooling as privilege are faced with one of the most intractable problems of educational sociology: to demonstrate a 'school effect'. Halsey and his colleagues use data from the Oxford Mobility Study (which is restricted to men) to make three points in a succinct review on the debate (Halsey, Heath and Ridge 1984: 21–38). The first point concerns entry into private schools. A meritocratic model of selection would suggest that entry to private schools is determined by ability. If it is assumed that the HMC schools recruit from the top of the ability range, the rough proportions of pupils from different social-class backgrounds who should enter them can be predicted on the basis of knowledge of the distribution of IQ by social class. Comparison of this model with evidence of what actually happens shows that selection is biased in favour of the upper social classes. Halsey's 'service-class' group have nearly twice the chance they would have on a strictly meritocratic basis to enter HMC schools whereas manual workers have about one-quarter (Halsey, Heath and Ridge 1980, Table 4.7).

If private school selection carries a class handicap, what of sixth-form education, A levels and the transition to higher education? As we have already noted, there is a tremendous concentration of sixth-form schooling in the private sector. Despite the sharp increase in the numbers of state school sixth-formers competing for university entrance over the last two decades, the private sector has more than held its own. The relative chances of a private as against a state school pupil leaving with the three A level passes crucial to university entrance have actually shifted in favour of the former. Further analysis of data from the Oxford Mobility Study shows that some 85 per cent of the difference between A level scores for private and state schools for those educated in the 1960s can be explained in terms of social background and length of sixth-form education. The time spent in the sixth-form is a far more important factor in accounting for A level scores than other differences between state and private schools. Thus the major school effect seems to be in the extra length of school careers in the private sector—crude resources, rather than some difference in kind in the education provided.

The third point continues the analysis to cover entry to higher education. In relation to university entrance, any school effect is again negligible compared with social background and length of sixth-form schooling: 'The schools as such are largely transmitters of pre-established inequalities' (Halsey, Heath and Ridge 1984: 34). Much discussion of private-school privilege has focused on Oxbridge entrance. The historic link between the most prestigious universities in the UK (and possibly the world) and independent schools is strong. In 1938/9 almost exactly three-quarters of male entrants and two-thirds of female entrants came from the private sector. By the 1960s the proportion had fallen to slightly over a half for both groups. At this level the challenge of the state sector had been held. By 1985 the proportion was almost exactly half.

The emphasis on Oxbridge entrance, the close ties with particular colleges and the effort devoted to devising a strategy to maintain the school's reputation are vividly documented in Walford's report of Oxbridge entrance planning meetings at one private school (Walford 1986). Both Robbins (1963) on Oxbridge and Franks (1966: 88) on Oxford indicated that entrants from private schools secured places at Oxbridge on the basis of lower average A level scores than those from state schools. In addition, traditional private boarding school entrants gained the highest proportion of third-class degrees, whereas state entrants gained the lowest proportion. However, progress towards securing a more even balance of able young people was made in the 1970s. In 1983 the Dover Committee at Oxford recommended the ending of special scholarship exams requiring a seventh term of sixth-form schooling, a procedure currently being adopted by Cambridge. Closed scholarships confined to pupils of particular HMC schools have been abolished.

The Dover Report shows that 62 per cent of university applicants with A level grades of two As and a C or better came from the state sector in 1982. However, this sector contributed only 51 per cent of Oxford entrants. This suggests that entry is not simply meritocratic.

None of this evidence is conclusive. It may be the case that the difference between private and state school output is simply the result of an untraced quirk in the distribution of scholastic ability in a particular social-class direction. However, there does seem to be a strong circumstantial case for suggesting that the superior performance of private school pupils results mainly from social background and the extra time spent in the sixth-forms. In the case of Oxbridge entrance, an additional 'social contact' factor may well be operating. The advice to prospective parents seems to be: 'It's too late to alter your class position. Enter the child into the sixth-form of an HMC school to get the sociologically attested advantages.'

Halsey and his colleagues conclude that, while the balance between parental class, school characteristics and sixth-form schooling is undecided, the appropriate programme for the reformer is to press for equalization of resources between state and private sectors. This might at least isolate school and extra-school effects. In contrast, Salter and Tapper argue that reformers are misguided. They claim that 'public schools provide a convenient institutional context for the obtaining and augmenting of social capital'—access to an influential network of social relations and connections (Salter and Tapper 1984: 199). Thus schooling is a 'catalyst rather than a crucial determinant in its own right' (p. 200). In this they range themselves against those who argue for the abolition of private schooling on the grounds that it perpetuates privilege: privilege comes from social class outside the school system, and will find ways of perpetuating itself whatever happens in schooling. From this perspective the evidence used in analysis of access, A level passes and Oxbridge entrance, can be accepted while its force is denied. Social background is the most important factor. This simply means we should focus our attention on social background itself, and not on one of the less important institutions through which it is expressed.

Since the existence, extent and nature of privilege existing within or transmitted by the private school system is a matter of uncertainty, we move on to consider other issues of debate in relation to provide schooling. The discussion of the development of state intervention stressed the capacity of the upper-class private sector, unlike the lower-class sector, to insulate itself effectively from direct governmental challenges, and to hold its own against indirect market challenges from the state sector.

If the history of state schooling has been largely a story of attempts by the state to gain control over the socialization of the working-class men and women as workers and parents (Arnot 1986; Birmingham Centre for Contemporary Cultural Studies 1981) and the story of working-class attempts to achieve self-expression in resistance to that system (Willis 1977), the story of the private sector is more a story of upper-class success in gaining power over state-mobilized resources while resisting attempts by government at interference.

POWER AND PRIVATE SCHOOLING

The slow encroachment of state schooling on the distinctive private education systems of, first, the working class at elementary level, then of the middle class at secondary level, has already been discussed. The power of the private education system for the upper class (power defined as the capacity to achieve effects in one's own interest against opposition) can be illustrated in its success at the major turning points of the development of British education. These are the settlement of the 1860s culminating in the Foster Act, which created an eclectic and incomplete education system for the working class by filling the gaps in private and voluntary schooling; and the settlement at the close of the Second World War, which extended state secondary education to all. The attempts of the Labour government of the late 1960s to reform examinations, introduce comprehensive education and radically restructure higher and further education in order to achieve greater social-class equality of access and outcome, constitute a further but somewhat inconsequential settlement.

In the two major settlements, private schooling for the working class was absorbed. The 1870 Act, the introduction of compulsory education in 1880, the extension of state grants and Education Board schooling resulted in an effective state take-over of elementary schooling by the end of the century. The state's penetration of working- and middle-class secondary schooling was not completed until the second settlement of the 1940s. 'In 1932 the Chuter Ede Committee on Private Schools recommended Board of Education inspection and registration of all private schools, those failing to reach minimum standards to be closed. This was not implemented until 1944' (Thane 1982: 203). Private education for lower social groups thereafter becomes of little importance.

The Newcastle, Clarendon and Taunton commissions had provided an overview of education needs and provisions in the 1860s. In response to the Taunton Report, Foster proposed legislation in 1869 to enable a substantial measure of state intervention. In a standard history, Musgrave writes that 'many of the public schools took fright, and ... formed the Headmaster's Conference to organize opposition to the Endowed Schools Bill' (Musgrave 1968: 39). However, under the version of the bill that became law, Charity Commissions were empowered to reorganize endowments to make the most efficient use of available resources for the education of both boys and girls: 'By 1873 over 300 schemes had been drawn up.... There was a tendency for these schemes ... to direct monies from the provision of working-class education to the establishment of new secondary schools for the middle-class' (Musgrave 1968: 39). Of these schools, some succeeded in establishing themselves as private institutions in the next century, while others ultimately joined the state sector as grammar schools. Educational opportunities for middle-class girls were expanded (David 1980: 118). For the main public schools, the danger of state interference was averted. The net result was more freedom to use endowments to meet changing upper-class needs.

Further struggles to gain concessions from state law turned on the question of charitable status. While charitable status, which carried with it relief from rates, corporation tax and tax on profits, had been available to the major public schools since Peel's 1842 Income Tax Act, the concession was only grudgingly extended until a test case brought by Brighton College in 1915 resulted in a clause in the 1927 Finance Act making all non-profit making charities tax-exempt (Jones 1982: 11). Tax relief on life-insurance-based savings schemes was an important subsidy to parents until it was abolished in 1984. The total value of the relief was in excess of £1 billion in 1983/4. These schemes were, of course, devoted to many other objects besides education (Taylor-Gooby 1985: 84; Wilkinson 1986: 33).

The second major education settlement was contained in the Butler Act of 1944, which embodied a broad inter-party consensus on mass secondary schooling. This was modified by the 1964–70 Labour government, which pushed for comprehensive rather than selective secondary schooling and attempted various reforms in examinations, curriculum, further and higher education designed to achieve greater equality, especially between social classes. Butler set up the Fleming Committee in the period of educational inquiry leading up to the 1944 Act as a response to pressure from the HMC. The brief was, 'to consider means whereby the association between the Public Schools ... and the general educational system of the country could be extended and developed'. The committee proposed a variety of schemes for LEAs to nominate children as day or boarding pupils to private schools. These proposals foundered for two reasons. First, the committee was unable to propose a selection procedure which met the private sector's requirement that it retained control over entry and the state sector's desire not to lose the most able pupils: 'any attempt to make use of the schemes which we propose in order to segregate abler children and to send them to Boarding Schools would be socially and educationally wrong'. However, 'the first task ... should be to remove ... the names of those for whom an education at the school applied for would not seem suitable. ...... It can never be satisfactory for a child to be educated at a school where the work is above his powers' (quoted in MacLure 1974: 213). Second, LEAs were unable to meet fees at two or three times the cost of state education. The problems of control and cash have undermined all subsequent attempts to alter the status of private schools.

The impact of the Fleming Report was minor—the DES extended the direct-grant list, authorities were encouraged to 'increase somewhat' the numbers of children for whom private school fees were subsidized and some (such as Hertfordshire) set up experimental 'bursary' schemes. Its real significance was that at a time when all-party concensus on the extension of secondary education to all with 'equality of opportunity' and 'parity of esteem' between the different types of state secondary schools (Spens 1938: 376–81; Norwood 1943, ch. 1) had been laboriously constructed, the issue of the role of the major private schools was confused (Thane 1982: 228) and a small additional subsidy in the shape of state sponsorship of a few extra able children obtained. As Butler put it, 'to use a railway metaphor, the first-class carriage had been shunted into an immense siding' (Butler 1973: 22)—or as Silver writes, 'The English public-school has never become amenable to the pressures of national policy-making ... it was untouched by Government-sponsored enquiries and reports during the Second World War and at the end of the 1960s' (Silver 1980: 18).

The next attempt to couple the private school carriage to the national train, and even to alter the seating arrangements within it, was the Public Schools Commission (1965–70) set up by Labour as a response to a 1964 manifesto commitment. The original terms of reference of the committee reflect the Labour Party's ambivalence on the issue (see Corbett 1978: 39). While they mention the social selectivity of the schools and explicitly refer to 'the divisive influence they now exert', the main task is 'to advise on the best way of integrating public schools within the state system of education', not to explore the possibilities of abolition or of the removal of fiscal and other privileges. Despite this, concern about the political climate led the HMC to appoint for the first time a public-relations firm in 1967 (Sampson 1983: 147). The first report in 1968 collated much useful information on the social status and subsequent career of private school pupils and on the financial relationship between school and state. Its recommendations had little effect. These called for the broadening of academic intake and a massive extension of state-sponsored pupils to fill something like half the places in integrated private schools. As in the Fleming Report, the issues of selection and cost were not resolved, and the net result was again the extension of local authority sponsorship and the removal of some minor fiscal advantages which were restored by the 1970 Conservative government. Vaizey's note of dissent argued that the commission had avoided the real issue of abolition, and instead proposed a different kind of recruitment. Labour policy on education has continued to evade the issue.

The commission was reconstituted in 1968 with a new chair (Donnison) and terms of reference that included direct-grant schools. These schools received grants from the DES in return for making at least 25 per cent of places available without fees. The arrangement gives them virtually complete independence from LEAs and a quasi-private status. The report (in 1970) provided a detailed defence of comprehensive education. The committee favoured the ending of the direct grant in order to integrate the schools into the state comprehensive system. However, the Conservative government, returned in 1970, gave a full commitment to supporting the private sector. In 1976 the next Labour government ended the direct grant, with the intention of strengthening state secondary education by integrating some 200 well-resourced and successful schools into it. The net result, however, was to reinforce the private sector and widen the gap between it and the state. Of the 174 schools, four closed, fifty-one became comprehensive, and the remaining 119, including some of the most successful schools in the country in terms of examination success and university entrance, became fully private. The schools who opted to go comprehensive were mainly controlled by the Roman Catholic Church, located in northern cities, and had a high proportion of free-place pupils. The shift was consolidated by the Assisted Places Scheme in 1981, designed to restore state subsidy for bright but poor pupils at these and other private schools (Finch 1984: 48). Whereas the net cost of the direct-grant scheme in 1974 was about 0.25 per cent of the education budget, the cost of the Assisted Places Scheme by 1988, when it is fully operational will be 0.35 per cent of the then budget.

The subsidy to private schools will slightly exceed that provided under the old direct grant (calculated from DES 1975, vol. 5, Tables 1 and 5; Treasury 1987 vol. II: 194). The result of the abolition of the direct grant—the most strenuous attack on private education to date—has been identical to that of all other official challenges: the expansion of the private sector and an increase in state subsidy to it.

Recent changes include the ending of endowment insurance relief in the 1984 budget. However, it is likely that home-owners' equity finance plans are providing an equivalent route for tax-derived subsidy.

Power is difficult to define. The development of private education in the UK is a story of state encroachment on and assimilation of the minor private schools for lower social groups. However, the major schools of high social status have been for the most part ignored and, when challenged, have not only been well able to resist attacks, but have, if anything, succeeded in deriving advantage from them. The private sector as it exists now appears to enjoy a high degree of immunity from state power, perhaps most strikingly illustrated in the confusion and ambivalence which have characterized even the Labour Party's pursuit of egalitarianism. The issue of private power has arisen most pointedly in the debate about state subsidy to private schooling.

SUBSIDIES TO PRIVATE SCHOOLING

The central question concerns the flow of money between state and private education. On the one hand, it is argued that private schools, by charging fees to finance education which education authorities would otherwise be compelled to provide under their duty to ensure 'that efficient education ... be available to meet the needs of the population' (Education Act 1944, part 11.7), save the tax-payer money (ISIS 1986a: 14; Salter and Tapper 1984). On the other hand, critics of public schools point to a range of open and concealed subsidies from direct payment of fees to staff training and tax reliefs (Field 1981, ch. 10; Glennerster and Wilson 1970). Analysis of this debate is bedevilled by a number of difficulties.

First, the value of private schooling to state education is hard to estimate. It seems reasonable to suppose that the overnight abolition of private schools would compel the state to provide for their pupils at tax-payer's expense. It is a moot point how many pupils would continue their education in the UK, and how many would remain at school. In addition, the marginal cost of the extra schooling is likely to be much lower than the actual cost of private schooling.

Similarly, the size of state subsidy to private schools is partly a matter of definition. The elements usually considered include the full or partial subsidy of fees at private schools by the army, diplomatic corps, LEAs and other government bodies, including the DES under the Assisted Places Scheme; the charitable status of most independent schools which renders them exempt from rates and many forms of taxation; tax arrangements which allow tax relief on earnings by individuals for school fees; exemption from Value Added Tax (VAT); and the effective payment of training costs for most teachers in private schools through state subsidies to teacher training colleges, the payment of fees and maintenance grants for trainees. Some of these costs might be met by government in any case. Boarding education would probably be necessary for the children of some state employees. It may also be questioned how far training costs are a specific subsidy. After all, many people are trained at the state's expense, partly to develop their skills. Table 3.2 summarizes some recent evidence. It also reminds us of the practical difficulties. Good information is simply not available on many of the important issues. Two points about current changes may be made. First, the practice of saving for school fees through endowment insurance is no longer subsidized through a relief at half the standard rate on individual premia. However, it seems that 'more parents are using the equity value of owned houses to provide for fees' (ISIS 1986c). Since mortgage interest payments and building society deposits carry effective tax relief, taxation on the annual value of owned housing was abolished in 1963 and capital gains on the sale of owner-occupied housing carry tax exemption, it is possible to argue that this form of accumulation is heavily subsidized (Le Grand 1982: 91). The second point suggests a reduction in one form of subsidy. While Assisted Places Scheme subsidies are substantial and likely to more than cancel the effect of the abolition of the direct grant, local authority sponsorship has fallen sharply as an unintended effect of government spending policies. Such subsidies to individuals designed to enhance opportunities are in any case a minor part of the overall picture.

The statistics given in the Table 3.2 show the degree of vagueness in current estimates. The overall impression is that the crude exchequer saving occasioned by private schooling far exceeds the subsidy. However, a number of issues arise. First, the estimate of the cost of transfer of private pupils to the state sector assumes that these individuals would pursue similar school careers. This may not be so, because state sixth-form provision is generally more limited, and because a proportion (3.2 per cent in the ISIS 1986 census) of pupils are of foreign nationality and might not enter British state schooling.

Second, the discrepancies between ISIS and Labour Party figures in the second part of Table 3.2 may be explained partly by the fact that ISIS confines attention to the two-thirds of private schools covered in its statistics, and partly by the fact that its estimate of tax relief is based solely on an estimate of the subsidy to school-fee saving schemes as equivalent to 1.5 per cent of fees derived from Glennerster and Wilson (1970). Rate relief, VAT exemption and the benefits of charitable status in relation to covenanted gifts and the proceeds of endowments are not included in these. As fees have risen, assistance with fees from the schools themselves has increased. In 1982 this covered about 7 per cent of pupils in the ISIS survey. By 1987 the proportion had increased to over 10 per cent. Tax relief on funds also contributes to this subsidy. The proceeds of covenants were estimated at £35 million in 1978/9 (Field 1981: 176).

Third, teacher training is an important item. The value of training to the private sector was put at between £170 and £255 million in 1978/9 by Rogers. The ISIS pamphlet estimates the cost at £300 to £400 million in 1980/1 (1986b). If each teacher lasts forty years, this is equivalent to an annual subsidy of just under £10 million. Fourthly, the creation of the Assisted Places Scheme provides a major new source of income,

Table 3.2   Subsidies and private schooling

(1) *Cost of transfer of private pupils to state sector* (£ millions)

	Cost, 1979/80
Current	
Primary	94.2
Secondary	131.0
Sixth-form	65.5
	290.7
Capital	
Cost of purchase of private buildings	£1,500

Sources: ISIS 1986b: 7; Hansard, Written Answers, col. 43, vol. 989, 1979/80.
Note: The current cost figure is updated to £750 million at 1985 prices; Mintel Market Intelligence, October 1985, quoted by ISIS 1986b.

(2) *Subsidies to private sector* (£ millions, cash)

	a 1980/1	b 1980/1	c 1986/7
Boarding school allowances for children of diplomatic and military personnel	56	43	150
Local authority sponsorship	62	22	46
Assisted Places scheme	—	—	50
Charitable status:			
tax relief	37	15	36
rate relief	1.5	—	6
	156.5	80	288

Sources: (a) Labour Party 1980, (b) ISIS 1986b, (c) author's calculation from ISIS 1986a figures and Hansard, Written Answers, col. 259, vol. 84, 1984/5.

scheduled to cover some 10 per cent of pupils by 1987.

Private schooling clearly applies large resources to the education of small numbers of pupils. Total fee income for 1986 was of the order of £1.2 billion. Most of these resources came from private pockets. State subsidies are unlikely to exceed a quarter of this. The issue of subsidy flow is confused and discussion must be inconclusive. Two points emerge. First, private schooling is not the simple product of individual choice in spending one's own money as one wishes: it does carry state subsidy. Second, the amount of that subsidy is not central to the existence of the system, although it may affect the viability of some schools at the margin. In judgements of the significance of the system, class power may be of more importance than cash flows.

The interaction of state and private schooling has become an issue of debate through discussion of recent proposals for voucher systems and through controversy over the Assisted Places Scheme. To these we now turn.

VOUCHERS AND ASSISTED PLACES

The idea of an education voucher is simple: the state education budget is divided up between parents who allocate it to particular institutions by sending their children to the schools they prefer, thereby endowing those schools with the relevant budget amounts symbolized by the voucher. Essentially, the market principles of resource allocation by consumer demand and consumer sovereignty are underwritten by state finance.

The voucher proposal involves numerous practical problems: the speedy provision of extra classrooms and teachers in response to fluctuating demand; the conflict between professional and consumer interests; the cost of transportation to make school choice a reality (seen as the final stumbling block to a proposed Kent County Council Scheme in 1986); the proportion of budget to be allocated to schools directly to cover fixed costs; the limits to parental choice to be imposed by inspection of standards. Its educational impact depends on political choices. Three are of most importance. First, is the voucher to be flat rate or income-related? An income-related voucher could serve to make the children of poor parents highly attractive to schools and counter the bias in resources towards already privileged children that undermined the practice of the egalitarian reforms of tripartitism in the 1940s and the introduction of comprehensives in the 1960s. In the USA, concern about the access of poor children from racially disadvantaged groups to good state education and the extent to which their parents could exert control over schools led to a proposal for income-related vouchers by Jencks (1970). A modified version of such a scheme was put into practice in a five-year experiment in Alum Rock, California, between 1972 and 1977, with the effect of integrating race and class-segregated schools (Cohen and Farrar 1977).

The second and third choices concern the issues of privilege that have provided the keynote to the discussion of private schools. These are: should parents be allowed to supplement basic vouchers and should the state redeem vouchers spent at private schools? Supplementation would enable middle-class parents to buy places at high-demand schools and would widen the resource gap between such schools and those with a poorer clientele. The activities of Parent Teacher Associations, Friends' groups and others already ensure that a substantial gap exists (Her Majesty's Inspectorate 1981, para. 38). The application of state vouchers to private schools would presumably direct some of the state education budget to those schools, increase fees at existing private schools as the available resources rose and call forth a supply of private schools in relation to the pattern of effective demand. It is also likely that such vouchers would not ensure open access to private schools for applicants further down the class ladder. The Kent feasibility study found that all of the twenty-three local private school head teachers contacted were willing in principle to accept state vouchers as payment for all or part of the fees. They would also be able to increase capacity by about a sixth to accommodate extra demand under the scheme. However, the most important safeguard stipulated was the wish to control admissions to the school as at present by their own testing and selection procedures (Kent County Council 1978: 23).

The experience of the Assisted Places Scheme by which the state supplements fees for the able children of poor parents indicates the importance which private schools attach to control over entry. This scheme was set up by the 1980 Education Act as a substitute for the direct grant system abolished by the previous government in 1976. It followed a model originally put forward by the HMC in the early 1970s. Pupils are selected by participating schools, parent or parents means-tested according to a national scheme by the school, and the appropriate proportion of the fee remitted by DES direct to that institution. Some 5,500 places have been offered in each year but only 4,243 taken up in 1981 and 4,417 in 1982 (Whitty and Edwards 1984: 164). Originally, many of the most prestigious private schools were unwilling to participate, probably because they were uncertain of the effect of admitting working-class assisted pupils on demand from their traditional entrants. However, by 1988 when the scheme is fully operational, it is anticipated that it will cover 229 schools with about a fifth of them taking more than 40 per cent of their pupils under it; 33,200 pupils will be included. Most HMC schools, including many former direct-grant schools, now participate.

The preliminary results of research sponsored by the Economic and Social Research Council into the scheme indicate that it has failed to extend educational opportunities in the way originally envisaged. It seems probable that most assisted places have gone to 'submerged middle-class' parents, often those whose family income has fallen as a result of divorce, sickness, disability or bereavement rather than to children of lower social groups. Roughly a third of 157 children in assisted places covered by the study came from single-parent families, only 9 per cent of fathers and 4 per cent of mothers were in working-class occupations, and 25 per cent had siblings who were in independent schools (Whitty, Fitz and Edwards 1986: 8). According to a survey carried out by the Independent Schools Joint Council in 1982, the biggest single group of beneficiaries was children in one-parent families; a high proportion of places go to children already established at a school whose parents suffer a loss of income. In fact about a third of the pupils assisted by the scheme had previously attended private schools (Hansard, Written Answers, vol. 99, col. 536, 1985/6). The upshot is that educational opportunities are extended while social-class barriers are not breached. This may explain the private sector's support for the scheme after initial hesitation (Whitty and Edwards 1984: 178). Private schools would be able to manage a voucher scheme to achieve similar results, especially if current selection procedures remained. The Kent feasibility study implies that the schools would make this a condition of participation.

Discussion of vouchers in the UK has turned largely on issues of class privilege and state subsidy to private education, whereas the debate in the USA has mainly been concerned with class and race privilege and the integration of disadvantaged groups (Cohen 1982: 1; Blaug 1984: 161). After some initial support, Sir Keith Joseph, Education Secretary from 1983 to 1986, dismissed the idea as impractical at the 1985 Conservative Party Conference and at a Conservative local government conference in March 1986. However, a leak to *The Times* (10 March 1986) that Mrs Thatcher was actively considering the idea, and the replacement of Sir Keith by Kenneth Baker in May 1986, may foreshadow an attempt to resurrect it. A campaigning pamphlet from the Institute of Economic Affairs (IEA), which has exerted more influence on the present Conservative government than on any of its predecessors, coincided with the new appointment (Seldon 1986). The policy of allowing state schools to opt out of LEA control and depend instead on the DES for a grant based on the number of pupils outlined in the 1987 Conservative Manifesto is seen by many commentators as presaging the resurrection of the direct grant combined with what will be effectively a voucher scheme (Conservative Party Manifesto 1987: 20).

Vouchers may well prove popular with parents. The Kent feasibility study found that 10 per cent of parents would wish to move their children within the state sector and some 20 per cent to transfer from the state to the private sector. A survey sponsored by the IEA also found willingness to supplement a voucher among some two-thirds of their sample (Harris and Seldon 1979: 91). However, this study suffers many methodological weaknesses (Judge, Smith and Taylor-Gooby 1983: 471). A major obstacle to the development of vouchers is the opposition of teachers' unions, who are concerned to resist the extension of non-professional control in education (Kent County Council 1978: 37). The power of teachers' unions has recently been undermined by their initial failure to achieve a substantial pay advance despite a bitter nine-month dispute in 1985–6. The time of the voucher may have come. Whether the scheme will make much difference to the principles of private schooling and whether its practice will be hamstrung by an expenditure constraint which denies transport subsidies remains to be seen.

POLITICS AND PRIVATE SCHOOLING

The policies of Labour and Conservative parties on private schooling are at first sight diametrically opposed: The emergence of education as a major political issue in the mid-1970s has brought dissensus on issues of freedom to choose and the unfairness of the sale of privilege, state support for private schooling and abolition of fee-paying education, the irresponsibility of the market and the self-interested power of unionized state sector professionals to the forefront of debate. Analysis of policy statements indicates that the opposed positions both contain ambivalences.

Labour's discussion document *Private Schools* is heavily critical of the private sector's restricted social-class recruitment, its links with the most powerful, prestigious and wealthy groups in society and of the 'arrogance' instilled by a system that is seen as designed to inculcate a sense of superiority (Labour Party 1980). The ambivalence of Labour attitudes is expressed in two factors. First, there is a striking contrast between the attack on the sale of privilege in education — 'the superior facilities that parents can buy ... in many of the public schools' — and the rejection of the claim that public-sector education is in any sense inferior (Labour Party 1980: 13–14).

Secondly, the experience of the failure of the recommendations of the Newsom Commission to achieve progress (Newsom 1968) and, even more damaging, the perverse result of the attempt to integrate the direct-grant schools into the comprehensive system in 1976, has led to an interesting contrast in the policies stated in the 1987 manifesto. The document proposes to end the diversion of 'precious resources through the public subsidies to private schools' (Labour Party 1987: 9). On the other hand, and unlike the two previous Labour manifestos, it makes no demand for the ending of private schooling. This ambivalence may reflect awareness of public sentiment in favour of the retention of private schools, both for their own perceived merits and on the grounds that they do the public sector no harm (Witherspoon 1986. Appendix H. q89A and B). In addition, as Salter and Tapper point out, the obstacles that any attempt to abolish school fees by legislation would face, and the financial pressures imposed by the education demands of private-sector pupils, may well make such a move impracticable (Salter and Tapper 1984: 202). Removal of subsidies might simply make the private sector an even more exclusive preserve of the wealthy by buttressing the fee barrier.

The ambivalence in Conservative policy is less clearly apparent. The Party's successful 1987 election platform defends 'the right to independent education as part of a free society' and claims that the Assisted Places Scheme is an egalitarian policy because it allows bright working-class children access to a superior quality of education than they might otherwise get. The traditional commitment of Conservatives to private schooling enacted in the 'ritualistic' reiteration of 'the principle that parents should have the right to purchase schooling for their children at party conferences' (Salter and Tapper 1984: 186) had two main foundations. First, inequality is assumed to be natural and legitimate, underlying the view that superior education is necessary to develop the aptitudes of the 'talented tenth', as Sir Edward Boyle, Conservative shadow education spokesman, put it at the 1965 Party Conference. The decrease in state grammar school and scholarship direct-grant school selective places has added impetus to the campaign for state-supported access to private schools.

Second, private schools are seen as innovative, freed from bureaucratic and trade-union restrictions and directly responsive to parental preference. Rae, in his spirited defence of private schools, stresses the changes in emphasis on intellectual performance and cultural activity over the post-war period (Rae 1981: 31). Research such as that of Walford (1986, chs 8 and 9) and Fox (1984: 45) supports the view that these changes have occurred largely as a result of parental demands. Parents' willingness to pay fees that increase more rapidly than inflation is also cited as evidence of popular support for the schools (ISIS spokesman, *Times Educational Supplement* 1986).

Conservative support for private schools is probably enhanced by their close links with influential groups in the Party. The ambivalence arises because recent policy has not been entirely supportive of the intellectual case for developing access to high-quality selective private education. The Assisted Places Scheme is an undoubted benefit to the private sector and the possibility of the establishment of direct-grant 'Crown Schools' (in a policy document considered by the Cabinet in March 1986 and reported in the leak in *The Times* of 10 March 1986) together with Education Secretary's flirtation with the idea of a voucher scheme constitute moral encouragement at least. The direct grant has been effectively restored, albeit on a smaller scale, with the announcement in September 1986 of twenty City Technical Colleges to be funded by charitable capital in partnership with the DES outside local authority control. The manifesto proposals to allow state schools to opt out of local authority control, possibly reintroducing selection and fees may extend the private sector downmarket. However, public attitudes to private schooling display a great deal of ambivalence (Taylor-Gooby 1985: 46). It is uncertain in what form these policies will be enacted. The power of the private sector is displayed in the failure of Conservative attempts to change the pattern of access as it is in the failure of Labour to face up to the problems of integration. Treasury policies have also generated problems.

As in other areas of policy, a combination of expenditure constraint and the expansion of the private sector is often self-contradictory. Thus, while the proportion of pupils at the 1,300 schools covered by the ISIS survey receiving help with fees from the Assisted Places Scheme increased from about 1 per cent in 1982 to about 6 per cent by 1987, the proportion receiving LEA assistance fell from about 5 per cent to less than 2 per cent as a result of government spending policies. As the ISIS survey concludes, 'gains in assisted places under the Government's new scheme ... are to a large extent offset by the drop in assisted places being taken up by local education authorities' (ISIS 1983: 4). Similar difficulties apply to a voucher scheme. The Kent feasibility study concluded that this would require a considerable state commitment to transport subsidy to be effective. This is unlikely under present spending policies.

The SDP-Liberal Alliance, perhaps wisely, omits any reference to private schooling from its 1983 manifesto, although it emphasizes 'creating one community' as a major aim, to be achieved through attacks on the social divisions of poverty and poor community services (*Times* 1984: 340–3). Discussion of education focuses on the link between schooling and employment and on policies to increase the supply of technically skilled workers. The 1987 Manifesto proposes the ending of the Assisted Places Scheme and the restriction of charitable status to charitable objectives, echoing in minor key Labour policy without the rhetoric; at the same time the rights of those who wish to pay for private schooling are upheld (SDP-Liberal Alliance 1987: 15).

Both major parties underestimate the problem of effecting a fundamental change in the private sector, either by integration or by widening access. Salter and Tapper argue that both approaches are mistaken (Salter and Tapper 1984: 202–3). Labour policies are based on the premise that private schooling creates privilege rather than the more plausible view that it simply acts as a convenient channel for the intergenerational transmission of privilege which has its main source in social background. One response might be that the Labour Party's concern is precisely to attack intergenerational transmission. However, legal and practical obstacles to abolition are likely to prove insuperable. The ending of subsidies would simply weed out weak private schools and have the effect of raising the fees (and therefore the barriers to non-élite access) at the academically strong and socially influential. Privilege would be even more secure in its regeneration. In the event of abolition, élite groups would develop other means of protecting their interests.

Conservative policies of benefiting the able by widening access are similarly misguided. These are based on the assumption that educational standards in state schools are low. As Halsey demonstrated, the educational attainments of private scholars are much more a function of background and length of schooling than of any separable 'school effect'. Assisted Places Scheme entrants will probably do well, because selection procedures capture those who would do well in state schools. There is no reason to assume that private schools provide an appropriate avenue for the academically talented. Similarly, it is unreasonable to suggest that the pace and diffusion of innovation in state schools, with major curriculum changes, orientation towards technical and vocational training, examination restructuring and striking increase in the average length of schooling and in examination pass rates over the past twenty years, is necessarily slower than it is in private schools.

CONCLUSION

The future of private school education is uncertain. Examination of the record of past attempts by politicians to influence the private sector implies that any changes achieved will be far smaller than the rhetoric of manifestos suggests.

The state has been highly successful in assuming control of private education for the lower and middle classes. It has been entirely unsuccessful in intervening in upper-class private education. The failure of Labour to overcome its ambivalence between integration and abolition equally with the capacity of the private sector to turn aside the class implications of the Conservative policy of extension of opportunity, demonstrate that private schooling is well able to resist attempts to change its character. The private sector possesses considerable power expressed in its ability to resist attempts to alter its role within the British class system. Whether the operation of that power had an effect on the individuals who pass through the schools that may be attributable to their specific characteristics as schools rather than to their class location as institutions or the crude fact of longer sixth-form courses, remains an open question. It is entirely possible that the wealthy are wasting their money, and that if it is education they want, they should send their children to state schools and invest in extra private schooling only after the age of 16. Like many ideological arguments, much of the debate may be about nothing.

4 Occupational and Private Pensions

BACKGROUND

The provision of pensions is the most costly of all welfare benefits. Its significance has been highlighted by recent attempts to phase out the State Earnings Related Pension Scheme (SERPS) under the so-called Fowler proposals—an initiative aimed at reducing costs, heightening public awareness and improving the rights of contributors to pension schemes as well as anticipating a greater reluctance on the part of the working population to fund those in retirement. Some of the proposals have been interpreted as an attempt to alter radically the balance between public and private provision. The situation is far more complex. Occupational pension schemes (as opposed to the basic state pension) already held an entrenched position within the existing consensus (Disney 1985: 62), and can be traced back to the nineteenth century.

In order to come anywhere close to understanding the complex intermeshing of state and private initiatives, this chapter considers the historical development of pension schemes (e.g. the role of friendly societies and the creation of group schemes); state intervention, both to provide minimum provision and to prevent abuses of occupational schemes; and the limits to the effectiveness of government policies. These include the creation of incentives (via tax relief) for people to save towards their retirement, the curtailment of costs and the promotion of freedom of choice and more flexible arrangements. We also consider the extent and nature of pensions coverage—its complexity and heterogeneity—as well as the social and political bases of support for current policies.

STATE AND PRIVATE INITIATIVES

This section examines the background to the development of pension schemes. The main reasons for the involvement by the state and other institutions in social security provision for retirement include the increasing complexity of social structures; the process of industrialization; corporate paternalism (both by monarchs and employers); attempts to control and restrain mobility of labour in the context of competition between employers; the rise in popular expectations and demands; the efforts of individual and groups of reformers; and the efficient organization of insurance on the basis of a collective undertaking such as a company or a public agency. The post-war growth in occupational pensions arose partly because of the vacuum between public welfare and private affluence. This generated rising expectations (and the capacity to pay for these) in the form of better provision for retirement.

The role of central government and large institutions in the provision of pensions is a relatively recent phenomenon. In previous centuries the elderly usually depended on charitable acts by others to support them in their old age. In Tudor times it was assumed by the state that the aged would receive assistance from voluntary alms, although society was gradually becoming 'too complicated for individual action in relieving the needs of the helpless and the aged' (Wilson and Mackay 1941: 3). Hence the statutes of Edward VI and Mary sought to persuade whilst those of Elizabeth compelled people to contribute towards the needs of these groups. The framework provided by the Poor Relief Act of 1601 lasted until 1834, although it was subject to modifications, particularly though the transition from mercantile to liberal and industrial capitalism. Provision of care for the old and infirm was facilitated not only by the creation of workhouses but also of working-class friendly societies and box clubs.

In 1796 William Pitt as chancellor of the exchequer, put forward proposals for a 'parochial fund to be raised by voluntary contributions and supported by the rates, to be applied to the relief of old age or chronic sickness, and the support of widows and children of deceased members' (Wilson and Mackay 1941: 5). The Friendly Societies' Act of 1819 gave legal sanction to societies that

> intended to provide contributions, on the principle of mutual insurance, for the maintenance or assistance of contributors thereto ... in ... advanced age, widowhood, or any other natural state or contingency where the occurrence is susceptible of calculation by way of average.
>
> (quoted in Wilson and Mackay 1941: 5)

From 1834 onwards a new system of Poor Law authorities was created. However, the Victorian welfare system—based on the Poor Law, charity and collective self-help—came under increased pressure, and by the end of the nineteenth century it was widely recognized that the friendly societies were becoming increasingly insolvent and often defrauded their working-class clients. Membership of the societies had grown rapidly in the last quarter of the century and most working men were contributing to some form of collective self-help.

Initiatives for change came from various quarters. Some employers realized 'the shortcomings of a system which could render an old servant destitute simply because of the untimely death of the employer upon whom he was dependent for his pension' (Pilch and Wood 1960: 18). Another initiative was the vigorous campaign conducted by Canon Blackley, who in 1878 advocated contributions by the workforce to a self-supporting national insurance scheme. This provoked strong criticism from both friendly societies and insurance companies. According to Wilson and Mackay, Canon Blackley 'brought the whole question of old age pensions, almost single-handed, before the public' (Wilson and Mackay 1941: 16). In 1885 the government appointed a select committee which examined the social measures being proposed by Bismarck in Germany in his attempt to take the wind out of the sails of the socialist movement.

Provision for the elderly had become a widespread social problem in Britain. According to Canon Blackley, 47 per cent of all old people over the age of 70 in the UK died as paupers in workhouses. Evidence gathered by Charles Booth showed that poverty was greatest in old age and he advocated pensions for all those over 65. A paper presented in 1891 by Booth to the Royal Statistical Society is generally acknowledged as the 'turning point in the argument for old age pensions in Great

Britain' (Goodin 1985: 148). The lack of interest shown by political parties over this issue and the opposition of the friendly societies to any state scheme was bound to be short-lived—because of the increasing evidence of poverty among the elderly and the financial difficulties confronting the societies. By the 1906 elections the issue of a state pension scheme was on the political agenda. Widespread poverty, highlighted by research findings and coverage in the popular press all contributed to a greater interest in collective forms of action to tackle social problems. The earliest state pension scheme was introduced in 1908, and provided pensions to people aged 70 or over. However, access to this first nationally financed social security scheme was subject to certain economic and moralistic constraints: it was means-tested and limited to a maximum of £31 per annum and it was denied to anyone who had been in prison within the last ten years or had 'habitually failed to work according to his ability, opportunity or need'.

Certain groups of employees had long enjoyed some sort of pension cover. As early as 1834 a Superannuation Act gave statutory definition to a non-contributory pension for male civil servants (Pilch and Wood 1960: 19). In the private sector, joint-stock banks were paying 'retiring allowances' in the mid-nineteenth century; and the railway companies and a few other large enterprises had superannuation schemes before the First World War. However, the schemes spread slowly in private commerce and industry until after the Second World War, and were regarded as a form of 'employer benevolence' (Wiseman 1965: 171). It was only later that they evolved into part of the contract of employment to attract certain grades of staff. A survey of 117 large firms in 1958 showed that pensions accounted for more than half of total company expenditure on fringe benefits (Wiseman 1965: 171).

In 1918 there were about 400 staff schemes, paying mostly pensions and nearly another 400 provident funds paying lump sums only. Most of the schemes were run by single firms. The aftermath of the First World War resulted in a considerably improved system of pensions for those who had suffered casualties in the conflict, which was in sharp contrast with the fate of those who had suffered industrial accidents. The main avenue of progress was in the extension of the 1911 Health Insurance Scheme advocated by Beveridge. The Widows, Orphans and Old Age Contributory Pensions Act of 1925 introduced contributory pensions for people between 65 and 70 who were covered by the Health Insurance Scheme. The means-tested, non-contributory old-age pension remained from age 70 for those who had never been insured. In 1940 supplementary means-tested pensions were introduced to bring pensions up to what was then considered the necessary minimum. As with many other innovations and reforms, the impact of war proved to be decisive in the development of pension schemes. The Beveridge proposals helped to broaden the scope of pensions following the reforms introduced after the First World War. The demands by the modern state on the individual during times of war appear to necessitate compensation through the social or political reform in the aftermath.

Another crucial factor in the development of pension schemes was the system of tax reliefs on savings for retirement. Life-insurance payments were allowed tax relief when income tax was introduced in 1799. This was later withdrawn and reintroduced in 1853. Until the 1921 Finance Act, schemes which were run like trust funds did not enjoy any special privileges in contrast with insured schemes, which offered employees tax relief on their contributions. With the new Act the ordinary annual contributions of both employers and employees qualified for full tax relief as allowable expenses, and the investment income of the fund was freed from all tax liability (Pilch and Wood 1960: 19). The 1922 Local Government and Other Officers Superannuation Act allowed local authorities to provide for the superannuation of employees. This contributed to greater interest in pension schemes and the creation of more superannuation funds.

A major innovation, influenced by a scheme introduced in the USA in 1928, was the Group Life and Pensions Scheme. It was the first type of scheme which tackled the problem of providing pensions for groups of, as opposed to individual, employees through insurance cover (Pilch and Wood 1960: 20). A group of employees was therefore insured under a single policy, issued by the insurance company to the employer and not through separate policies with each employee. This led to large savings in the expense of establishing a scheme: lower premium rates could be charged, and a more efficient system of administration was introduced for the employer.

In the years leading up to the Second World War, another type of pension scheme based on endowment assurances (usually called provident funds) became highly popular. Whereas provident funds provided a lump-sum benefit, the new scheme offered a 'guaranteed annuity option at maturity'. Thus, a lump-sum benefit could be exchanged for a pension based on a rate of exchange which was guaranteed in the original contract. Major legislative action to control many abuses of pension schemes was passed in the Finance Act of 1947. The Income Tax Act of 1952 (s. 378) had a significant impact on the further development of pension schemes. The schemes were not allowed to provide tax-free lump-sum retirement benefits; at death there was a pension (or a lump sum) for the dependant; investment income was not taxed; tax was deducted from pensions as in Pay-As-You-Earn; and tax would be levied at a quarter of the standard rate on contributions withdrawn by employees. For schemes covered by section 388 of the Act, a quarter of retirement benefits could be taken in tax-free lump sums; there was no predetermined upper limit to pensions and it would depend on earnings and length of service; investment income would be taxed; and no tax was payable on contributions which were withdrawn (Wiseman 1965: 180).

This illustrates how, once pension cover was extended under the umbrella of the state, the development of schemes, both in the public and the private sectors, could be strongly influenced by centralized measures. The initiatives taken by individuals, employers and insurance companies were channelled into a framework with the state as a central actor. Despite this, there remained scope for variability in schemes and the post-war growth in occupational pensions reflected the gap that emerged between the minimum provision of public welfare and private affluence.

LIMITS TO CHANGES IN POLICY

The current attempts by the Conservative government to alter radically the arrangements for state, occupational and private pensions serve as an example of the difficulties involved in uniting different policy objectives. Much of the literature on the accumulation and legitimation 'crisis' of the welfare state suggests a powerful connection between pressures on policy-makers and a situation of economic downturn. However, these accounts tend to ignore how the pressures are exacerbated, in the current economic context, by attempts to realize conflicting principles. Hence, the 1985 Green Paper on social security reform represented, in the words of one commentator, 'the most sophisticated expression to date of the present Conservative Government's liberal theory of the state' (Weale 1985a: 321). The purpose of this section is to highlight the complex nature of any attempt to fulfil policy objectives by focusing on the gap between goals and outcomes, notably between the original proposals to phase out SERPS and the package that was approved under the 1986 Social Security Act. We need first, however, to consider some of the complexities inherent in modern pensions schemes.

The cost of pensions and SERPS

One of the central issues in the debate over pensions has been the cost of maintaining the payments promised by SERPS. As with all previous schemes, this one will never reach full fruition for the majority of the population. To some extent, this is a legacy of the way in which the Beveridge proposals were implemented to create a comprehensive social security system.

A basic pension was paid on retirement from work which would provide a subsistence income without a means test. The initial intention was to fix the rate of contribution actuarially in order to cover the cost of the pension. However, popular pressure led to the rejection of the original plans, which had foreseen a transitional period of twenty years before the payment of full pensions in favour of instant payment of increased pensions. Thus, in the 1950s a system was introduced whereby people in employment paid contributions to meet the immediate cost of pensions for those who were in retirement.

Various authors (Disney 1985; Reddin 1982) have argued that the public has therefore become deluded into thinking that what it now contributes to state pension schemes will determine future entitlements. The 'insurance principle' does not apply in practice; and all amendments to the state scheme do not escape from this basic flaw, even if they graft on an earnings-related component in order to supplement flat-rate contributions, for instance in the National Insurance Act 1959. Fourteen years later, the Social Security Act aimed to introduce earnings-related contributions in return for a basic flat-rate pension as well as the possibility of a second-tier pension either through a company or the state which would be funded on the basis of a return of investment. The 1974 election stood in the way of this scheme. The Social Security Act 1975 introduced SERPS, which created an earnings-related pension as an addition to the basic pension. The scheme came into force in 1978, though its full impact will be felt in 1998, when contributors receive an additional pension equal to a quarter of their average revalued earnings between the lower- and upper-earning limits. For those retiring after 1998 the pension would be based on the best twenty years of earnings. The contributor would receive 1.25 per cent of his or her earnings between the lower and upper limits for each year in the scheme. Occupational schemes were allowed to 'contract out' of the state scheme on condition that they provided a guaranteed minimum pension as well as other benefits. They must guarantee an amount broadly corresponding to the state additional pension based on the number of years contracted out since 1978.

In its review of pensions the Conservative government regarded SERPS as too costly and complex. It also argued that employers would be reluctant to create occupational schemes because of the risk involved in promising a particular benefit. A further criticism which it might have made, but did not, was that SERPS enabled occupational pension schemes to attract a substantial segment of contributors on high incomes and with steady employment from the state scheme. In his study of state pensions, Creedy shows how the state pension scheme as a whole has a limited redistributional effect (Creedy 1982). In brief, SERPS appears costly, complex and of little benefit to employees on low or variable earnings.

As will be shown later, the government has focused mainly on the costs of SERPS over the next fifty years, particularly as a result of the likely rise in the number of pensioners and the decline in the ratio of working people to pensioners (on the assumption of an improvement in the longevity of the elderly and of a reversal in the decline of the birth rate over the past twenty years). Whilst some critics of the new proposals argued that SERPS is financially viable (Piachaud 1985; Disney 1985) and that the government has been too pessimistic about future prospects for economic growth, there has been a tendency to ignore two major reasons for the attempt to reform pension schemes: the belief in greater freedom of choice and the anticipation of a greater reluctance by those in employment to fund those currently in retirement. We begin by examining the issue of freedom of choice and the substantial limits to the rights of contributors to pension schemes.

Freedom of choice and the rights of contributors
In the preface to a consultative document on personal pensions, Norman Fowler stressed the importance of giving people 'more choice in the way they save for their old age' (DHSS 1984c: 1). The 1985 Green Paper focuses on three issues: better protection against inflation for members' pension rights if they leave a scheme before retirement; the right when they leave a scheme to a transfer value, representing the value of their deferred pensions rights, which they can put into a new employer's scheme or personal pension; and access to information to take informed decisions about their pensions (DHSS 1985a, vol. 1: 25; DHSS 1984b).

Economic change and occupational mobility mean that at least a million people every year leave pension schemes. Until recently there has been little support for the claim that they may be just as entitled to benefits derived from pension contributions as those who remain with the same employer. Trade unions, for instance, have generally been involved in negotiations on behalf of their members currently in the employers' service (who, by definition, were not early leavers from a scheme). Prior to the 1973 Social Security Act early leavers often lost all their pension rights or obtained a refund of their own contributions. The Act required these rights to be preserved until pension age, although no provision was made for revaluation of deferred pension in the period up to retirement. The 1975 Social Security Act offered protection to early leavers for part of a scheme's pension: the guaranteed minimum pension of contracted-out employees is effectively revalued annually in line with national average earnings up to pension age. Members of non-contracted-out schemes, and of schemes whose pension rights exceed the guaranteed minimum pension often lose out substantially when they change jobs.

In a Gallup survey of members of occupational schemes aged 21 to 55, 10 per cent of the sample wanted to change their current job but decided against it because they felt they would lose too much pension if they moved to another employer, and 2 per cent turned down an actual offer of employment because of this (Gallup Report 1984). Almost half (44 per cent) felt it was unfair for employees to be compelled to join a particular scheme, whilst the other half (52 per cent) felt it was fair. Eighty-five per cent felt that if people were able to make their own pension arrangements and were not obliged to join their employer's scheme, this choice should be available to both people starting a new job and existing employees. Overall, members of occupational schemes were satisfied with existing arrangements (26 per cent were very satisfied; 55 per cent, quite satisfied; and 13 per cent, not very or not at all satisfied).

In drafting its case for a reform of pensions, the government highlighted some of the risks to which the rights and expectations of an employee may be vulnerable. For instance, if an employer becomes insolvent or there is a take-over bid for a company the accumulated contributions from employees may not be sufficient to finance the pension based on a percentage of final salary. Where promised rights are not met in full, the benefit priority rules of a scheme decide in what order the liabilities are to be met. Low priority benefits may therefore be left unpaid even though both employer and trustees have carried out their tasks in the proper manner. A further difficulty is that the rate of return on the pension fund, after allowing for real increases in earnings, could be less than the valuation made by the actuary. It may be difficult to obtain an increase in contributions and, if the scheme is terminated, members' rights are limited to what the assets in the scheme will provide. Another aspect is that private-sector pensions are often at the discretion of the employer. If the generosity of a former employer ceases, a pensioner may suffer as a result. The government made several proposals to reduce these risks: (1) since many employees are not aware of their occupational pension rights and of the risks involved, compulsory disclosure of information would improve understanding; in addition, a register of pension schemes (which contained the main deeds and documents) should be available for inspection; (2) state funding control should be introduced, or pension guarantees backed by credit insurance against insolvency could be made mandatory in order to provide greater security; and (3) a Public Registrar might supervise schemes along the lines of supervision over insurance companies, banks and building societies (DHSS, 1984a: 6).

The last point highlights the limited supervision of pension-fund management. All funds are subject to trust law and many are managed by licensed dealers in securities who must adhere to certain legal standards: some are managed by 'exempted dealers'; and others by stockbrokers under the scrutiny of the Stock Exchange. About 15 per cent of schemes, namely those which are contracted-out and represent about 90 per cent of all schemes' members, are subject to supervision by the Occupational Pensions Board. However, this is only to ensure that they are financed on a scale which makes it possible for them to provide guaranteed minimum pensions. The government decided not to establish supervisory machinery comparable to that applied to other financial institutions. It argued that there was a considerably greater number of pension funds (100,000) than banks, insurance companies and building societies; the employer who runs a pension scheme has a vital interest in running it efficiently in order to limit his own contribution to it; and employees normally have some means of exercising pressures on the trustees or the employer to maintain adequate standards (DHSS 1984a: 17–18).

Employers are legally required to provide employees with a written statement of conditions relating to pension arrangements, but are under no obligation to clarify whether the pension promise is a conditional one and if so on what it depends, or to what extent it is enforceable as a term of the contract of employment. In general, neither the contents of a pension booklet nor the trust deed which usually governs the pension scheme are terms of the contract of employment. In general, neither the contents of a pension booklet nor the trust deed which usually governs the pension scheme are terms of the contract of employment. It is unclear how far they commit the employer. Whilst the trustees of a scheme are legally obliged to administer it in the interests of all members, an employer can be and often is either one of the trustees or the sole trustee. Conflicts of interest could arise, particularly where the trustee is the employer or one of his subsidiary companies or one of his directors. Situations can (and apparently do) arise in which pensions are judged to be 'overfunded'. This often happens because assets have risen in value at a far faster rate than inflation as a result of the boom in the Stock Exchange of the past few years. Apparently, it is possible for employers to take the surplus out of the funds (if they can find a complaisant actuary) and put it into the business. Overall, the employer has 'the dominant voice in most of the decisions' (DHSS 1984a: 22) — for instance, on whether to have a pension scheme, wind it up, use it to contract out of part of the state pension scheme; which employees are to be covered by it; and whether employees must join. Of course, employees and their respresentatives might be consulted about all these decisions. Those who have the least say are, as the government has stressed, the early leavers.

Long-term planning, rising expectations and the pensions lobby

The second and less obvious reason for the proposed reforms was the desire by the government to reverse the growing gap in the 'actuarial link between contributions made and benefits received' (Weale 1985a: 324). According to Weale, the attempt by the government to narrow this gap has two principal aims:

first, to respond to what may become 'a growing resentment at increased contributions for which, from the point of view of the individual contributor, there was no reasonable expectation that the savings would be returned in later life'; and second, to score a major political victory over the pensions lobby.

Complex changes underlie both these perspectives. Drawing on our study of attitudes to state welfare, he points to the perception by high-income respondents that low-income groups benefit most from state pensions. In a situation where pensioners' incomes have increased both in relative and absolute terms since the 1940s (and when many pensioners have been replaced in the bottom quintile of income distribution by families with children), 'the motive for making increased contributions through the tax-transfer system correspondingly weakens' (Weale 1985a: 325). In addition, the successful resistance by the pensions lobby to the original Fowler proposals tends to confirm the notion of a Conservative attempt, embodied in the Green Paper, to undermine it and 'reduce expectations about future improvements in state benefits' (Weale 1985a: 324). Before examining the resistance by the pensions lobby, we consider further the background to the 1986 Act.

Apart from the regular catalogue of electoral promises, the major political parties have, until recently, never initiated a major debate on the issue of state and occupational pensions. The 1983 general election manifestos of the Conservative and Labour parties signalled their preparedness to engage in such a debate, even if the dialogue has failed to address some of the principles and issues underlying social security provision. Both parties did address the issue of early leavers from occupational schemes and of information about pension rights. The Labour Party also stressed the importance of members' 'rights to participation'.

In its plans for the abolition of SERPS, the Conservative government stressed the future economic and demographic pressures on state pensions, as well as the importance of freedom of choice in order to allow greater occupational mobility. Complete freedom of choice in deciding on whether or not to join an occupational scheme or to contribute to a personal pension would be subject to some restrictions. People would be free to choose within a framework of compulsory occupational or personal pensions, and the concept was extended in a manner designed to answer (unsuccessfully) criticisms about the creation of a dual society:

> The Government believe that it is important for everyone to have that security by building up at least a minimum additional pension to what they will receive from the state. Otherwise we should perpetuate "two nations" of those with and those without additional pensions.
>
> (DHSS 1985a, vol. 2: 4)

The government felt that the new arrangements should be extended to a wider range of employees with the possible exception of casual, part-time workers and young people up to 18 years of age. It proposed a minimum level of contribution to occupational or personal schemes of 4 per cent of earnings (with the employer responsible for at least half of this amount). The 4 per cent is a very low level of contribution when compared with the approximate average in most schemes, and as a percentage of a low income, it would do little more than cover costs for administration. Despite the greater variability, flexibility and freedom of choice, those on higher incomes would still be able to make a greater contribution and to benefit more from tax reliefs, and it is not obvious how individuals on lower wages or with fluctuating employment prospects — let alone with no employment at all — would benefit from these arrangements.

The proposals did not aim to abolish the basic National Insurance pension, and they would be introduced over a transitional period: people whose pensions expectations were closely linked with schemes like SERPS would, according to their age group, either remain fully in that scheme or be offered extra rights in the new arrangements. The rate of National Insurance contribution would be reduced by around 3 per cent to offset the minimum occupational or personal pension contribution required under the new arrangements. The basic justification for this was that people 'will know how much their retirement investment is worth as it builds up over the years' and that freedom of choice between employers' occupational schemes and personal pension arrangements would be established by law (DHSS 1985a, vol. 2: 9). The one definite advantage of the government proposals was that they would ensure greater occupational cover for some full-time employees in the agriculture, construction and distribution sectors (DHSS 1985a, vol. 2: 6). However, this would not necessarily improve the lot of those who would pay less to the state and more to occupational pensions at the minimum legal level.

These proposals represent a fairly novel attempt by a government to combine long-term planning (on the cost of pensions over the next fifty years) with the realization of its principles (on freedom of choice and to dampen rising expectations) and to link these to a potential reluctance on the part of wage-earners to fund those in retirement. Not surprisingly, they met with considerable resistance from most influential organizations accross the political spectrum. To reiterate some of the central themes of this book: ideology had to concede to pragmatism; incrementalism rather than rapid change remained the norm; and even when privatization was a major policy goal, it had to contend with a host of other objectives. The government had recognized that pension savings, an immense source of assets, are to a large degree distributed by the state. The proposals to shift some control over these assets to individuals represented a conflict between two principles: 'one which asserted that economic resources were in the ultimate ownership of society which through government could choose to distribute them as it chose, and the other of which asserted that resources were the property of individuals to which government only has access for limited purposes' (Weale 1985a: 329–30).

The outcome

First, the outcome, as embodied in the 1986 Social Security Act, was a retention of the SERPS scheme with the following drastic modifications. The pension will be related to an average spread over all lifetime earnings instead of the best twenty years of earnings. Years in which a person is involved in care for children or for an elderly or disabled person will not be included in the calculation. Although time spent out of work due to illness will not be included, the reverse applies to any period of unemployment. Persons intending to return to low-paid or part-time work—particularly women—might, in many instances, reconsider this move if they are to receive a smaller pension because of the reduction in average lifetime earnings. The additional pension equal to a quarter of average revalued earnings will be reduced to one-fifth; and a widow will only inherit half instead of the entire pension rights of her husband. These reductions in benefit will, according to the Government Actuary, reduce the cost of SERPS from £35.3 billion to £16.3 billion by 2053/4.

Second, the legislation, and the data used to support it, highlights the problems of long-term planning: assumptions have to be made about the growth of the economy (in this case, 1.5 per cent per annum) and levels of unemployment (at 6 per cent per annum); there are difficulties in predicting the size of GNP to fund firm commitments or rising expectations; and any change in government could have affected some aspects of the package (particularly since the changes in the 1986 Act were only to be implemented in April 1988; the reforms will not affect people retiring this century; and a transition period, up to 2010, is anticipated). This point is aptly illustrated by the declaration of the Labour shadow social services secretary, Michael Meacher, that certain incentives to personal pension schemes would be abolished by a Labour government, for instance the payment by the state of an additional contribution of 2 per cent of a person's earnings on which contributions are payable, for the period 1988–93.

A similar 2 per cent incentive will also apply to occupational pension schemes where employers establish money purchase schemes for their employees in order to contract out of the state scheme. A further incentive to the expansion of such schemes is the removal of the requirement that contracted-out arrangements must offer a guaranteed minimum pension (based on the minimum offered by the state). However, contributions must not be below the National Insurance contributions rebate. In order to broaden the choice of investment outlets, banks, building societies and unit trusts will be permitted to offer personal pensions.

Even if we were to accept some of the assumptions on which the restructuring of SERPS has been based, the impact either in distributional terms or on public attitudes is unlikely to be of major significance and will certainly fall well short of the intentions expressed in the original Fowler proposals. We now examine the extent and nature of contemporary pensions coverage which may provide clues to the sources of resistance to any rapid alteration in the current complex structures.

THE EXPANSION OF OCCUPATIONAL PENSIONS

Complexity and heterogeneity

Depending on how the calculations are made, one can arrive at different results on the extent of occupational pensions coverage; and even those do not take into account the variability between different schemes. In addition, these may only comprise the 'tip of the iceberg' in terms of benefits and perks available with particular occupations (Reddin 1982: 132). Since the early 1960s the overall proportion of full- and part-time employees covered by occupational pension schemes has remained fairly static at around 50 per cent (Table 4.1). The greatest advances were made between the 1930s and 1950s. Since 1971 the main area of expansion has been in the provision for women employees, especially in the public sector. Most of the decline in recent years has occurred in the private sector. In terms of the proportion of adults covered by schemes out of the total adult population, there has been a slight increase over recent years: from 36 per cent in 1966; 37 per cent between 1974 and 1977; to 40 per cent 1978 and 1981 (Board of Inland Revenue 1981: 61; 1983: 51).

Although for the population as a whole there has occurred little change over the past few years, a significant increase has taken place in coverage for full-time employees, from 49 per cent in 1972 to 65 per cent in 1982. (Table 4.2). This is mainly related to the position of women in the occupational structure of full-time employees where coverage has increased from 34 per cent in 1972 to 57 per cent in 1982. As I shall point out later, these extensions of occupational welfare do not necessarily correspond with the level of social welfare for the population as a whole. A further area of expansion has been in the number of pensioners covered by schemes: from 200,000 in

Table 4.1 Employees (full time and part time) in pension schemes, 1936–83

Year	Private Sector (millions)			Public Sector (millions)			Overall (millions)	Scheme members as total proportion of all employees (%)
	Men	Women	Total	Men	Women	Total		
1936	1.3	0.3	na	0.8	0.2	na	2.6	na
1953	2.5	0.6	3.1	2.4	0.7	3.1	6.2	na
1956	3.5	0.8	4.3	2.9	0.8	3.7	8.0	37
1963	6.4	0.8	7.2	3.0	0.9	3.9	11.1	49
1967	6.8	1.3	8.1	3.1	1.0	4.1	12.2	54
1971	5.5	1.3	6.8	3.2	1.1	4.3	11.1	49
1975	4.9	1.1	6.0	3.7	1.7	5.4	11.4	49
1979	4.6	1.5	6.1	3.7	1.8	5.5	11.6	50
1983	4.4	1.4	5.8	3.4	1.9	5.3	11.1	52

n.a.: not available
Sources: Government Actuary 1981: 6; DHSS 1985a, vol. 1: 21; CSO 1987: 100.

Table 4.2 Employees covered out of total (full-time) labour force (%)

	1972	1973	1975	1976	1979	1982
Men	55	57	63	65	68	69
Women	34	39	47	50	55	57
Total	49	52	59	61	64	65

Source: CSO 1985b.

1952 to 300,000 in 1956. By 1971 nearly two and a half million former employees and half a million widows and other dependents were receiving pensions (Government Actuary 1972: 13).

Whilst the proportional coverage of full- and part-time employees has remained steady, there has been a rapid increase in the number of schemes from 37,500 in 1957, 56,000 in 1967, 96,000 in 1979 to over 100,000 at present. This partly reflects the desire by most firms to make their own arrangements. However, the most extensive coverage is provided by larger firms, particularly those with over 1,000

Table 4.3 Private-sector cover, 1979

Number of employees in establishment or group	Number of employers	Number with a pension scheme	Percentage of employers with a scheme	Percentage of employers who are members
1–9	430,000	30,000	7	6
10–99	165,000	55,000	33	15
100–999	12,000	9,000	80	40
1,000–9,999	1,260	1,250	99	57
10,000 and over	150	150	100	64
Totals	608,410	96,000	16	39

Source: Government Actuary 1981: 7–8.

employees (Table 4.3). Coverage in the private sector (around 10 per cent) does not compare well with the public-sector cover: 60 per cent of local authority employees, 78 per cent in central government and 93 per cent in public corporations (Government Actuary 1981: 5). A far higher proportion of private-sector schemes have not contracted-out (75,000 out of 90,000) in comparison with the public sector (30 out of 130), although this applies mainly to small companies (Government Actuary 1981: 23). Coverage of central and local government employees was most extensive for civil service and other central government employees (98 per cent), members of the armed forces (98 per cent), regular firemen (100 per cent), regular police officers (100 per cent) and local authority teachers and lecturers (88 per cent) (Government Actuary 1981: 9). Women in part-time employment are twice as likely to be covered if they are employed in the public rather than private sector. Overall, only 7 per cent of part-time employees are in a pension scheme (Government Actuary 1981: 11).

These figures reflect the complexity and heterogeneity of pensions coverage. They reveal little, however, about differences between schemes and the level of coverage of particular groups. The question of variability between schemes in different sectors is a source of controversy (Reddin and Hodges 1982: 131). In some instances no scheme at all is available, in others the coverage, generosity and duration of the scheme fluctuate in relation to different grades of staff, sex, full- or part-time status and variable accrual rates of benefits. Schemes are also subject to the potential dangers cited earlier in this chapter. Thus any figures we provide on the extent of cover should be treated with caution because of the possible variations in the precise benefits provided by each scheme. As Reddin points out, it is hard to evaluate how far a pension scheme will deliver its promises and 'the wage or pension trade-off is rarely sufficiently explicit to permit rational decisions (Reddin 1982: 141). Attempts to establish the costs and benefits of a scheme lead to circular arguments about the relationship between wages, contributions, wage demands, the price paid by the consumer and taxation (e.g. see Reddin 1982: 142).

Demographic and socio-economic factors
None the less, it is possible to identify certain demographic and socio-economic features which have fostered continuity and change in pension arrangements. Whilst the coverage of full-time employees rose between 1972 and 1982, the Conservative government was particularly concerned about the lack of expansion of occupational pensions for the total workforce. Between 1971 and 1985 the proportion of pensioners' income from the state rose by 25 per cent, whilst from occupational pensions it remained almost static (DHSS 1984d: 16). This is particularly true of certain sectors of the economy. In manufacturing industries (excluding engineering) the proportion of scheme members as a percentage of the total of full-time employees is 53 per cent. In other sectors the figures are even lower: distribution (41 per cent), construction (37 per cent) and agriculture (23 per cent) (DHSS 1985a, vol 1: 23). The government argued that SERPS has done nothing to encourage the spread of occupational pensions in these sectors, especially because of its complexity and the open-ended commitment that is required of employers.

Apart from the importance of employment sectors, three other factors influence the extent of pension coverage: sex, occupational status and income. The gap in coverage between the sexes has narrowed considerably, particularly in the 25–65 age group. In their 1982 survey, Ritchie and Barrowclough found that 60 per cent of males and 53 per cent of females in this age group were covered by occupational schemes (Ritchie and Barrowclough 1983: 23). In this age group the gap between men and women was narrow only in professional, managerial and technical occupations. However, in other occupations the pattern was similar to the results of an earlier survey which revealed a consistent under-representation of full-time women employees (Table 4.4).

Occupational status is clearly an important indicator. In 1956 the proportion of salaried male employees covered by schemes run by firms in the private sector was 71 per cent in comparison to 38 per cent of male 'wage earners'. Among women the proportions were 34 per cent and 23 per cent respectively (Government Actuary 1958: 5). Although not directly comparable with the 1965 survey, evidence from surveys in 1967 and 1971 suggests that the gap among non-manual and manual male workers had become slightly narrower, whereas among female workers it has widened slightly. In 1967 the proportion of non-manual males covered by schemes run by firms in the private and public sectors was 73 per cent and 88 per cent respectively. Among manual men the proportion was 58 per cent in the private sector and 64 per cent in the public sector, and among women 16 per cent and 13 per cent respectively. In 1971 the proportion of non-manual males covered by these schemes was 75 per cent in the private sector and 94 per cent in the public sector, and among women 36 per cent and 60 per cent respectively. Among manual males 45 per cent were covered in the private sector and 68 per cent in the public sector, and among women 19 per cent and 25 per cent respectively (see Government Actuary 1968: 7–8; 1972: 6, 8). If we focus solely on the 25–65 age group, we find that 67 per cent of non-manuals are covered by an occupational pension, 11 per cent by a private pension and 30 per cent by other financial arrangements for retirement. Among manuals, however, coverage in these three forms extends to only 47 per cent, 8 per cent and 24 per cent respectively (Ritchie and Barrowclough 1983: 23). A further indicator of provision for retirement is the gross household income of families and individuals. Evidence from the Family Expenditure Survey highlights the extreme gap between high-, middle- and low-

Table 4.4 Coverage of different groups in occupational pension schemes

	Full-time males (%)	Full-time females (%)
Managers	73	38
Supervisors and foremen	75	51
Engineers, scientists, technologists	79	63
Technicians	70	53
Academic and teaching	95	95
Medical, dental, nursing and welfare	90	77
Other professional and technical	73	65
Office and communications	72	41
Sales	54	11
Security	78	69
Catering, domestic and other services	33	22
Farming, forestry and horticulture	26	3
Transport	50	24
Building, engineering, etc.	39	15
Textiles, clothing and footwear	25	8
Other occupations	52	19
All employees	55	36
Of whom: manual	46	18
non-manual	75	47

Source CSO 1972: 94 and based on sample numbers in the New Earnings Survey 1970, which excluded members of the armed forces, employees in Northern Ireland and, possibly, some members of pension schemes whose benefits were lump sums only.

income households of similar size in relation to the amount they contribute to employers' pension funds and to life assurance (including industrial policies and mortgage endowment policies) (Table 4.5). This is hardly surprising, although it

Table 4.5 Contribution to employers' pension funds and to life assurance, 1985

Type of Household	Gross normal weekly income of household	Average weekly contribution to pension funds and life assurances
One man and one woman and two children	Under £175	£3.89
	£175 and under £250	£9.58
	£250 and under £350	£15.77
	£350 or over	£24.56
Average		£13.18

Source: Department of Employment: 1986: 49.

does raise the issue of the social and political bases of support for pension arrangements now and in the future.

SUPPORT FOR AND FURTHER CONSTRAINTS ON PENSION POLICIES

The social bases of support for occupational pensions

The notion that the advantage of an occupational pension arises out of advantageous socio-economic location and educational background is confirmed by data from the national survey on attitudes to welfare (Taylor-Gooby and Papadakis 1985b), (Table 4.6). For instance, 77 per cent of those with degrees or postgraduate qualifications and 61 per cent of those in non-manual occupations were members of occupational pension schemes. Support for Conservative and Alliance parties related more closely to membership of a scheme (57 and 62 per cent respectively) than support for the Labour Party (49 per cent). Among members of schemes, owner occupiers predominated over public and private tenants by a ratio of more than 2 : 1. The most striking aspect, however, is the lack of correspondence between membership of occupational schemes and attitudes towards expenditure on welfare and taxation. It has been suggested that the existence of occupational schemes will tend to diminish the demand for stable or better state benefits (Reddin 1982: 147). Although 68 per cent of those who did want a reduction in taxes were members of occupational schemes, they only represent a minority. Eighty-seven per cent of members of occupational schemes either favoured continuity in current levels of expenditure or wanted an increase.

As we mentioned earlier, the Beveridge scheme aimed to provide a basic minimum. Despite the real increase in the value of state pensions, higher-income groups that have shared in the prosperity generated by post-war economic growth have either sought to invest their surplus themselves in private pensions or have had it invested for them by their employers in occupational schemes. (The survey by Ritchie and Barrowclough 1983 shows the varying degrees to which manual/non-manual, owner-occupiers/tenants and people on different incomes have invested in private pensions or other financial policies.)

Tax relief and the limits to privatization

Ever since the last war, governments of all political persuasions have actively encouraged occupational pensions by offering generous tax relief on schemes and many other concessions. A recent estimate of tax relief on pensions arrives at a figure for 1983/4 of between £1.85 billion and £3.35 billion—the latter being far more realistic (Wilkinson 1986). The extent of the subsidy raises, once again, the issue of a clash between social policy goals: on the one hand, the encouragement, through subsidy, of provision for old age, and on the other, the aim of greater distributional equality. The former is advanced not only through tax relief on the value of the employee's contribution and on the value of the employer's contribution, but also 'the exemption from tax of the investment income and capital gains of superannuation funds, the exemption of lump-sum payments from tax, and the treatment of pensions from superannuation as deferred pay —as earned income (Wilkinson 1986: 34). Over a four-year period, 1979–80 to 1983–4, tax relief on pensions doubled in real terms. This further illustrates the limits of government control of social expenditure. As with mortgage interest relief, tax relief on pensions implies a 'limitless commitment' which

Table 4.6 Characteristics of members/non-members of occupational pension schemes

| | Total in Employment | | | |
	Member of an Occupa-tional Pension Scheme (%)	Not a member of an Occupa-tional Pension Scheme (%)	No reply (%)	Base N =
Educational qualifications				
None	48	52	—	262
CSEs/O Levels	44	55	1	151
A Levels	56	44	—	36
Degree or post-graduate qualification	77	23	—	57
Other qualifi-cation	64	35	1	130
Occupational status				
Non-manual	61	39	—	345
Manual	44	55	1	291
Tenure				
Owner-occu-piers	57	42	1	445
Tenants (either council or private)	43	57	—	174
Political party				
Conservative	57	42	1	212
Labour	49	50	1	209
Alliance parties	62	38	—	127
Attitude to spending on health, education and pension and taxes				
Reduce taxes	68	32	—	34
Same level	53	47	—	287
More spending	55	45	—	258

Table 4.6 Continued

	Total in Employment	
	Member of an Occupational Pension Scheme (%)	Not a member of an Occupational Pension Scheme (%)

Educational qualifications

	(%)	(%)
None	37	45
CSEs/O Levels	19	28
A Levels	6	5
Degree or post-graduate qualification	13	4
Other qualification	24	15
Other, no reply	—	2

Occupational status

Non-manual	62	45
Manual	38	53
Other, no reply	—	2

Tenure

Owner-occupiers	75	62
Tenants (either council or private)	22	33
Other, no reply	3	4

Political party

Conservative	36	30
Labour	30	35
Alliance parties	23	16
Other, no reply	11	19

| Base N= | 340 | 300 |

Table 4.6 Continued

	Total in Employment	
	Member of an Occupational Pension Scheme (%)	Not a member of an Occupational Pension Scheme (%)
Attitude to spending on health, education and pensions and taxes		
Reduce taxes	7	4
Same level	45	45
More spending	42	39
Other, no reply	7	13
Base N =	340	300

Source: Taylor-Gooby and Papadakis 1985b.

will vary according to the number of investors multiplied by the level of investment eligible for relief, and contrary to any egalitarian distributional aims of social policy, the prime beneficiaries are the high-income groups, who can invest more than low-income groups.

The policy of privatization, though open to public influence, is largely worked out on the basis of bargains made between corporate bodies and of subsidies made to them by the government, rather than by the liberalization of market forces. Governments have thus lent powerful support to those companies and organizations that seek to restrain labour mobility, engage in corporate paternalism and increase their popularity by offering occupational schemes. More recently, many companies have actively sought to involve staff in the running of such schemes. The Confederation of British Industry has argued that participation by employees in the management of the schemes can lead to improved staff relations and a greater sense of 'partnership'. However, under the prevailing institutional structures, where there is no standardization of employee involvement, it could place further barriers on occupational mobility, let alone reinforce mechanisms of control, whereby conformity to employer guidelines becomes a precondition for the realization of benefits from such a partnership.

There is clearly widespead support for occupational pensions. As shown in our national survey, 57 per cent thought they were very important and 32 per cent fairly important. However, support for state pensions is even stronger, with 91 per cent affirming that they were very important and 7 per cent fairly important. The pattern of consensus in support for state and occupational pensions is not repeated over the issue of satisfaction with state pensions. Whilst 45 per cent of the sample were either fairly or very satisfied with state pensions, 49 per cent were either not very (30 per cent) or not at all (19 per cent) satisfied. Yet in recent years the trend has been towards a rise in pensioners' income from state rather than occupational pensions. In an analysis of the growth in spending on state pensions between 1951 and 1978, Judge argues that the increase in the number of pensioners resulted in 43.3 per cent of the total growth and that the major proportion, 56.7 per cent, was the outcome of a considerable improvement in the real rate of the state pension (Judge 1981). This leaves considerable scope for conflict in the future over whether to spend more on state pensions or make further concessions to occupational and private schemes.

Demographic change, politics and inequality

Projections about future rates of expenditure and demographic change can be used to predict either an increase or a levelling off in the cost of pensions to the population. Judge, for example, uses the time-scale of 1978 to 2001 to predict that the number of elderly people at or above the retirement age will remain unchanged and, therefore expenditure on state pensions will decrease. The Conservative government adopted a fifty-year time-scale to emphasize the demographic pressures that will add to the cost for the state which is already overloaded with its commitment to SERPS. In the 1985 Green Paper it stressed how the number of pensioners will rise by four million and the ratio of working people to pensioners will decline steadily, thus imposing a huge cost on those still at work and contributing to National Insurance (Table 4.7). This has allowed the government to work on a broad foundation in its attempt to extend occupational welfare: on the argument of the cost of state pensions accentuated by demographic changes; on the prevailing consensus of support for private and public welfare; and on the encouragement of occupational welfare by all previous governments.

Table 4.7 Demographic factors affecting pensions

Year	Pensioners (millions)	National Insurance contributors (millions)	Ratio of National Insurance contributors to pensioners
1985	9.3	21.8	2.3
1995	9.8	21.9	2.2
2005	10.0	22.2	2.2
2015	11.1	22.4	2.0
2025	12.3	21.9	1.8
2035	13.2	21.8	1.6

Source: DHSS, 1985a, vol. 2: 4.

In addition, its action follows a tradition of politically calculated decisions on pensions. As Judge suggests, under both the government of Harold Macmillan in 1958 and the Labour government in 1974, major increases in state pensions were granted in the context of powerful political pressures (Judge 1981: 525–7). The Conservatives under Margaret Thatcher have not revised the basic consensus over welfare but have chosen to politicize particular aspects of it, especially the idea of freedom of choice. In contrast to government policies on state expenditure and welfare as a whole, the attempt to remind people of the dual nature of pensions provision may strike a powerful note of approval above all among those who benefit most from occupational schemes.

A critique of the government from the standpoint that its policies may increasingly lead to a dual society — with some people covered extensively by occupational welfare and others who depend mainly on an impoverished public sector —would appear more valid than one which focuses on a conspiracy to mislead people about the merits of belonging to pension schemes. Very few people seriously believe that they are getting something for nothing. (This should be contrasted with the scenario painted by Reddin 1982: 146 and Disney 1985: 63.) According to a recent survey, 38 per cent of employees regarded their pension as a means for the employer to compel them to save; 25 per cent saw it as deferred pay: 19 per cent as a reward for loyalty; and 10 per cent as a means for the employer to recruit staff (Gallup Report 1984). A simple interpretation of these figures would suggest that those who regard it as a form of compulsory saving (63 per cent of the sample) are aware of their entitlement to the pension and do not regard it as a gift. This interpretation conflicts with that of Reddin, who argues that employers' contributions 'conceal costs from employees, creating the illusion that somebody else is paying for benefits' (Reddin 1982: 183) rather than, ultimately, the employees themselves. At most, 29 per cent of the sample harbour this illusion.

Contrary to Reddin, we find that pensions does not fit snugly into the traditional perception of British industrial relations since pensions, unlike wages, have been an issue of low 'class struggle'. This is not to deny that pensions and wages are interrelated and that there is a need for a social base, broader than occupation, to determine the level of income in retirement. However, the implied notion of false consciousness is difficult to sustain: most people are aware of their overlapping role as both consumers, earners and tax-payers. Reddin may be confusing the general reluctance of people to talk about their pension rights with what he considers to be an illusory perception of these rights. The system of occupational welfare merely provides them with a further opportunity to pursue their own interests. The unintended consequence of the framework in which they operate is that it perpetuates and develops the dual society—of insiders who are increasingly able to enjoy occupational or private pensions, health care and education, and outsiders who rely almost entirely on state benefits.

CONCLUSION

An immense effort was made by the Conservative government to review pensions arrangements, to assess the long-term prospects of schemes and to put into practice some of the principles it cherishes most of all. However, confronted by highly complex and entrenched institutional arrangements and by the ambiguities of public opinion, it had to settle for far less than it had originally intended. Its attempt to project into the middle of the next century both economic costs and social and political changes in attitudes implies an overestimation of the capacity of a single government, over a limited period in office, to bring about rapid changes. Politically, the appeal to freedom of choice was an attempt to gain support for new arrangements for occupational and private pensions, yet it appeared to underestimate popular awareness of the real benefits to be gained under SERPS —comprising, as it does, both state and private initiatives. The attempt to enhance freedom of choice was itself highly ambiguous. It arose not as a result of any popular movement or self-organization but was initiated from above, by government agencies, and, although open to suggestions by individuals for reforms, was dominated by the established lobby groups: employer and worker organizations and powerful financial institutions.

Although most people, who could afford to, would prefer to belong to a private pensions arrangement which did not mix 'their fate with the fates of those less fortunate or well placed than themselves' (Weale 1985a: 329), support for state pensions remains very high. Criticism of state pensions is based almost exclusively on the premise that they are inadequate (and therefore should be improved) rather than on any desire to abolish them altogether. As Weale suggests, one of the covert aims of the 1985 Green Paper on Social Security may have been to prepare the ground for a transfer of control over savings for retirement from the state to the private sector — hence the allusion to the fact that pensions savings could represent for many people a far bigger asset than ownership of their homes (Weale 1985a: 330). However, whereas ownership of a house or of British Telecom shares represents an asset that is either more tangible or realizable in the short-term, this does not apply to retirement pensions. Above all, the prospect of being responsible for successfully investing their savings towards retirement via a private pension arrangement would be far too daunting for most people—or, at least, most are not prepared to consider it and continue to place a high value on the guarantee of a state pension. Conservative policy, whether it sought to pander to electoral wishes or to steer the electorate in new directions was constrained by the ambiguities of public preferences and by the institutional setting—both public and private.

5 Private housing

BACKGROUND

In terms of the restructuring of the state involvement in welfare, the housing sector has witnessed some of the most dramatic changes in recent years. The reason for this lies in the massive state-sponsored privatization of council housing. The rationale underlying these policies has been characterized by its supporters as the extension of freedom of choice and by its opponents as the demotion of public housing to a residual role. In order to test these claims we examine the crucial role played by the state in regulating the development of both public and private sectors; the nature and extent of support for owner occupation by the major political parties; the weaknesses of the private rented sector (notably, the high proportion of older dwellings, poor rate of return on investment and the conflict between landlord and tenant); and the provision of public housing and its limitations. Equally relevant is an assessment of the development of mass private ownership—its social characteristics and the power of the building societies and other financial institutions; and the various interpretations of these changes, especially in terms of their distributional consequences, the incorporation of the working class and the impact on voting patterns, the apparent advantages of owner occupation and the alleged polarization between owner occupation and other forms of tenure. The straightforward division of the population into different tenure groups is central to some of these interpretations. These, however, should be treated with caution because of the importance of state intervention for all forms of tenure; housing provision does not enjoy the same universalistic status as other forms of public welfare; and the complexities are becoming more marked as a result of the extension of owner occupation.

STATE INTERVENTION IN HOUSING

The origins of extensive state intervention in the housing sector can be traced to the development of nineteenth-century capitalism linked to industrialization and urban expansion. The outcome, in terms of housing, was immense overcrowding and the outbreak of epidemics as a result of poor sanitation. The first legal measures adopted by the state to clear slums (the Artisans and Labourers Dwellings Act of 1868, or 'Torrens' Act, and the Artisans and Labourers Dwellings Improvement Act of 1875, or 'Cross' Act) were largely ineffective due to ratepayers' resistance to fund these measures or, when the measures were enacted, they simply forced the poor to move elsewhere. Local authorities at the time provided very little alternative accommodation. When legislation was passed to house the working class (1890, 1894 and 1900), local authorities based many of their criteria of eligibility and tenure on the approach of philanthropic societies. Accommodation was offered mainly to those who would more likely conform to management attitudes and practices. The alternative aspects of local authority accommodation, both in terms of design and the rules imposed, can be traced to and vividly illustrated by practices at the turn of the century. Tenants of the Peabody Trust, for instance, faced numerous restrictions once they did gain access to the 'barrack-like' dwellings: they 'could not sublet, take in washing, undertake outwork, keep pets, paper their rooms, hang pictures on their walls or stay out after 11 p.m.' (Burke 1981: 4). Whilst the early initiatives by the state were a reflection of the failure of the market to provide suitable accommodation, later interventions were also determined by political pressures. Local authority housing did not 'take off' until after the First World War (Balchin 1981: 105). Whereas in the late nineteenth century slum clearance partly occurred in anticipation of social unrest from among the poorest and most disaffected (Burke 1981: 6), involvement in the First World War created a much greater potential for change and social protest.

The state referred to its post-war initiatives as an attempt to create 'Homes fit for heroes'. In reality, the bargaining position of the majority of the population had been greatly enhanced by the massive casualties it had suffered and sacrifices it had made during war. In exchange for military obligations it was in a powerful position to demand concessions in terms of greater welfare and socio-economic security (Giddens 1985). The aftermath of the Second World War was, similarly, a time in which the state responded to political pressures for good quality council housing and placed severe restrictions on speculative building.

More fundamentally, perhaps, the failure of the market to meet housing needs has acted as a spur to state provision, subsidy and regulation. A major regulatory move was the Rent and Mortgage Restrictions Act of 1915, which imposed rent controls on the private sector and paved the way for state provision of housing for the working class. The Housing and Town Planning Act of 1919 foreshadowed massive state-sponsored housing programmes which would provide local authorities with subsidies so that they could charge rents below the market level. Yet state intervention in the housing market was unable to meet the demand for suitable accommodation so that subsidies soon had to be extended to the private building industry to try and make up the shortfall. Neither state nor market, even through co-operation, were able to achieve this. None the less, the role of the state had become firmly established with local authorities controlling 10 per cent of the housing stock in 1938. The private rented sector remained the largest with 58 per cent of the stock, followed by owner occupation (32 per cent) (Table 5.1).

The war reinforced these trends and gave shape to a policy of much greater control over the private sector. The Ridley Report (1945) argued strongly against the principle of decontrol on vacant possession, pointing to the many hardships which it had caused. The difficulties encountered by

Table 5.1 Housing stock and tenure, England and Wales, 1914–84

Year	Owner occupied (%)	Local authority[a] (%)	Privately rented[b] (%)	Total housing stock (Millions)
1914	10	—	90	7.9
1938	32	10	58	11.4
1960	44	25	32	14.6
1971	53	29	19	17.1
1981	59	29	13	19.1
1984	63	26	11	19.7

Notes: (a) Includes new towns.
(b) Includes minor tenures such as housing associations.
Sources: DoE 1977, 1980 and 1985.

tenants in the private rented sector help a great deal to explain widespread support for other forms of tenure. By the mid-1960s, despite repeated efforts to decontrol the private rented sector, even the Conservatives accepted the need for controls in London at least (Duclaud-Williams 1978: 78). The background to this was the Milner Holland Report (1965) which found evidence of widespread harassment and evictions. Insecurity of tenure rather than high rents appeared to be the major problem, though both issues were the subject of legislation from the 1950s onwards: on the one hand, through measures of radical decontrol introduced by the Conservatives (1957) (which were partly aimed at encouraging private landlords to repair and maintain their properties and partly to facilitate evictions) and, on the other hand, through controls of rents and tenure arrangements introduced by the Labour Party (the Protection from Eviction Act of 1964 and the Rent Act of 1965). Control of private renting was a major election issue in the mid-1960s ably exploited by Harold Wilson with the concern about Rachmanism. It is in the late 1960s that housing pressure groups (e.g. Shelter), squatting campaigns and support for Homeless Persons' legislation began to make an impact on the agenda for change. However, any attempt to protect tenants simply made private landlordism less attractive as an occupation, whilst measures aimed at encouraging repair and maintenance failed to halt the decline both in quality and quantity of the houses available. The returns on an investment in this sector were, apart from the top end of the market, simply unattractive. By 1960 owner occupation had overtaken the private rented sector as the most popular form of tenure. Despite their different approaches on how to protect tenants and develop the private rented sector, neither of the major parties were able to halt its decline. Choice became increasingly restricted to council housing or owner occupation.

In the aftermath of the war, council housing was accorded the highest priority and the annual rate of construction rose from 200,000 in the last year of the Attlee government (1951) to 300,000 in 1954 under the guidance of Macmillan as housing minister. To some, such a policy reflected an intensification of pre-war trends (Donnison 1967; Burke 1981) rather than a qualitatively different approach. Although housing 'lacked the dimension of universality' (Kirwan 1984: 135) apparent in the fundamental alterations to the health and social security systems, one can hardly ignore the rejection of the dominant role of private landlordism through

the firm establishment of the twin principles of 'housing as of right' (which was embodied in the concept of the waiting list and permanent tenure irrespective of changes in household need), and of 'non-profit provision' (embodied in the historic cost-financing system)

(Kirwan 1984: 134)

Whilst Labour policy implied a commitment to these new principles, Conservative policy was ambivalent. It supported the new consensus, yet was prepared to undermine it: by decontrolling the advantageous interest rates offered to local authorities via the Public Works Loans Board and allowing them to rise to a market level in 1956 (Burke 1981: 19); and by reducing subsidies to council housing (Duclaud-Williams 1978: 237). Politically, the Conservatives anticipated later support for owner occupation by publishing a White Paper on housing (1953) which argued that people prefer 'to help themselves as much as they can rather than rely wholly or mainly upon the efforts of Government, national or local' (quoted in Burke 1981: 18). The theme of creating a 'property-owning democracy' was developed around this time by

Macmillan. Conservative politicians did remain generally in agreement with the Labour Party over the 'need principle' for the allocation of housing. They were, however, critical of the 'ineffficiency' of local authorities who 'built their own estates rather than contract with private firms' (Duclaud-Williams 1978: 157). The Conservatives undid some of the controls over the housing industry, lending a new lease of life to speculative building. The turning point in the number of housing completions in the public and private sectors occurred in 1958. In the previous decade public-sector completions enjoyed a 2.6: 1 advantage over the private sector, after which the balance was tipped the other way (Duclaud-Williams 1978: 177).

However, it was the failure of both major parties to develop suitable policies for the private rented sector that increasingly limited the choice of consumers either to a council dwelling or to becoming an owner occupier. In times when 'freedom of choice' has become a popular slogan, a glimpse into how choice has been limited (partly as a result of state policies on public renting, private renting and owner occupation) helps to explain contemporary enthusiasm for some forms of tenure and not others.

PRIVATE RENTING

As far back as in the 1930s a chairman of the Building Societies' Association stated, 'The new owner occupiers were so by necessity rather than choice ... the main source of the increased demand for building society mortgages came from people forced to become owner occupiers because there were no houses to let' (quoted in Ball 1983: 39, and Boddy 1980: 15). The faith of the post-war Labour government in council housing and the impact it would have on meeting needs meant that it more or less ignored the private rented sector, only to be jolted into action by Conservative policies of decontrol (1957–65). However, neither policies which favoured land-lords nor those which favoured tenants went anywhere near tackling the problems faced by this sector. Statistically, the decline can be charted as follows: from a situation of almost total domination in 1914 (90 per cent of tenures), to one of supremacy in 1947 (61 per cent), to one of marginalization from 31 per cent in 1960 to 11 per cent in 1983. The dramatic decline is more noticeable when expressed in terms of relative rather than net losses of dwellings. A major weakness of the private rental sector is that it comprises some of the oldest and least maintained housing stock. On every measure of housing standards, it fares worse than all the other tenures (CSO 1985b: 125). As a consequence it has assumed a marginal role serving specific social groups at different stages of the life-cycle. For the young the furnished sector has frequently been a stepping stone before they sign up for a mortgage (Kemeny 1981: 133). Two-thirds of tenants in this sector were under 29 years old, whereas those aged over 65 comprised well over half of the tenants in the unfurnished sector (OPCS 1985: 71).

The decline in private rented accommodation has occurred in the latter, where conditions of tenure have been more secure. However, the decline cannot simply be blamed on rent control legislation but rather on the increasing appeal of public housing and owner occupation as a result of massive state subsidies; and on the long-term weaknesses of the housing market. The rents that landlords would have to charge on newly built or recently repaired and maintained dwellings in order to acquire an attractive return on their investment leave them with little chance of competing with the other heavily subsidized sectors. Where landlords have been able to improve their property, they have opted for a quick return on their investment by selling it for owner occupation. Both the age of rented properties and changes in public preferences may also play an important role. The demolition of hundreds of thousands of old dwellings in the slum clearance programmes (from the 1930s onwards) meant that demand was met either by the state or by the expansion of owner occupancy. The same applies to policies which tackled overcrowding (the Housing Acts of 1961, 1964 and 1969) and thereby reduced the number of private tenants, and to housing rehabilitation programmes whereby landlords, having im-proved their properties with state suppoprt, then sold them (Balchin 1985: 92–3). These factors may have engendered a dif-ferent and more negative attitude towards private renting: in countries where private renting faces little competition from public renting (USA), where rent controls are minimal and combined with subsidies (France, West Germany, Denmark and the Netherlands) and where private renting has hitherto enjoyed widespread popularity (Sweden), there has been a decline in this sector (Harloe 1979; Balchin 1985: 95; Kemeny 1981: 111).

Other options for renting are through housing associations or local authorities. Yet, here too the limits of choice are becoming increasingly apparent. Housing associations have never controlled more than a marginal proportion of the housing stock: about 1 per cent from 1971 to 1980 and 2 per cent from 1981 to 1983. Their main advantages are that they have often been managed less bureaucratically than local authority housing and provide shelter to disadvantaged groups such as the elderly, single people, single-parent families and the unemployed. The main weaknesses are that their rents are often far higher than council rents; standards are often poor; they are insufficiently accountable to public authorities despite receiving substantial subsidies; their screening procedures may discriminate against prospective tenants; tenants have limited protection from eviction; and they are generally inefficient because of the high turnover in management and administrative staff (Balchin 1985: 130–3). Whereas in the 1960s the Conservatives attempted to stimulate the expansion of private rented accommodation by providing assistance to housing associations so that rented accommodation at cost might expand (Duclaud-Williams 1978: 91), in the 1980s they introduced legislation granting housing association tenants the right to buy their homes. Any discussion of the limits of choice needs to consider the complex ways in which state policies may influence citizens to opt for particular tenure arrangements. In the case of private renting many of these options have gradually been eliminated—at least for the foreseeable future— partly to the benefit of public renting and owner occupation.

PUBLIC RENTING

The influences of state policy on decisions by citizens to opt for or out of public housing can occur at the following levels:

retrenchment or reallocation of state expenditure; popular myths about the inefficiency of the public sector; genuine failings in the public rental system; and the inability of the state to cope with long-term problems.

The most well-known failure of state policy has been its inability to provide rental accommodation both to those on waiting lists and to those registered as homeless in England and Wales. From 26,000 households in 1976, the ranks of the latter had swelled to 73,000 in 1983. Those on waiting lists in 1983 numbered 1.6 million; and, according to one estimate, those joining this queue would have to wait twenty-one years before gaining access to a council dwelling (Balchin 1985: 172). Even when access is gained, it does not necessarily match expectations: a considerable number of dwellings lack basic amenities and are in serious need of repair; others are either difficult-to-let or simply left empty because of neglect and deterioration. What Kemeny describes as the 'social organization' of council housing may also exert a powerful disincentive effect on public support for council housing: tenants have very little choice in the type of dwelling they are allocated; they enjoy little or none of the relative control exercised by owner occupiers in security of tenure and residential mobility; and they are often confronted by a vast bureaucratic system of management that takes a patronizing and authoritarian stance towards them (Kemeny 1981; Kilroy 1979; Ball 1983; Balchin 1985).

The acuteness of these problems has been acknowledged by all major political parties, though each has interpreted them differently. The Conservatives, in the 1980 Housing Act, introduced a Tenants' Charter which emphasized freedom of choice and opportunity (Burke 1981: 154): this meant allowing them to repair and redecorate their dwellings and to take in lodgers; making it easier for them to have greater say in management of the council estate and to apply for improvement grants; and strengthening their security of tenure. Many of these proposals formed part of a Housing Bill which the previous Labour government had planned to introduce and are supported by the Social Democrats and Liberals. However, some critics would argue that as far as the Conservatives are concerned, the main motive for these changes is to reduce public expenditure rather than enhance democratic participation (Balchin 1985: 180). Arguments over retrenchment or reallocation of state expenditure are central to whether the public sector is increasingly becoming a residual one and being sacrificed on the altar of owner occupation or not.

The most pertinent reply by Conservatives to criticisms of their policies of retrenchment is that there is nothing novel about them and they simply reflect continuity with a trend begun by Labour governments. Between 1974/5 and 1979/80, under the Labour government, public expenditure on housing was reduced by 25 per cent in real terms, whilst strict limits were placed on local authority house-building programmes (Balchin 1985). Capital expenditure on land and new dwellings was reduced in real terms by 4.2 per cent between 1975/6 and 1976/7 and 17.5 per cent in the following financial year (Lansley 1979: 124); in 1981 real capital expenditure on dwellings was 15 per cent of that in 1976 and the number of new dwellings started 20,600 in comparison with 107,600 in 1976 (Ball 1983: 8).

However, since coming into office the Conservative government has intensified this process. In real terms public expenditure on housing was reduced by 45 per cent between 1979/80 and 1984/5. Measured in 'volume input' terms, the reduction is closer to 52 per cent (Robinson 1986: 8). The major cutbacks were in current expenditure subsidies to local authority housing (by 79 per cent over that period) and in expenditure on new dwellings (by 68 per cent). Yet some of these reductions have been offset by increases in other areas: in the case of subsidies to local authorities (mainly for council rents), tenants are now able to apply for rent rebates via the social security system—indeed the number of eligible applicants rose from 1.2 million to 3.8 million—and there appear to have been limited negative distributional con-sequences. Similarly, the decline in expenditure on new dwellings—leading to a reduction from 70,000 completions in 1979/80 to less than 30,000 in 1984/5—may have been offset by massive increases (over 300 per cent) in expenditure on improvement and insulation grants. In the latter example, however, the distribution may have favoured the better-off since the grants, taken up by over a quarter of a million people in 1983/4, were not related to income. The final outcome of these changes may entail not so much a real reduction in expenditure on housing, but a fundamental restructuring of it, which is turning local authority housing 'into a residual, welfare sector catering for only low-income households and those families with special needs' (Robinson 1986: 7).

Although new rights and freedoms were being granted to council tenants, pressures were being applied on them to reconsider their position in the public rented sector. For the more prosperous, the inducements are twofold: the right to buy their dwelling at a considerable discount or to remain as tenants paying much higher rents. Poorer tenants generally have little option but to join the ranks of the millions of recipients of rent rebates and supplementary benefits. Those receiving such benefits rose from 40 to 48 per cent of all tenants between 1979/80 and 1982/3. The better-off tenants had to meet the full cost of their rent, which rose by 109 per cent between 1979/80 and 1982/3, in comparison with a 70 per cent rise in gross earnings (Balchin 1985: 164–5). Clearly, some tenants had in the past benefited from relatively low rents in the public sector, which on average comprised only 6.4 per cent of gross average wages in 1979/80 and subsequently rose to 8.8 per cent in 1982/3—the highest since the Second World War (Balchin 1985: 169). Although the new system of allocation had the potential to enhance both economic equality and social justice, these advantages may have been cancelled out both economically (through massive subsidies directed towards owner occupation) and politically (through the creation of a residual, socially distinct public housing sector).

There is little doubt that the state has been either unable or unwilling to tackle some of the weaknesses of the housing sector. However, many of its achievements are ignored in an attempt to justify the alleged superiority of owner occupation as an ideal form of tenure. One of the most popular myths is that of the uncontrolled public housing debt: 'In money terms it did increase, 1965–80, but in real terms fell continually from 1968, and inflation eroded the existing debt. In contrast the mortgage debt increased eightfold in money terms, and doubled in real terms over the same period' (Balchin 1985: 29). Above all, because local authority housing is not constantly subject to revaluation and exchange, it does not generate the same 'remarkably high degree of indebtedness' (Kemeny 1981: 142) as the owner-occupied sector. Local authority housing has the added advantage of being organized on a collective basis: losses incurred in rents from new, more expensive dwellings can be offset by gains on older ones where most of the debt has already been paid off. Although, as indicated earlier, the condition of many of these older dwellings is far from ideal, poor housing standards are also a problem confronting the owner-occupied sector; in proportionate terms there are as many if not more owner-occupied dwellings which are unfit, lack basic amenities and are in serious disrepair as council dwellings (Balchin 1985; CSO 1985b: 125). Critics of the failure of state policies to deal with long-term problems of economic change and social justice (Ball 1983; George and Wilding 1984) have also mentioned the vast improvement in housing conditions and standards, the demolition of slums and the net annual gain of around 200,000 to 250,000 dwellings between the early 1950s and 1980. This figure has fallen below 200,000 for the period up to 1985.

Changes in demographic structure, the need to build, repair and maintain houses as well as changing expectations are, none the less, posing a continued challenge to state policy. Lansley, referring to the period 1976–86, estimated that 6.27 million dwellings were required to meet 'current' and 'future' needs (Lansley 1979: 96). To meet current shortages (particularly the replacement of unfit, substandard dwellings) would have required another 2.73 million dwellings; to meet future shortages (particularly due to the formation of new households and to replace housing that would be unfit or in disrepair) would have required another 3.54 million dwellings. This implied, for England and Wales, an annual rate of 627,000 completions: yet the total number of dwellings built in the UK dropped from 320,000 in 1975 to 180,000 in 1982, with a slight recovery to nearly 200,000 by 1985. Local authorities were the worst-affected with falls to levels recorded previously in the 1920s, from 130,000 in 1975 to 40,000 in 1982 and 30,000 by 1985 (CSO 1987: 143). The number of completions fell to less than 10,000 in the first half of 1986/7 (Treasury 1987 vol. II: 153). The consequences for the construction industry have been disastrous: hundreds of thousands of workers have been made redundant and many firms have gone bankrupt. The state is faced with the additional cost of attempting to provide massive subsidies both to owner occupiers and to council tenants (Ball 1983: 10). The strategy for the 1980s is to favour the former at the expense of the latter. We now explore some of the initiatives taken by the state to encourage owner occupation and, in some respects, to direct attention away from some of the more fundamental problems faced by both producers and consumers of housing.

OWNER OCCUPATION

Although there is nothing new about state encouragement of owner occupation, it has been argued that the shift during the twentieth century of state subsidies (and other independent sources of finance) away from investor landlords to middle-income households is 'little short of revolutionary' (Kemeny 1981: 73). Ball mentions four key aspects of state legislation to encourage home ownership: the creation of preconditions for market exchange; lowering the income threshold to owner-ship; supplying subsidies for rehabilitation and selling land at low prices; and the introduction of tax reliefs (Ball 1983). He also makes the distinction between capital and current expenditure subsidies. The former refers to preferential tax treatment of wealth in the form of owner-occupied housing, improvement grants, expenditure on the built environment and providing builders with opportunities to make windfall gains. The latter refers mainly to mortgage interest tax relief to owner occupiers. Our main concern is with those aspects of legislation which have recently begun to tilt the balance even more in favour of owner occupation. Although it is difficult, if not impossible, to quantify the effects of some of the legislation, one can arrive at an estimate of some tax reliefs and their distributional impact.

We refer first to the abolition of Schedule A tax and the

exclusion of owner occupiers from capital gains tax. Schedule A was introduced in 1803. It was directed at income from land and buildings and based either on the revenue received from rented houses or the estimated rental value of owner-occupied houses (minus costs such as interest payments on a mortgage, repairs and maintenance)—hence, a tax on 'imputed' income for owner occupiers. In an attempt to gain electoral support prior to the 1963 elections, the Conservatives abolished the tax. At the time this seemed to be a minor change since 'the tax loss involved in abolition was relatively small' (Cullingworth 1979: 100–1). Yet owner occupiers now enjoyed a double advantage: even though its 'rationale had disappeared', deduction of mortgage interest payments from taxable income was not terminated (Le Grand 1982: 91). The major political parties had all supported the abolition of Schedule A tax and have never since advocated its re-introduction even though it has added significantly to the privileged position of owner occupiers (Duclaud-Williams 1978: 239; Le Grand 1982: 88–93).

Second, we note the importance of mortgage interest tax relief to home-owners. It was introduced, before the Second World War, at a time when most people did not pay any income tax. However, in the post-war context of increasing affluence, the creation of the welfare state and the broadening of the tax base, it has become a crucial determinant in encouraging owner occupation. Although the subsidy is not in any way directly related to housing needs, many people would be unable to purchase a house without it. This, however, may be a perverse effect of tax relief in increasing prices. Until 1983 interest payments on mortgages could be deducted from income for tax assessment purposes, which meant that the higher your tax bracket, the more you benefited from tax relief. Since then, with the introduction of Mortgage Interest Relief at Source (MIRAS), mortgagors pay the building societies or other lending institutions the full interest rate minus the basic rate of tax. The subsidy is so large that even the Conservative government, when it came into office in 1979, might have considered abolishing it (Burke 1981: 38; Balchin 1985: 256). Although subject to a ceiling of £30,000 (which has not been uprated in line with inflation), the subsidy represents a 'limitless commitment' (Ball 1983: 11) which, according to some estimates favoured high-income owner occupiers compared to lower-income occupiers by a ratio of over 6 : 1 (Le Grand 1982: 92). The mortgage interest relief subsidy in 1980/1 was five and a half times higher in real terms than in 1970/1 (Ball 1983: 9). A significant number of studies have also found 'no evidence for the claim that public housing tenants are more heavily subsidised than owner occupiers' (Kirwan 1984: 139). As Ball points out, some of the major subsidies to council housing have not been housing subsidies but income maintenance subsidies (Ball 1983: 341) and this has been 'recognized' by the recent measures to pay rent rebates via the social security rather than housing subsidy system.

Government subsidies for renovations in the 1970s and 1980s have provided another incentive for owner occupation, particularly in older dwellings. Studies suggest, however, that the main recipients of these grants were young households with above-average incomes; that younger people would not have been willing to purchase older houses had they not been aware of the possibility of getting assistance to improve their condition; that for many this was the only type of house they could afford; and that private landlords would have had little economic incentive to compete with owner occupiers for such grants (Le Grand 1982: 90 refers to Whitehead 1977: 46 and DoE 1979: 21). In the 1980s reductions in local authority expenditure on new dwellings were partly offset by such grants. From a peak of about 240,000 grants to private owners and tenants in 1974, the number allocated solely to owner occupiers fell from 74,000 in 1975 to 55,000 in 1977 and had only recovered to 76,000 in 1981. In 1982 and 1983 there was a massive boom (122,000 and 279,000 respectively), partly fuelled by the offer of a 90 per cent grant for applications submitted to local authorities by 1 April 1984 (CSO 1985b: 133), which was then severely curtailed. Although undoubtedly helping to rehabilitate and maintain a large number of houses, the grants probably secured a long-term capital gain for better-off owner occupiers since they were not specifically targeted towards those on low incomes.

Owner occupation among low-income groups has been

encouraged by measures such as the Option Mortgage Scheme and the sale of council housing, although here too the distributional effect has been uneven. The Option Mortgage Scheme, introduced by the Labour government in 1968, was aimed at low-income households that were unable to gain as much (if any) mortgage interest relief as owner occupiers who paid tax at standard or higher rates. Through the scheme low-income households were not permitted to deduct interest from income for tax purposes but paid lower mortgage interest rates.

The government paid the loaning institution the difference between the lower rate and the standard rate. Within a year 200,000 people had joined the scheme and the numbers fluctuated thereafter: the peaks were in 1972 and in 1982 (when high tax rates improved the comparative advantage of the scheme), accounting for around one-fifth of all mortgages—about 217,000 mortgages in 1982. (Estimates are based on Balchin 1985: 222; Cullingworth 1979: 102; and DoE 1985: 126). This source of funding was later complemented by the efforts of Labour governments to increase the number of loans offered by local authorities to low-income households, particularly their own tenants. The proportion of option mortgages out of all local authority loans rose from about 13 per cent between 1969 and 1971 to 33 per cent in 1973 and to over 45 per cent from 1974 to 1979, with a peak in 1975 when 48,583 out of the 101,952 loans were option mortgages (DoE 1980: 144).

The most forceful attempt by government to boost home ownership in recent years has occurred through legislation introduced by the Conservatives in 1980 and 1984. The 1980 Housing Act compelled local authorities to sell dwellings at a considerable discount (up to 50 per cent) on the market value. The 1984 Act raised the possible discount to 60 per cent and the 1986 Act further increased it to 70 per cent. The sale of council houses has been permitted ever since 1925. However, the emphasis was on building rather than disposal, at least until the Housing Act of 1957, introduced by the Conservatives and allowing, under certain conditions, discounts of up to 20 per cent on sales of council dwellings. The Act did not open the floodgates, although in the early

1970s Conservative Party dominance did steer sales to five figures (Table 5.2). Control by the Party of several metropolitan local authorities again boosted sales from 1977 onwards, although resistance and reversal of such policies was still liable to occur, for instance, through the re-acquisition of dwellings in Manchester (at the cost of £1 million per month in 1977) (Balchin 1985: 182). The 1980 and 1984 Acts not only offered substantial discounts but sought to prevent any resistance by Labour-controlled local authorities enabling the government to intervene and carry out sales if necessary. The impact was without precedent: sales rose from 42,460 in 1979 to a peak of 207,050 in 1982.

Table 5.2 Sale of dwellings by local authorities and new towns, England and Wales, 1970–86

Year	Number	Year	Number
1970	6,231	1978	30,620
1971	16,851	1979	42,460
1972	45,058	1980	85,700
1973	33,720	1981	106,485
1974	5,394	1982	207,050
1975	2,950	1983	146,450
1976	5,895	1984	107,230
1977	13,385	1985	95,300
		1986	101,500

Note: Numbers for 1970 to 1973 are for sales by local authorities; for 1974 to 1986, for all sales by local authorities and new towns.
Source: DoE 1985: 101; Balchin 1982: 182; Treasury 1987 vol. II: 154.

Demand in 1982 and 1983 was high: 9 per cent of tenants had taken active steps to buy their dwellings and a further 13 per cent had considered buying but not taken any action (OPCS 1985: 92). Between 1983 and 1986 around 400,000 tenants, 8 per cent of the total, bought their dwellings. According to a recent survey, 25 per cent of tenants said they probably would purchase their dwelling (Building Societies Association 1986a). It is hardly surprising that the number of sales, from 1979 onwards, easily outstripped the number of new dwellings being built by local authorities. The greatest interest in the scheme had been expressed by skilled manual and semi-skilled manual groups: though comprising 23 per cent of tenants, 43 per cent of the former had considered buying their accommodation; the latter, comprising 13 per cent of tenants were overrepresented by 5 percentage points, whilst the economically inactive heads of household (50 per cent of all tenants) were underrepresented by 31 percentage points (OPCS 1985: 70, 93).

The rapid growth of owner occupation from 55 per cent of all tenures in 1979 to 64 per cent in 1986 has been influenced to a significant degree by the sale of council dwellings: between 1981 and 1984 such sales contributed to about 40 per cent of the growth of owner occupation from 56.4 per cent to 60.9 per cent of all tenures (DoE 1985: 100–1).

State policy, in promoting the shift towards owner occupation, has both shaped and been influenced by popular notions of the superiority of this form of tenure and the constellations of power that have emerged around it. The following sections therefore explore, first, its advantages and pitfalls and whether it has responded to or helped to create a consistent ideology and, second, the development of mass private ownership, its socio-economic characteristics and the formation of particular interests, notably in and around building societies.

THE 'IDEOLOGY' OF OWNER OCCUPATION

The 'advantages'

Among the advantages commonly attributed to owner occupation are considerably enhanced security of tenure (Burke 1981: 37) and, for existing owner occupiers, greater flexibility over the timing of a move from one house to another (Ball 1983: 324). Kemeny (1981) refers to studies of owner occupation as a popular form of tenure (Couper and Brindley 1975; Sutcliffe 1974); or as one that encourages repair and maintenance of the housing stock (Alderston 1962; Grigsby 1963). The arguments can be linked to the notion of housing as a private rather than a merit good, whereby the benefits to the individual consumer arise from his or her capacity to select a particular 'mix, and level, of the wide range of attributes that make up the good housing' (Whitehead 1984: 116). However, when choice is dependent on state subsidies, it becomes a 'freedom' which is directed by state paternalism. The Conservative critique of state paternalism has not removed it 'but changed its nature' (Whitehead 1984: 131). Heavy-handed public-sector management has not been replaced by a more efficient, less alienating market-based structure.

On one issue at least, Conservative ideology converges with criticism of the adverse distributional effects of housing policy: both play down some of the disadvantages of private ownership for home-owners themselves. In the case of the Conservatives this is hardly surprising given their long-standing commitment to home ownership for its own sake or in order to improve political stability rather than as a model of successful free-market enterprise (Duclaud-Williams 1978: 247; George and Wilding 1984: 191).

Emphasis on the superior 'moral' value of house ownership can be traced back to nineteenth-century notions of social reform based on 'thrift and forethought' (Burke 1981: 39); to pledges by the Conservatives in the 1950s to create a 'property-owning democracy'; and to official policy statements in the 1960s and 1970s under both major parties. For the 1965 Wilson government the expansion of public housing was 'born partly of a short-term necessity, partly of the conditions inherent in modern urban life', whereas the expansion of building for owner occupation was 'normal' and reflected 'a long-term social advance which should gradually pervade every region' (*Housing Programme* 1965: 8). Under the Conservatives, owner occupation was regarded as the 'most rewarding form of tenure', satisfying 'a deep and natural desire on the part of the householder to have independent control of the home that shelters him and his family' and providing 'the greatest possible security against loss of his home; and particularly against price changes that may threaten his ability to keep it' (*Fair Deal for Housing* 1971: 4). Recent policies on private ownership have built on this tradition and widened the gap between free-market ideology and paternalist practice:

state subsidy not only establishes a form of 'home ownership "monopoly"' which eliminates 'real choice in housing tenure' (Kemeny 1981: 145), it also reflects 'market failure in the sense of an inability to satisfy housing needs cheaply or adequately' (Ball 1983: 338).

Any thought that may have been given to abolishing subsidies to owner occupation have been undermined either by political expediency or by arguments about the need to maintain political stability. Both these factors are central to any analysis of the 'ideology' of owner occupation. By abandoning any reservations it had towards owner occupation and through its unquestioning attitude, the Labour Party has been less able to focus on the disadvantages of this form of tenure. To a large extent, however, this reflects not so much the persuasiveness of a coherent ideology of owner occupation but what Ball refers to as the haphazard, passive and *status quo* orientation of policy: 'a fear by successive governments of undertaking any fundamental reform that includes owner occupation because of the perceived threat of a political backlash' (Ball 1983: 336). To some writers this fear reflects the adoption by governments of an ideology aimed at the incorporation of the working class.

Owner occupation and political consciousness

One of the most prevalent arguments is that workers, as owner occupiers, have a vested interest in the established order and are less likely to become involved in radical protest: an emphasis on wages to pay off the mortgage (linked to employment and career prospects) develops into an acceptance of established norms and values (Bassett and Short 1980; Harvey 1973). Others argue that owner occupiers have become, both in the interests they defend and their behaviour, a distinct 'housing class' (Rex and Moore 1967), and willing to engage in collective action to defend these interests (Saunders, 1979), for instance, in distinct forms of electoral behaviour (Dunleavy 1979a).

The incorporationist approaches have been criticized for their crude instrumentality and for their identification of 'a lack of organized political protest amongst owner occupiers with ideological acceptance of the political *status quo*' (Ball

1983: 284). The attempts to link owner occupation with electoral support for the Conservatives have been criticized for their ahistorical approach and terminological imprecision. The party preferences of owner occupiers are likely to be determined more by particular policies at a given time (hence by consideration of self-interest) than by inherent support for a particular ideology. Furthermore, the distinction made by Dunleavy between 'collectivized' public tenure and 'individualized' private ownership is not supported by the data used in his analysis (Ball 1983: 290). The complex nature of state intervention in all housing sectors makes such a distinction all the more implausible.

These approaches fail to consider both the variation in advantages or disadvantages experienced by consumers and the structure of the housing market. Among the long-term structural factors are the general crisis in the housing sector, particularly since 1973, when there was a significant drop in building starts and the collapse of many firms; the volatility of the housing market—from a situation in which house prices rose at a slower pace than the rate of inflation (1950s), to a boom period (1960s) and to sharp rises and falls (since the 1970s) (Ball 1983: 99); and the lack of supply of housing for those who wish to move into better and more expensive accommodation (Ball 1983: 334). The inability of the housing market to respond to demographic changes and the movement of population is another factor; for instance, between 1971 and 1981 the total population in Greater London declined by 0.75 million in contrast with a gain of 1.75 million in non-metropolitan, non-city districts, where 'there is a strong demand for new housing and pressure is often highest for family or retirement accommodation (Ball 1983: 248).

The gains to be made from investing in private home ownership tend to receive more attention than the less profitable aspects. This may be related to the increase of investment in land and housing as a proportion of personal wealth, for instance from 23 per cent in 1960 to 47 per cent in 1974 (Diamond Report 1976). Yet investment in housing, life insurance and pension funds, while accounting for 90 per cent of personal savings, reflects the favourable tax treatment given to these sectors (Balchin 1985: 243 refers to Kilroy 1980).

However, housing is a necessity which we cannot do without. Any gain that might be made on the sale of a house is mostly used to fund both the purchase of a more expensive one and the move itself (removal costs and solicitors', surveyors' and estate agents' fees) (Stow Report 1979; Ball 1983). The transactions involved in moving from one dwelling to another (particularly for existing owner occupiers) can be protracted (since a completed purchase frequently depends on a series of others in the 'chain' of moves by different households) and demoralizing (when someone breaks the chain). For prospective owner occupiers the major obstacle is to acquire sufficient funds, particularly in situations of price rises well above the rate of inflation. They are also likely to be using a high proportion of their wages to pay off their mortgage debt. Although comparative data is only indicative of trends (and is not adjusted to compensate for variations in taxation and mortgage interest relief), it shows that the ratio of initial mortgage repayments to average earnings has fluctuated from 25 per cent in the 1960s, to between 30 and 40 per cent in the 1970s, to 45 per cent in 1980 and 38 per cent in 1981 (Ball 1983: 367).

Though nowhere near as high as the proportion of council tenants, significant numbers of owner occupiers receive supplementary benefits. Their numbers have risen from 413,000 in 1979 to 603,000 in 1983, whereas the percentage increase of local authority tenants on supplementary benefits (from 1.266 million to 1.656 million) has been lower: 31 per cent in contrast with 46 per cent among owner occupiers (DoE 1985: 129). Unemployment has forced a small, yet increasing, number of households out of private ownership: the number of repossessions has risen from 2,350 in 1979, to 5,320 in 1982, 7,320 in 1983, 10,870 in 1984 and 16,770 in 1985 (Building Societies Association 1986b).

The ideology that emerges out of this complex situation may be the outcome of the unintended consequences of state policy rather than successful planning. This may help to explain why there is a tendency to arrive at diametrically opposed conclusions over the impact of owner occupation on the working class. The more pessimistic view (Kemeny 1981; Bassett and Short 1980; Harvey 1973) is that it is being distracted from the more fundamental struggle in the sphere of productive employment. The optimists, however, argue that private ownership extends working-class power in a sphere over which it had much less relative control than other social groups (Stretton 1974).

Residualization and the politics of pragmatism

In attempting to assess the nature of the ideologies surrounding housing provision, we first consider the issue of residualization, which emerges most acutely in the debate over the sale of council houses. Again, we find that neither of the major parties have consistently opposed the notion of public housing as a residual sector. Labour, never as anxious as the Conservatives to sell off council houses, none the less gradually played down and undermined the 'needs-oriented' role of public housing in favour of its residual 'welfare' role (Balchin 1985). Residualization is encouraged by measures that increase the dependency of public tenants on welfare benefits; for example, rent increases (in a time of high unemployment) meant that by 1985, 3.8 million tenants had to apply for rebates (Robinson 1986). The sale of council houses has increased the concentration of poor and disadvantaged persons in this sector. Between 1980 and 1983 the proportion of economically inactive heads of household (those least likely to buy their dwelling) rose from 42 per cent to 50 per cent of all tenants, whereas that of skilled manual heads of household (those most likely to buy it) dropped from 27 to 23 per cent (OPCS 1982: 51; 1985: 74).

The creation of an infrastructure for a residual sector was anticipated by a House of Commons Environment Committee (1981) which criticized the government for underestimating the financial losses to local authorities as a result of the sales; for the exacerbation of inner-city problems as waiting lists became longer; and for the gradual depletion of the council housing stock (by about one-third in ten years) (Balchin 1985: 196). In addition, the sales comprise mainly the best and most sought after stock. Though improving the housing prospects of a minority, these quantitative and qualitative reductions in local authority accommodation reinforce its residual aspects by limiting the choice for those left in or waiting to enter it.

Second, the unequal nature of the struggle to maintain possession of a home is likely to persist even in a situation where nearly all households are in private ownership. For some immigrants ownership of very poor quality accommodation is the only available option. These factors serve further to reinforce the critique of any notion of a housing class with a coherent ideology. Socio-economic location, race, gender and education transcend the distinction between different tenure groups. Although in our exploration of the characteristics of owner occupation, socio-economic variables are significant, a further distinction has to be made, namely between outright owners and mortgagors. On-going changes also need to be considered, such as the influx of low-income households: manual workers comprised 40 per cent of house buyers in 1979 in comparison with 33 per cent in 1973 (Balchin 1985: 211).

These changes may provide clues to the nature of support for owner occupation and the inconsistent approach of the major political parties to this issue. To some extent, the success of the Conservatives in capturing the working-class vote can be explained in terms of their positive attitude towards owner occupation. In 1983 a majority of owner occupiers (59 per cent) voted for them and only 19 per cent for Labour. Among working-class home-owners 47 per cent voted Conservative and 29 per cent Labour (Balchin 1985: 211). Yet, in promoting owner occupation, the Conservatives have actively fuelled a massive increase in mortgages which is 'contrary both to the spirit of the government's medium-term strategy and to the letter of its original financial targets' (Congdon 1986). The reflationary impact of such a policy (through 'private' rather than public borrowing) prompted Congdon to ask whether the British economy was entering a 'new era of Thatcherite Keynesianism'.

The housing policies of Conservative and Labour governments suggest that the only consistent state-initiated ideology is that of pragmatic acceptance and furtherance of the notion that high rates of owner occupancy are inherently beneficial. It has been easy to downgrade public housing since it has never enjoyed the same support as public health or other universally provided services. It would be mistaken to assume that the attraction for the working class of Conservative housing policies is inevitable. First, many who voted Conservative in order to obtain a generous discount on the purchase of their dwelling will no longer have the same incentive to repeat this. Second, the Labour Party has been as motivated as the Conservatives by short-term electoral gains and is as unlikely as them to develop a consistent 'hegemonic' ideology of home ownership. State intervention in the provision of housing is an inescapable feature of the existing social structure. Any attempt by political parties to advance an ideology of home ownership may therefore be regarded as a distraction from the issues and problems of the housing sector, and likely to be inconsistent with actual practice—be it in the form of state subsidies and reallocation of expenditure or in concessions to electoral pragmatism. The following examination of changes in mass private ownership of housing highlights the lack of homogeneity among owner occupiers and suggests that it would be difficult to promote or achieve ideological unity on the basis of tenure location.

THE DEVELOPMENT OF MASS PRIVATE OWNERSHIP

Many of the preconditions for the development of mass private ownership have been considered already. Table 5.1 (see p. 138) charts (for England and Wales) changes in tenure, especially the steady increase in owner occupation, the demise of private renting and the emergence of mass public housing after 1945 followed by its decline in the 1980s. The inter-war period was crucial to the development of private ownership: the construction of houses for private renting had become much less profitable; the price of houses fell during the depression (especially between 1930 and 1934); and the withdrawal of investment from the manufacturing sector was channelled into housing. The shortage of rental accommodation rather than any particular set of values acted as a major catalyst.

Regional variations are particularly striking in the development of owner occupation. In the prosperous south east and south west of England 66 per cent of all tenures were owner occupied in 1983 in contrast with 36 per cent in

Scotland, 48 per cent in the northern region and 57 per cent in Yorkshire and Humberside (OPCS 1985: 62). The pattern of home ownership is subject to a further variation: between 1971 and 1983 owner occupiers with a mortgage increased at three times the rate of outright owners as a proportion of all tenures—from 27 per cent to 33 per cent in contrast with 22 per cent to 24 per cent respectively (OPCS 1985: 67). Outright owners tend to be older than mortgagors (Table 5.3). The significantly lower proportions of mortgagors among the aged clearly reflects the limited scope for private ownership for their generations. Outright owners have fewer educational qualifications and comprise a very high proportion (59 per cent) of economically inactive heads of household. Their incomes tend to be significantly lower than local authority tenants. It is striking, however, that a high proportion of owner occupiers, 43 per cent, have manual occupations. Having a job at all, rather than the kind of job, is obviously an important precondition for access to home ownership, although there is great variation in the proportion of owner occupiers in each occupational group: among professionals, 90 per cent; employers and managers, 86 per cent; intermediate non-manual, 78 per cent; junior non-manual, 66 per cent; skilled manual, 62 per cent; semi-skilled manual, 42 per cent; and unskilled manual, 28 per cent (OPCS 1985: 74).

People with no educational qualifications are under-represented (by 18 percentage points) among mortgagors, whilst high-income earners are, not surprisingly, more prominently represented than those on low incomes. Among economically active heads of household, mortgagors with a gross income over £160 per week outnumbered local authority tenants by a ratio of 3.5 : 1, and a similar pattern emerges among economically inactive heads with an income of £80 per week or more. The mean income of mortgagors in 1983 was £243 in contrast with £110 among local authority tenants. Among heads of household with an income of less than £30 per week, 35 per cent are owner occupiers; rising to 47 per cent for those with incomes of between £100 and £120; 68 per cent for incomes of between £140 and £160; 83 per cent for incomes of between £200 and £250; and 92 per cent for higher incomes (OPCS 1985: 76).

Table 5.3 Characteristics of various tenure groups (heads of household), 1983 (%)

	Owner occupiers		Local authority New town renters	All households including other tenures
	Outright owners	Mort-gagors		
Age				
Under 25	0 (-4)	4 (-)	5 (+1)	4
25–9	1 (- 7)	12 (+ 4)	7 (- 1)	8
30–44	8 (-19)	50 (+23)	19 (-8)	27
45–64	40 (+7)	32 (-1)	34 (+1)	33
65–74	30 (+13)	2 (-15)	20 (+3)	17
75 and over	21 (+10)	0 (-11)	14 (+3)	11
Highest educational qualification				
Degree or equivalent	5 (-)	8 (+3)	0 (-5)	5
Below degree or higher education	7 (+1)	10 (+4)	1 (-5)	6
GCE A level	5 (-2)	10 (+3)	2 (-5)	7
Other	33 (-2)	43 (+8)	27 (-8)	35
None	49 (+2)	29 (-18)	69 (+22)	47
Socio-economic group				
Professional, employers and managers	11 (-4)	31 (+16)	2 (-13)	15
Intermediate non-manual	4 (-7)	12 (+ 1)	3 (-8)	11
Junior non-manual	4 (-2)	8 (+2)	4 (-2)	6
Skilled manual	15 (-8)	33 (+10)	23 (-)	23
Semi-skilled manual and personal service	6 (-4)	9 (-1)	13 (+3)	10
Unskilled manual	1 (-2)	1 (-2)	5 (+2)	3
Economically inactive	59 (+23)	5 (-31)	50 (+14)	36

Note: Figures in brackets indicate percentage points below the percentage for all households including other tenures.
Source: OPCS 1985: 70.

Gender divisions in access to and control of tenure are less easy to evaluate since official data are usually collected on the assumption that among married couples, males are automatically heads of household. Hence much of the subsidy to men is actually to households consisting of men, women and children. Of the 87 per cent of married mortgagor heads of household, 86 per cent are male and only 1 per cent are female. However, single, widowed and divorced or separated males and females make up similar proportions (7 per cent and 6 per cent respectively) of the remaining mortgagor heads of household. Among outright owners, married males comprised 60 per cent of heads and household. However, women comprise a far higher proportion of heads of household than men among single, widowed and divorced or separated outright owners: 30 per cent in contrast with 10 per cent. This is largely on account of the high proportion of widows (22 per cent) (OPCS 1985: 73).

Much of this data should be treated with caution and placed in the context of changes over several generations in prosperity and access to particular forms of tenure as well as changing attitudes and life-styles. Although patterns of association between income, education, occupation and tenure do emerge, the data also suggest variety in circumstances. Global averages on either the distribution of income or conditions of dwellings may conjure up a false impression of homogeneity in circumstances. Such trends may be important in directing the attention of policy-makers towards inequalities, which is not to imply that the complexity in life circumstances (e.g. variations in levels of indebtedness and living conditions in relation to the ability to change these) will be matched by the instruments available to policy-makers. Above all, it would be hazardous to draw conclusions about the constitution of political power directed towards change in society solely on the basis of such data.

THE BUILDING SOCIETIES

A cornerstone of the development of mass private ownership has been the activity and influence of building societies. Their origin can be traced to the eighteenth century when members of different trades pooled both their skills and financial resources together to construct dwellings for each other. However, financial pressures, legislation on the health and safety of dwellings and the disincentive impact of taxes on home ownership led to their collapse during the nineteenth century (Burke 1981). None the less, the principles of 'thrift and self-help among artisans' (Burke 1981: 11) did survive in building societies which were formally recognized as limited companies under the 1874 Building Societies Act. Though exerting limited influence in the housing market, they consolidated their position and established a method of funding home purchase that has ever since remained central to the development of private home ownership. In the words of Nevitt, 'the nineteenth-century invention of the amortised loan was of such importance in housing economics it should rank with the steam engine in changing the face of Britain' (Nevitt 1966, quoted in Burke 1981: 35).

Building societies were originally non-profit organizations, run independently of governments. They began to influence the housing market in the inter-war years, although for a time, after 1945, their expansion was constrained by government policies in favour of local authority housing. However, controls on speculative building did not alter the structure of this sector (Ball 1983: 41) and were lifted by the subsequent Conservative government. Encouragement by the Conservatives of owner occupation did not lead to any new forms of direct state intervention. Only from 1964 onwards did the state issue advice on interest rates (Duclaud-Williams 1978: 241), and in 1973 the Conservatives attempted to back this with a £15 million grant. The failure of this measure to suppress interest rates led to the formation of a Joint Advisory Committee comprising the societies, the Department of the Environment and the Treasury. In the following year, the Labour government lent the societies £500 million and again the impact on interest rates was short-lived. Governments have tended to accept that they 'cannot compel societies to hold mortgage rates, cannot firmly control the number and size of mortgages, nor the type of borrower who can receive them, nor the type of house on which societies will lend'

(Balchin 1985: 229). Such structures will tend to preclude effective state intervention, forcing it to react to change rather than develop a coherent long-term policy (Ball 1983: 344–5). Yet, without state intervention, the societies are even less likely to solve the problems that confront them.

A major difficulty lies in the fluctuation of funds available to the societies from three sources: repayments of mortgage debt by existing borrowers; interest credited to investors' accounts; and net receipts (i.e. the net gain from the flow of withdrawals and additions to accounts). Rapid alterations occur in the sources of funds; for instance, for the period 1977 to 1981, and as a proportion of building society funds, mortgage capital repayments and interest credited to investors' accounts rose from 31 per cent to 45 per cent and 15 per cent to 28 per cent respectively, whereas net receipts dropped from 53 per cent to 27 per cent (Ball 1983: 310). The instability of the housing market is further reflected in the competition between societies and the banking industry. Since 1981 the latter have captured a much larger share of the market (Table 5.4). They have been assisted in achieving this by the removal of government restrictions on bank lending in 1980 and by the narrowing gap between the bank rate and minimum lending rate on the one hand and building society share rates on the other. Building societies have, however, made impressive gains in their share of the market for personal liquid assets. In 1970 deposits with banks accounted for 34.6 per cent and, after peaking at 40 per cent in 1974, dropped to 33.6 per cent in 1981; over the same period the share of building societies rose from 34.5 per cent to 46 per cent, mainly at the expense of National Savings, which dropped from 22.8 per cent to 14.8 per cent (Ball 1983: 304).

Other difficulties arise from factors which are beyond the control of the societies: the state of the construction industry, the level of incomes, and demographic changes. The structure of building society finance is another factor—one which 'generates its own volatility' (Ball 1983: 312). The sale of houses leads to substantial withdrawals of money from the housing market. These funds become the major source of personal liquid assets available for investment and much of it returns to the societies. Hence 'mortgage advances help to

Table 5.4 Main institutional sources of mortgagors: net advances per annum, 1970–84

Year	Building societies (%)	Banks (%)	Other sources (%)	Total
1970	87	3	10	1,245
1971	88	5	7	1,823
1972	80	12	8	2,783
1973	71	11	18	2,831
1974	68	4	28	2,420
1975	76	2	22	3,632
1976	93	2	5	3,870
1977	96	3	1	4,250
1978	94	5	1	5,413
1979	82	9	9	6,461
1980	78	8	14	7,333
1981	67	26	7	9,491
1982	56	36	8	14,152
1983	76	25	—	14,407
1984	86	14	—	16,536

Sources: DoE 1985: 108; 1980: 125.

finance the movement of funds out of house ownership (possibly via a chain of sales), so part of building society receipts paradoxically are financed by their own net advances' (Ball 1983: 312–13). Building societies are also increasingly dependent for business on the moves of existing owners: 'As the ability of existing owners to move depends on the existence of an active housing market, building society business becomes increasingly locked into the cycle of boom and slump in the housing market' (Ball 1983: 310–11).

The societies have none the less enjoyed several advantages in addition to the ones mentioned so far. Ball highlights these advantages, the challenge to them and the innovations that the societies are considering in order to retain control over the private housing market (Ball 1983). He argues that, as 'market monopolists', the societies could, until they faced competition, charge high prices. They then concentrated on the expansion of branches, capitalized on the fact that comparatively low numbers of adults in Britain held bank accounts, and offered different returns to small and large investors with share accounts (Table 5.5). The other major advantage has been the preferential treatment they have received from the government, enabling them to offer investors higher interest than other financial institutions. Two aspects merit attention: first, the 'composite tax' arrangement, whereby the societies pay, on behalf of investors, much less than the basic rate of tax on share interest. In 1979–80 it stood at 21 per cent in contrast with the basic rate of 30 per cent. Second, the societies pay a much lower rate of corporation tax than other financial institutions—40 per cent instead of 52 per cent.

These advantages have come under strong challenge from the banking industry (Wilson Committee 1980)—adding, therefore, a political dimension to the economic difficulties facing the societies because of a volatile housing market. A number of strategies have been adopted by the societies: greater centralization (Table 5.5) has produced economies of scale, whilst branch expansion plus the offer of term shares forms part of a more aggressive marketing strategy aimed at winning new investors. However, attempts to expand their functions (into banking and other consumer services) will strengthen the calls by other financial institutions for an abolition of the advantages enjoyed by the societies because of their specialist role (Ball 1983).

Like other major financial institutions, the societies are characterized by a low level of accountability. There are not only clear limits to government intervention in the societies' activities but also very little direct control by the membership and no organized representation of the interests of owner occupiers as a group (Duclaud-Williams 1978: 263). Those in control of the societies form, to a large extent, a 'self-perpetuating oligarchy ... of estate agents, builders, solicitors, surveyors—who stand to gain from their position' (Lord Young, quoted in Balchin 1985: 236) and who 'benefit considerably from an increase in home ownership' (Kemeny 1981: 69). Yet the survival of the societies will depend not so much on the capacity of the powerful interests that run and derive high incomes from them to adapt to changing circumstances, but on the very group of people who are hardly represented in them at all: the majority of owner occupiers and

Table 5.5 Building societies, 1900–84

Number of societies

1900	1930	1940	1950	1960	1970	1981
2,286	1,026	952	819	726	481	251

Number of branches

1968	1970	1972	1974	1976	1978	1980	1981
1,662	2,016	2,552	3,099	3,696	4,595	5,716	6,203

Number of borrowers (000s)

1940	1950	1960	1970	1975	1981
1,503	1,508	2,349	3,655	4,397	5,484

Numbers of loans (000s)

1968	1972	1974	1976	1978	1980	1981	1982	1983	1984
498	681	433	732	802	675	736	861	949	1,083

Number of share accounts (000s)

1900	1920	1940	1960	1977
585	748	2,088	3,910	22,536

Mortgages outstanding (£000s)

	1960	1970	1973	1975	1977	1979	1981
	2,647	8,752	14,532	18,802	26,427	36,801	48,854
Actual deflated to 1975 (RPI)	7,272	16,207	21,122	18,802	19,590	22,900	22,400

Sources: Ball 1983: 297; DoE 1985: 108; Lansley 1979: 52–3.

members. Any attempt to abolish mortgage interest relief would meet with widespread resistance from those who perceive owner occupation as the best available form of tenure.

CONCLUSION

The ambiguities of Conservative support for private ownership are particularly evident in housing policy, where expansion has been dependent either on direct and substantial discounts for the purchase of public housing or 'hidden' support through the retention of tax reliefs. As a result public housing has been accorded a much lower priority and an infrastructure has emerged to sustain public housing as a residual rather than slowly expanding sector. Conservative emphasis on the moral and political value of owner occupation has been met by suspicion in other quarters as attempts to incorporate the working class and distract from more salient conflicts in the sphere of production. It has also prompted numerous studies into the uneven distributional effects of policy. The common link between these approaches, the notion of some form of political hegemony, frequently distracts attention away from some of the disadvantages experienced by many owner occupiers and their diverse social and economic characteristics. In such an atmosphere it is easy to forget that recipients of mortgage interest relief comprise about one-third of all households since nearly half of all owner occupiers are outright owners. The only consistent ideological aspects, therefore, appear to be the general unpopularity of private renting, the lack of commitment to public housing and the channelling of these negative attitudes into electoral platforms focused on the furtherance of owner occupation.

Several factors are likely to inhibit the further expansion of private ownership: the most obvious one is that of low incomes and poverty, whilst the less publicized ones are the pressures on the construction industry and the uneven quality of housing. The creation of a property-owning democracy will not, in the existing social context, make any significant impact on differences in life circumstances and access to goods and services. The recent expansion of private ownership and broadening of its social base coupled with an increase in economic and social problems faced by owner occupiers may however prompt forms of interest articulation that have so far been absent in this sector. At the institutional level, the challenge to building societies from banks has already led to shifts in their proportionate share of the housing market and may undermine the basis for some of the state-sponsored advantages administered by building societies on behalf of owner occupiers. Attempts by powerful economic and political groups that may, at one level, constitute a form of manipulation and distraction of people from their 'real' interests, may also signify a hurried response to changes in preferences and demands for an improved quality of life. For the majority such improvements cannot occur in the context of public or private renting. Private ownership, however, remains intact as a dream, even though the reality is still a long way from meeting needs and expectations.

6 Conclusion

The debate over the private provision of public welfare has proceeded at a hectic pace in an atmosphere of controversy, partly fuelled by and contributing to a plethora of works on the 'crisis' of the welfare state. The instinctive reactions of those who accept some of the arguments, though not the 'solutions', advanced by the critics of the welfare state, has been to reply in kind (hence the description by Donnison of the Thatcher regime as 'barbaric'—Donnison 1984: 45); to mount a 'defence' of the welfare state (e.g. Bean, Ferris and Whynes 1985); and to suggest alternative strategies (Le Grand and Robinson 1984, esp. chs 1–5; Klein and O'Higgins 1985).

Some of the evidence and arguments presented in these reactions have been included in this study. The aim of this chapter is to examine more closely some of the assumptions underlying the work of the 'new' defenders and strategists of the welfare state both in the light of the overall picture presented in this work and of recent contributions to social and political theory. The chapter is divided broadly into seven sections: four that deal primarily with the limits to and contradictory nature of Conservative policies, followed by three sections on the impact of Conservative rhetoric on the debate over alternative strategies for coping with problems of the welfare state.

The following propositions are examined in more detail and may form the basis for further research:

(1) There is little doubt that the scope for the private provision of public welfare did expand between 1979 and 1986. This expansion however, can generally be linked to

long-term trends, has been incremental and has faced severe constraints even under Conservative patronage.

(2) Although there is sufficient evidence to support the idea that under Conservative rule the prevalence of dual structures of welfare provision—of private affluence and public poverty—were strengthened by attempts to privatize welfare services, much of this duality (reinforced by regional and socio-economic location as well as sex and demography) has always been a central feature of the welfare state in operation. What recent 'privatization' policies may have done is to reinforce some trends and diminish others, hence they have added to the complexity of, rather than uniformly exacerbated, pre-existing inequalities. Furthermore, in areas where the debate has been most intense (health care and, to a lesser extent, education) the private sector may be more important as a status symbol than in its material impact on anyone. Where it has had an impact on the poor (in housing) or on women (in pensions), the inequalities were already well entrenched and may have been exacerbated.

(3) Among the long-term structures and trends that preceded the Conservative attempt to alter the direction of the welfare state, we note the traditional ambivalence of major political parties over the importance of state-subsidized or marketed services; the problems involved in planning for demographic changes; and the unique impact of war and post-war economic growth on the development of the welfare state.

(4) Another major reason—perhaps the most important one—for the unspectacular growth of private welfare provision is the large number of constraints on policy-makers, however committed some of them might be to the goal of privatization. The rhetoric that supports this goal is not unimportant. It has channelled the debate over the welfare state into new directions and reflects the uncertainty over its future.

(5) The contrast that is frequently evoked between public welfare (dominated by bureaucracy and sectional interests) and free-enterprise market forces is often misleading since it masks essentialist and utopian notions of social

organization and may draw attention away from the most likely alternatives available to policy-makers.

(6) The absence of obvious public involvement in collective action to support or oppose new directions in policy cannot easily be interpreted as a lack of concern with such issues. However, there are difficulties involved in how the state can or ought to respond to pressures that may be contradictory, transient and unrepresentative.

(7) The current framework of policy-making is undergoing some modification, although not at the pace desired by proponents of new strategies. In response either to the rhetoric of the New Right or to problems that have arisen independently of this particular challenge, these authors have drawn up a long list of prescriptions. They focus on decentralization, 'mixed' economic enterprises and far-sighted planning. Some even consider wider issues such as the effect of social policy on women and on ethnic minorities as well as the interrelationship between welfare, economic growth, environmental destruction, technological change and demographic change. Their main weakness is to give little attention to the social and political context in which these strategies could be put into effect.

THE LIMITS OF PRIVATE-SECTOR EXPANSION

Most commentators agree that the Conservative governments elected in 1979, 1983 and 1987 have advocated more than any other previous post-war government the expansion of the private welfare sector. To a large extent, the context for this proposed expansion has been set by the successful denationalization of state-owned enterprises. The purpose of this short section is to highlight the ways in which 'privatization' has been achieved and to examine the complex nature of this development. The most striking aspect has been the expansion of occupational rather than privately purchased welfare. The major input into private health and occupational pension schemes occurred through this avenue. Moreover, the temporary boom in private health insurance in the early part of this decade and the rise in coverage for full-time employees in occupational pension schemes does not, in any way, appear directly related to the advent of the Conservatives. In other areas, government policy has made a significant impact on private-sector expansion, notably in the market for private residential care for the elderly and in the sale of council houses. In both cases the expansion could not have occurred without massive state subsidies either indirectly through the social security system or directly through massive discounts on the market value of houses. In the areas of education and pensions government policies have so far had only a marginal impact, although changes have been introduced—via the Assisted Places Scheme and social security legislation—which may have a significant impact on private-sector expansion. In the area of health care we also mentioned the changes to consultants' contracts; the effective privatization of optical and dental services as well as the increase in the cost of precriptions; and the contracting out of some ancillary services.

There are, however, a number of constraints on private-sector expansion. The most obvious is that of cost to the different income units. In addition, competition in private health care (between provident societies, commercial organizations and the NHS) and in the market for owner-occupied housing (especially between building societies and banks) introduces an element of volatility which does not necessarily benefit the consumer. In private health insurance the boom period of the early 1980s came to an abrupt end. In some respects, this sector is under constant pressure to innovate simply in order to survive. In addition, the content and impact of privatized welfare is often difficult to distinguish from that provided by the state—hence the uncertainty over the impact of private education on the skills a student may have had prior to entry into this sector; the poor quality of much owner-occupied housing; the limits to consumer control in private health consultations (Silverman 1984); and the uneven coverage offered by occupational and private pension schemes.

The critics of 'privatization' have, with some justification, argued that it has widened the gulf between rich and poor, and has exacerbated the unequal distribution of goods and services. A twofold process has developed: on the one hand there has been a general widening of the distribution of earnings under the Thatcher governments (Winyard 1985); on the other hand, constraints on welfare state services have taken place alongside the growth of private provision, thus widening inequalities. Yet in some respects privatization has augmented the complexity of, rather than simply added to, inequalities. Actual changes may also be far less radical than the rhetoric would otherwise suggest. Following on from Titmuss and his work on fiscal and occupational welfare, Hindess argues that 'what appears to be a system of equity serves as a smokescreen for the pursuit of sectional interests' (Hindess 1987: 46). A consequence of Conservative rhetoric about freedom of choice to opt for private welfare may have been to drawn attention to inequalities that have previously been less publicized. The massive real increases in subsidies to occupational pensions and owner-occupied housing since the early 1970s have of course contributed to this heightened awareness.

THE COMPLEXITY OF PRIVATE-SECTOR EXPANSION

The complexity of recent changes can partly be understood by examining redistributive outcomes, albeit in a highly differentiated manner, and partly by considering extra-distributional factors, such as notions of status and 'positional' satisfaction (Hirsch 1976). Any attempt to assess the distributional consequences of privatization faces, as an initial barrier, the heterogeneity and complexity of coverage. In the area of pensions there are over 100,000 schemes and coverage varies both within and between private and public organizations. In housing some inequalities may have been diminished and others exacerbated by the sale of council houses. The poorest have clearly not benefited from the discounts on council houses since they could not even afford the deposit. However, massive rent increases have, for the poorer tenants, been offset by increases in social security payments, whereas higher-income groups have often been forced to opt for owner occupation. The increase in owner occupancy among manual workers was given an added impetus by state-subsidized privatization initiatives. In some respects, however, inequalities may simply have been shifted from the public to the private sector—hence the increasing proportion of owner occupiers who depend on supplementary benefits and live in poor housing conditions.

The social and economic circumstances of owner occupiers —the level of indebtedness, the size of the household and the surrounding environment—vary immensely. All these aspects work against notions of a homogeneous 'housing class' or 'ideology of owner occupation'. Access to various forms of tenure may vary between age cohorts (for a number of historical reasons): the elderly are more likely to occupy private unfurnished dwellings on a long-term basis than the young; whereas the latter frequently occupy private furnished dwellings only as a prelude to owner occupation. Pension arrangements vary greatly from generation to generation, partly as a consequence of drastic changes in legislation. Interest in pensions obviously becomes more intense as a pensioner approaches retirement age. Official statistics, by highlighting male heads of household as owner occupiers, may give a misleading impression by failing to show how many women are joint owners of a house, let alone, in most circumstances, joint beneficiaries. Private health care, in terms of subscribers, relates strongly to full-time, therefore male-dominated, employment. Yet the coverage and actual benefits usually include women and children. Having any occupation at all—and this is a central issue in contemporary Britain—is an important precondition for gaining access to private health care.

In the area of occupational pensions, inequalities between men and women have certainly been increased by the reduction in benefits to widows as a result of the 1986 Social Security Act. This may, however, be partly off-set by the increase in occupational coverage for women, mainly because of their greater involvement in the labour force. Inequalities in access to housing have been exacerbated by the reduction in the supply of public housing for the poor who are on long waiting lists. In the area of health care the constraints imposed on parts of the NHS have made access for the poor much more difficult, yet the middle classes may also have emerged as losers, either because they too belong to the long list of people waiting for treatment or because of the cost of joining private health schemes as individual subscribers. Regional variations in access to private health care have been striking. Attempts by the Conservatives to counter these via the RAWP scheme have worsened the problems faced by areas that have been allocated 'too many' resources. These attempts at reallocation have, at the same time, been contradicted by the success of Conservative policy to encourage private health care, namely the expansion of private hospitals in the very areas that have 'too many' resources. At any rate, compared even to nations, like the USSR, with much more centrally planned economies, regional variations in Britain are far 'less conspicuous' (Klein 1983: 150, quoted in Hindess 1987: 94).

To assess the impact of privatization purely in distributional terms would be to omit other central areas of concern to the analysis of welfare provision. For instance, little attention has been given to the social control aspects of occupational welfare. Attempts to improve employee 'participation' in pension schemes under current heterogenous arrangements not only undermine occupational mobility, they might reinforce mechanisms of control which induce conformity by an employee to guidelines devised by the employer as a precondition for the realization of benefits. In health care, employer 'benevolence' in providing private coverage disguises a more pragmatic motive, namely to ensure the rapid return to work of high-status employees—a point well-illustrated in advertising campaigns by private health organizations. The latter often suggest that business can be conducted as usual from the hospital bed. Many employees would not resent this. Many of them attend health-screening clinics on their own initiative or take up the offer by an employer to do so. 'Human capital theory', based on the idea that the state has a vital interest in securing a healthy and well-educated workforce would appear to be less relevant in the current context of high unemployment (George and Wilding 1984). The restructuring of subsidies for public housing suggests that the state has reduced considerably its commitment to the creation of optimal conditions for the reproduction of labour power. Yet if the theory is applied selectively, to particular occupational groups, it does offer an explanation for the expansion of occupational welfare.

A further aspect, not captured by a purely distributional analysis, is the actual experience by people of services provided by the state. Public tenants often feel confronted by a vast impersonal system of management which allows them little choice or voice, let alone control. The consensus among all the major political parties over the need for improving tenants' rights reflects the acuteness of this problem. It may also be the case that expenditure on public housing is, in certain respects, misplaced. First, there have for a long time only existed limited, if any, incentives for tenants to repair and maintain their dwellings. Second, private ownership, may, for anyone who can afford it, have certain intrinsic advantages. Hirschman, in analysing the factors that generate consumer disappointment with durable and non-durable goods, refers to housing as one of the least 'disappointing' of personal belongings:

When owners have the opportunity, as with a house to furnish, arrange and rearrange it, to repair, improve or even add to it, they in effect make it into a reflection of themselves. The pleasure yielded by the house is immeasurably enhanced by the narcissistic contemplation of the result of their own effort and choices. Here is an important way of counteracting the loss of pleasure that would otherwise follow upon the permanent-comfort-producing acquisition of a house.

(Hirschman 1982: 37)

Exclusive emphasis on the advantages of greater equality via central planning would fail to account for the plausible arguments in favour of individual home ownership. Hirschman in fact provides a more comprehensive account that Hirsch (1976) of the pressure for public provision of services and the dissatisfaction that emerges in its wake. The work of Hirsch on positional goods has validity in some respects but not in others.

In our own work we have tried to demonstrate that satisfaction with public health, education and pensions is generally determined by perceptions of 'objective' standards of provision rather than positional comparisons (Taylor-Gooby and Papadakis 1986). However, our data also supported the argument advanced by Gershuny (1983) that positional awareness is a characteristic of middle- or upper- middle-class minorities who are more acutely conscious of a threat to their social privileges than of the remainder of the population. This positional awareness may help to explain the survival of 'islands of privilege' in health care and, even more so, in education. Powerful minorities have successfully resisted state interference in private education. As we pointed out earlier, the extent to which private schools provide a higher standard of education is open to dispute and the rich may well be wasting their money. The resistance by many parents to any threat to the private system may partly be explained by their belief in its 'superior quality'. It may also reflect its positional value—hence any attempt 'to equalize the distribution of positional goods threatens to make them less valuable to their possessors' (Hindess 1987: 30). Although positional awareness does not relate strongly to dissatisfaction with public welfare, it is important in understanding why people choose private services. In our own survey, respondents who had attended a private school were far more likely to show strong positional awareness than those who had not; a similar pattern was evident among those who were covered by private health insurance (Taylor-Gooby and Papadakis, 1986). As far as the latter goes, 'opinion polls consistently show more people claiming to be insured than is the case', whilst people chose private treatment partly 'because it had a higher social status, and because of a belief that the treatment would be better, although the industry never makes this claim' (Jenkins 1986: 7). One can understand why the proposals by Labour governments in the past to undermine private education or to phase out pay beds in the NHS led to such fierce resistance. For powerful minorities (who enjoy high levels of income, education and occupational status) exit from the system of collective provision is often preferable to exercising voice within it (Papadakis and Taylor-Gooby 1987). None the less, the notion of positionality by definition contradicts any impetus toward private-sector expansion since this would undermine its *raison d'être*.

LONG-TERM TRENDS AND STRUCTURES

It is hardly surprising that, in the context of resistance by powerful minorities and of widespread preference for the private appropriation of goods such as housing, political parties have developed ambivalent positions on the relative importance of collective provision and the operation of market mechanisms. Policy-makers also have to plan ahead on the basis of predictions about demographic change; and do battle with many of the contradictions inherited from a system of welfare shaped by the experience of the last war and the economic prosperity that followed it. This section focuses on these long-term features and anticipates subsequent discussion of the limits to and contradictions of public policy, the limited alternatives to existing arrangements, and issues of social organization which transcend the division between public and private welfare.

Evidence of ambivalence and difficulty in implementing policies has been presented in previous chapters. Whenever a major political party has adopted a strong ideological stance in relation to social service provision—for instance, the Labour Party on phasing out pay beds in the NHS and the Conservatives on privatization—they have only achieved marginal success. In addition, much of Conservative policy on constraining public expenditure had already been anticipated by Labour. Undoubtedly there have occurred major shifts in emphasis, but the continuities are as striking as the discontinuities. Support for owner occupation has been a major theme; for the Conservatives this commitment dates back to the 1950s, for Labour to the 1960s. Both have oscillated betweeen creating areas of residual welfare and emphasizing the importance of universal standards based on needs. The inequalities may have taken on different shape and become more complex under the Conservatives, yet they were neither absent nor radically altered by Labour dominance. Both parties have made concessions to sections of the population and organized pressure groups in order to secure either their political survival or re-election. When they have attempted to bring about long-term changes—as in the original Fowler proposals on pensions—they have been forced to back down.

Yet it is these long-term considerations that pose a major challenge to far-sighted policy-makers. Long-term planning cannot rely solely on statistical extrapolations of current trends. The impact on welfare services of changes in attitudes and preferences, the level of national wealth and employment structures is particularly hard to predict. Even if we use 'reliable' data on demographic change, the trends are anything but stable. Fluctuations in birth rates mean that between 1981 and 1989 the number of 5- to 15-year-old children in England will decline by nearly a million, only to rise by nearly the same amount in the following decade. As Klein and O'Higgins point out, 'such fluctuations are not uncommon' (Klein and O'Higgins 1985b: 226). They apply for instance, to the area of pensions (with substantial changes in dependency ratios, namely between people under school-leaving age or over retirement age and the working population); female employment (with increases in labour force participation); marriage breakdown, divorce and the formation of one-person households (the latter rising from 11 per cent of all households in 1961 to 22 per cent in 1980); and care of the aged (as the proportion of frail elderly continues to rise) (Rimmer and Wicks 1983).

Finally, in this section, we need to consider the mixed heritage of a welfare state created in the context of uncertainty after the last war and followed by unprecedented economic growth and expenditure on welfare. We elaborate here on earlier arguments about the trade-off between military obligations during war-time and the concessions made by the state in terms of increased welfare. In the area of housing one might add to this argument the fact that damage to the stock necessitated a radical initiative by the state to make good any losses. In the area of pensions the aftermath of the First World War provides an unequivocal example of the trade-off between military obligations and improved pension rights since these were not extended to those who suffered industrial accidents. The implementation after the Second World War of universal provision for retirement on a non-actuarial basis illustrates a different aspect of the mixed heritage—namely the difficulty, once such a commitment is made, of altering it at a later point in time. (The same applies to tax concessions to owner occupation which were made when it only represented a minority tenure.)

Heclo, in contrasting the wartime experiences of the European with those of the American population, argues that the latter did not suffer 'the kinds of dislocations and physical devastation that prevailed in Europe' (Heclo 1981: 390). There was also little political opposition to the creation of welfare programmes in Europe: many of them were approved of by coalition governments and may have emerged because of the strong bargaining position of the labour movement. Dryzek and Goodin offer two additional explanations: that 'war breeds attitudes such as "national unity" and "social solidarity" which are conducive to the growth of the welfare state' (Dryzek and Goodin 1986: 28), and that 'rare moments of deep and widespread uncertainty—war being the most dramatic example' helped temporarily 'to expand people's moral horizons' and forced people 'to imagine themselves in each other's place and to evaluate social policies accordingly, at least during most of the war' (pp. 30–1). The latter argument is particularly relevant to our later discussion of the extent to which 'uncertainty' prevails today and of how policy-makers might adjust to it. For the moment, however, we need only assume that at least one of these explanations is correct in order to establish a link between wartime experience and the creation of the welfare state. Even if the commitment to the welfare state took on a different shape in subsequent years, the nature of its expansion under the impetus of post-war economic growth forms the basis of contemporary conflicts over its future direction. According to Heclo, the very success of the welfare state helped to disguise 'a system of tolerated contradictions': between adequacy and equity; centralized 'standards for equality or local freedom of choice that produced inequalities'; and the balance between planned 'social services or market exchanges' (Heclo 1981: 392). Whilst these contradictions underlie many contemporary debates, we would argue that they have constantly been used by or served to hinder governments, although to a lesser degree in times of high economic growth and apparent political consensus. We move on to consider in more detail the limits to and contradictions of social policy.

THE LIMITS TO AND CONTRADICTIONS OF SOCIAL POLICY

The previous section has covered some of the issues that affect social policy. To these we add the following points made by Hindess in his critique of arguments on social policy: the use of planning measures as rhetorical or public relations devices rather 'than as serious instruments for pursuing their proclaimed objectives' (Hindess 1987: 28); the time needed to bring about the fruition of such objectives if they are wholeheartedly pursued; and, most importantly, and echoing the point made by Heclo, the problem of competing social policy goals and of having to accommodate diverse interests.

In the broadest sense the welfare state can be seen to have a range of goals: to ensure minimum standards of provision for all members of society; to maintain and regenerate workers necessary to the economic system; and to secure political legitimacy. More specifically, the conflict over goals has been illustrated with references to the role of women in the labour market and as principal carriers of community care; the conflict between attempts to reallocate public health resources and the encouragement of privatization policies which contradict this; the constraints on pensions policy as a conflict between principles of individualized and collective forms of ownership and control; and the tensions between socio-political and economic-rational goals in housing policy. The variety of objectives pursued by policy-makers means that decisions 'rarely point in a single, well-defined policy direction' (Hindess 1987: 96). Crouch argues that the Conservatives under the influence of the New Right seek 'to subsidize the élite service in order to make it more attractive and ... to run down the public sector so that it provides an unsatisfactory service from which people will want to escape' (Crouch 1985b: 419). In practice the pattern is both contradictory and inconsistent. It is perhaps not surprising that commentators have arrived at diametrically opposed conclusions, for instance over the impact of owner occupation on the working class.

In many instances the government has limited control over expenditure. The vast increase in real terms of tax relief on pensions and home mortgages can force a government into concentrating relief or subsidy on one sector rather than the other since it cannot do both effectively. Governments find it hard, if not impossible, to introduce long-term changes in the face of institutional constraints and the mobilization of interests. When changes have been implemented major concessions have been made (for instance, under Bevan, to medical professionals in the NHS); or the original proposals diluted almost beyond recognition (as in the recent Fowler proposals for the reform of pensions—DHSS, 1985a). Powerful lobbies within the state sector (notably, professional interests in health and education services) and the private sector (e.g. building societies and pension funds) are either competing for a greater share of resources or able to divert, in some respects, the potential impact of a policy perceived as contrary to their interests. Building societies, though dependent on tax reliefs, are able to avoid government controls over interest rates and many other aspects of access to mortgages. The limits to intervention in the economy (which impinges dramatically on welfare goals) are numerous and include the flow of international capital and the balance of trade (Hindess 1987: 25).

A major factor is the limited time available to a government in one or even two terms of office to consult, deliberate and legislate. The delay under the Conservatives in drawing up a comprehensive policy on community care is a case in point. Often, the most a government can achieve is to bring a new issue or perspective onto the political agenda. Although governments do have at their disposal a wide range of instruments such as the tax system and legislative powers, policies are usually 'based on the hope that the combination of climate, threat and promise' will achieve the desired objectives (Hindess 1987: 67). The Conservative government has certainly influenced the climate of debate over the welfare state. Yet in view of the less than spectacular changes that have occurred, its proposals have increasingly taken on a rhetorical character. Freedom of choice has only been made possible through direct sponsorship by state and corporate agencies. For it to have occurred in any other way would have been to undo the rhetoric and the power of the state to subsidize and regulate 'private' welfare. The rhetoric is not unimportant. As we show in the following sections, it has both channelled the debate over the welfare state into new directions and reflected the growing uncertainty over its future. Our analysis focuses, therefore, on the contrast between private versus public welfare, the possibilities for and difficulties of collective action and a range of strategies (based, for example, on decentralization or on a new 'mixed economy' or on new frameworks for public policy) in order to cope with past failure and on-going problems.

THE CONTRAST BETWEEN PRIVATE AND PUBLIC WELFARE

We have already demonstrated that one cannot easily distinguish between a monolithic state and an untrammelled market. Privatization does involve cuts in subsidy, regulation and provision by the state but this may only imply a restructuring and redirection of these three components: hence cuts in provision may be compensated for by increases in subsidy and so on. We have shown how in the area of housing massive subsidies, discounts and tax reliefs represent 'freedom of choice' directed by a new form of state paternalism—hence the characterization of housing policy as 'Thatcherite Keynesianism'. We have also noted that occupational pension or private health coverage is determined less by market forces *per se* than by heterogeneous corporate bargaining processes. There is little doubt that recent policies have brought private welfare to the fore and that theories of social policy have reflected this process with their own consensus of radical disenchantment. Frequently this disenchantment represents a reaction to Conservative rhetoric rather than a considered response to Conservative practice. Much of the literature on the crisis of the welfare state draws on a paradigm that contrasts state versus market. There has been, as noted in the introduction, a widespread acceptance, on the one hand, of a notion of crisis and, on the other, of the notion of 'market resurgence'. This in effect formed the basis of the 'new orthodoxy'.

The 'rediscovery of inequality' in the 1960s followed by economic decline in the 1970s meant that complacency gave way to a 'new pessimism' (Heclo 1981). Heclo may be going too far in the opposite direction when he suggests that governments have adjusted to the new situation and ceased 'trying to outbid each other in promises to continue rapid expansions in social policy spending' (Heclo 1981: 401). A glance at the 1983 Labour Party manifesto provides a striking example of an 'unprioritised menu of sundry pressure group demands' (Crouch 1985b: 415). However, we agree with the assessment by Heclo that 'the welfare state is more complex, its motive processes more dynamic than is credited by any version of the new pessimism' (Heclo 1981: 401). A central axis of this pessimistic response is the contrast evoked between public and private provision. The reduction of the problems facing the welfare state to a conflict between these two goals is dangerous to the extent that it evades or distracts from issues that could have dire consequences for the future of welfare: the consequences of demographic change; the growth of the economy and unemployment; and the global context of population growth, damage to the environment and changing expectations.

The reactions to the pessimists has been 'to show that the British welfare is not really in a severe state of crisis or to refute arguments that there is now a need to shift sharply towards market approaches to the delivery of welfare' (Hill 1986: 405). Many of these refutations involve, as Hill implies, considerable effort in trying to counter the pro-market, anti-welfare ideology which has swamped the political agenda. The tendency therefore is to focus on the public versus private debate and to treat Conservative policy-making as a coherent strategy of privatization without focusing sufficiently on its contradictions.

Clearly, Conservative policy does have a 'general commitment to the virtues of the market' (Hindess 1987: 152). However, these policies do not operate in a vacuum with social policy as 'a principle of organisation that is in conflict with the market' (Hindess 1987: 44). Such a juxtaposition would imply an essentialist perspective which analyses the market 'in terms of an essence or inner principle that produces necessary effects simply by virtue of its presence' (Hindess 1987: 8). Though valid in a general sense, this distinction between public and private provision masks, as we have shown in specific policy areas, 'extremely complex and heterogeneous sets of conditions' (Hindess 1987: 150). The problem with analyses that involve a principle as a single criterion for judging policies is their underlying utopianism. For market liberals it entails a 'utopian account of the "market" and its workings' (Hindess 1987: 43); for 'radical' social policy analysts, it leads to a one-sided focus on inequality and the pursuit of an 'egalitarian utopia' (Hindess 1987: 158) rather than an assessment of the 'most likely alternatives' (Weale 1985b: 321) to the welfare state. The point made by Hindess is that choices in political life cannot be reduced to a straightforward conflict between one principle and another.

We now appraise some 'alternative' approaches that have been proposed for tackling the problems of the welfare state, bearing in mind that they are responding in some respects to the rhetoric of the New Right and in others to problems that arose independently of this particular challenge.

COLLECTIVE ACTION

The absence of obvious forms of collective action to defend the welfare state against the threat posed by the Thatcher government could be interpreted in the same way as political sociologists have interpreted the growing importance of private market consumption in explaining patterns of political support—namely as a shift from collectivism to privatism in the political culture. Like most dichotomies this one contains some validity and much ambiguity. The valid aspect, which is explored through the work of Hirschmann (1982), is that the population tends to fluctuate between concern with public and private welfare goals. On occasion the concern with public welfare goals is clearly identifiable through the action of specific social movements. The ambiguous aspect is that it is very difficult to separate public from private goals: if the public does not 'take to the streets', it does necessarily reflect a lack of concern with public goals.

The problems with and obstacles to collective forms of representation and action (other than voting at elections) are numerous: they include problems of scale and definitions of geographical boundaries; the time needed to attend meetings and remain informed on current issues; the difficulty in achieving social representativeness; and the emergence of cliques within what may start out as a movement that practices grass-roots democracy (Weale 1983, 1985c; Papadakis 1984). A further issue is how the government and the state bureaucracy should respond to the preferences expressed by citizens or the needs and preferences of particular groups of consumers (Weale 1985c). Conflict can also emerge between professional interests (e.g. the pursuit of 'prestigious' research and experimentation in health care) and the immediate needs of consumers (Weale 1985c: 156). Whilst this may necessitate controls on professionals, in other areas there may be strong grounds for not acceding to consumer preferences 'that would be expressed in an open market', because 'we are worried by the distribution of the resources required to satisfy them' or 'we believe that consumers are not the best judges of their own welfare in complex areas of medical, educational or insurance practice' (Weale 1985c: 153).

There may also exist a number of obstacles to mass involvement in collective campaigns. One of the most well-known is the 'free rider' phenomenon identified by Olson (1965). In the words of Hirschman:

Since the outcome of the collective action (assuming it is successful) is a public good that can be enjoyed by all regardless of prior participation, the individual is tempted to withhold his contribution in the expectation that others will exert themselves on his behalf. As a result everyone waits for the next person to jump first—and nothing happens.

(Hirschman 1982: 78)

Whilst Hirschman has pointed out the inconsistency between this theory and the emergence shortly afterwards of the greatest wave of public protest to occur so far in the post-war Western world, one might also query the notion of 'public goods' whose 'goodness' is not all that widely accepted. This is not to say that an amenity affected adversely by, for instance, a new airport is not a public good. However, the amenity is not evaluted uniformly by the relevant population; the new airport (or whatever) may be evaluated positively by many of those affected, including some who value the threatened amenity, but who value it less than the prospects for more employment; and in many instances campaigns may relate to a range of particularist issues (such as the effects of airports on house prices). In other words, there may be many reasons, apart from the 'free rider' phenomenon, why mass involvement is absent from collective campaigns. In addition, many campaigns may be successful on their own terms, especially if they are targeted towards preventing new developments. A further aspect that would have to be considered is the large number of voluntary associations that both provide services and attempt to influence government policies. As Whiteley and Winyard point out, the size and effectiveness of this lobby has been underestimated in the past (Whiteley and Winyard 1987).

There is considerable evidence to show that the public does 'have increasing expectations of participation and of not being pushed around' (Crouch 1985b: 414). Our own survey of public interest in greater freedom of choice both within and outside the state sector and in wanting to be consulted on and gain access to information in major areas of welfare provision confirmed this (Papadakis and Taylor-Gooby 1987). It also provided further evidence of the tendency for the most articulate groups to become involved in collective action and, if they experienced frustration, to want to exit from the public welfare system altogether. Crouch in searching for plausible alternatives to current trends, makes a strong case for allowing articulate groups to express 'voice' within the public system: 'the damage done thereby to public provision will be less than if, because of their frustrations at limited opportunities for voice, these people seek exit altogether' (Crouch 1985b: 415). He goes on to argue that the state, whilst not openly supporting privatization of services, ought to increase or maintain opportunities for choice within the state system, for instance by retaining pay beds in the NHS. This would considerably reduce the potential for exit from the system, would ensure that privilege remained visible (and hence more open to challenge) and would retain within the public system articulate consumers who are most likely to provide feed-back to policy-makers. Naturally, the latter would also have to be more prepared to consult with citizens and consumers.

In contrast to Olson's 'free rider' phenomenon, Hirschman offers a convincing explanation for some of the attractions of public action. The very involvement in it provides certain gratifications, including a sense of community and belonging, the gaining of knowledge and a sense of fulfilment. Those who let others 'exert themselves on their behalf do not just cheat the community as is implied in the "free rider" metaphor; *they cheat themselves first of all*' (Hirschman 1982: 87). These incentives for participation in collective action are common to diverse social movements (Opp 1986). However, the outcome of such action can lead to great disappointment among participants mainly because of the gap between the 'expected result' and the 'sobering reality' (Hirschman 1982: 94). This reflects the 'deficiency of our imagination which leads time and again to the setting of utopian goals whose pursuit naturally turns out to be more time-absorbing than expected' (Hirschman 1982: 100). Utopian projects, once frustrated, are followed by a long bout of apathy and resignation.

We have therefore ascertained that collective action is difficult but possible; it may form part of a cycle of concern with public and private welfare goals; and it may frequently embark on utopian projects. To this we add the evidence available on the ambivalence of public attitudes (Taylor-Gooby 1985), the likelihood that the public is better-informed than ever before, and that levels of interest in consultation at various levels are increasing. The problem then emerges of how 'established' organizations can respond to the issues which are of prime concern to public opinion and new social movements. Political parties will either be tempted or compelled to take up some of these issues, whilst permanent bureaucracies will tend to highlight the difficulties of converting these into policies. It would be unrealistic to expect policy-makers to adjust to cycles of public opinion or action with great rapidity. They cannot vanish as easily as social movements do from the political landscape. There is, however, considerable room for improvement in coping with such uncertainties. We now consider other options that may be available.

LIMITED ALTERNATIVES

The debate over the private provision of public welfare has begun to move beyond the pessimism of previous theoretical accounts, although the tone remains cautious on the assumption that 'things can never be the same again'. Some approaches provide detailed prescriptions of how to make the best of the current situation—notably the essays by Walker, Donnison and Bosanquet in an edited collection on *Privatisation and the Welfare State* (Le Grand and Robinson 1984); others add to this a flexible framework for the setting of future objectives for public policy (Klein and O'Higgins 1985b). A third approach not only uses new social movements as models for change but tries to place social policy in a global context by focusing on issues of exploitation, overpopulation and ecological problems (Ferris 1985). These accounts contain two distinct elements: first, a response to the rhetoric of the New Right on how to tackle problems of the welfare state and, second, an appraisal of long-term contradictions and changes.

In their accounts Walker, Donnison and Bosanquet all accept that the public welfare services are seriously deficient, for instance in management, quality of service, accountability and efficiency. They also stress that private provision does not necessarily tackle these issues any better, and that it may increase inequalities whilst reducing efficiency and undermining the goal of social integration. For Walker the alternative would be based on universal provision 'distributed according to need rather than ability to pay'; local accountability through the creation of smaller administrative units; and de-professionalization, 'to enable clients to become less passive recipients of welfare and more active participants in social services' (Walker 1984b: 43). Without considering any objections that might be raised—for instance, the possibility of paternalism at a local level or the difficulties in and social control implications of encouraging 'participation' by clients—he simply asserts that 'this is a radical strategy'.

Donnison also favours greater decentralization of services, along with the development of economic opportunities and new forms of enterprise (e.g. co-operatives and non-profit companies) at a community level. He does acknowledge the problems of scale, standardization and constitutional structure that would need to be tackled. The basis for his optimism is to be found in 'the development of mutual aid, self-management techniques which are now being pioneered by groups up and down the country' (Donnison 1984: 55). Parallels to these activities can be found in new social movements in other Western nations. Donnison is rightly concerned about the 'ideology' that would bind together the diverse groups. Another major problem for such projects is that they frequently rely for their survival on a high level of self-exploitation. Often, they become torn between attempts to introduce a radical alternative and, because of their need for financial support, the possibility of co-optation by or providing new models of social integration for the centres of power. Decentralization of responsibility for welfare may also serve to direct attention away from the difficulties encountered by the state in meeting expectations (Papadakis 1986). The political implications of this strategy require much more careful consideration.

Bosanquet cites many good reasons why 'the old style of tax-financed, tax-owned, centralised bureaucracy is unlikely to be suited to the needs of the future': the relative scarcity of tax money; the need to recruit better management from the private sector; and diseconomies of scale, for example in managing large housing estates or achieving accountability and responsiveness in areas such as health care (Bosanquet 1984). The alternative, he argues, is to create new 'mixed' enterprises where private funding complements tax money; managers are no longer public employees but 'accountable to an independent committee or authority'; the 'organisation is responsible for setting its own pay and employment conditions'; and the managers 'make their own decisions on service patterns and on the range of clients to be involved' (Bosanquet 1984: 65). His choice of housing associations as a model for such 'mixed enterprises' is, in some respects, unfortunate. He argues that they 'avoid the problems of scale, social segregation and growing unpopularity with the public and with tenants that have affected the old public sector' (Bosanquet 1984: 66). However, as Balchin points out, they often have poor standards; are insufficiently accountable to public authorities despite receiving substantial subsidies; more easily discriminate against prospective tenants in their screening procedures; and are generally inefficient because of high turnover in management and administrative staff (Balchin 1985). The main advantage of some of the proposed changes is that they may be suited to a 'low-growth economy in which a large, inflexible public sector is faced with many new needs' (Bosanquet 1984: 68).

The theme of flexibility in a low-growth economy is central to the strategy advanced by Klein and O'Higgins (1985b). The past experience of governments making long-term commitments which they could not meet once there was a downturn in economic growth lies at the heart of this strategy of 'catastrophe avoidance' and 'coping with uncertainty'. Instead, they argue, governments should accept the inevitable, that surprises and unintended consequences will always be around the corner. They suggest that governments should be more openly or 'purposefully' opportunistic, that they be prepared for surprises which may, for instance, be the outcome of an unfavourable combination of demographic change, low economic growth and changing expectations.

Attempts by the Conservatives to be more flexible and to adopt long-term perspectives include a recent Green Paper (Treasury 1984) which 'takes a longer look into the future than any previous document published by the Treasury' (Klein and O'Higgins 1985b: 225); and their review of occupational and private pensions. However, the Green Paper has been criticized by alternative strategists for containing so little in the way of plans—for being a very weak anodyne document (Klein and O'Higgins 1985a). Alternative strategists aim to create a 'long-term framework of social policy' which 'should be less about programme *planning* (inputs) than about setting policy *objectives* (outcomes)' (Klein and O'Higgins 1985b: 227). This strategy would attempt to avoid the creation of a 'self-perpetuating interest group of service producers' and would try to run short-term programmes which can either be renewed or abandoned according to whatever resources are available (Klein and O'Higgins 1985b: 228). In some respects, the restructuring of public expenditure on housing is a prime example of 'purposeful opportunism'. Instead of a long-term commitment to building new houses, funds were channelled into repair and maintenance grants which could be much more speedily curtailed at short notice. The difficulty with this 'realistic' appraisal of the possibilities for social policy in the future is that it gives little attention to how the framework might be manipulated to suit specific political goals. None the less, there may be no alternative but for *all* governments to adopt such flexible and cautious strategies and to incorporate 'the inevitability of opportunism into the way we think about social policy' (Klein and O'Higgins 1985b: 229).

Some problems do not feature in the above framework. Ferris gives an account of these and offers a few more prescriptions. In his attempt to go beyond the conflict between public and private welfare, he refers, in part, to the work of Jonas (1972) on the dilemmas we face as a consequence of technological change, which includes the problem of how traditional ethics 'no longer correspond to scientific, social and political reality' (Ferris 1985: 65). He also uses the model offered by the West German Green Party and other new social movements that have 'absorbed the ecological critique of industrial society' and are tending towards 'local and decentralised participatory initiatives' (Ferris 1985: 71). These references require further clarification since they are both linked to arguments on social policy.

As we have already noted, the critique of centralization has become widespread and is in certain respects quite valid. It does, however, lead to an *a priori* assumption that decentralization is intrinsically good. It fails to examine some of the problems of sustaining such initiatives; the un-democratic tendencies that might emerge; and the necessity of resolving some, though not all, difficulties from the centre. For instance, large government departments may be able to exercise greater control than small local units over professionals in health care and education. What Jonas has to say in his more recent account of the problems that confront public policy may be both comforting and painful to those who regard new social movements as models for social change and policy (Jonas 1984). We also find some convergence between his analysis of the fragile basis for public policy and the concerns expressed by Klein and O'Higgins about the age of uncertainty.

According to Jonas, the foundations of public policy have become undermined by 'cumulative technological change'. It is not that uncertainty over the future has ever been absent from political action, rather that the swift advance of technological change has outpaced and increased the distance from our power to predict its consequences. In addition to the challenges posed by advances in cell biology which promise to extend considerably our life span, and methods of behaviour control which threaten individual autonomy, and genetic manipulation, he cites the even more pressing problems, caused inadvertently by economic growth and medical science, of population explosion and damage to the natural environment (Jonas 1984: 140). Taken as a whole they pose a major threat to welfare aspirations of the future. Even if we focus only on the West, we cannot discount the likelihood of an increase in dependency ratios (mainly as a result of an ageing population) at an even faster rate than predicted at present. In order for welfare aspirations—even for the minimal forms available to Western populations—to be fulfilled in the rest of the world, the West would have to accept a reduction in living standards, even if it continued 'to ever more recklessly plunder the planet' (Jonas 1984: 141). New social movements that call for low or selective economic growth as a means of protecting the environment and at the same time advocate greater expenditure on welfare are sidestepping this issue (Papadakis 1986).

Our main concern, however, is not with distributional issues but with alternative strategies that governments may pursue. For Jonas, our uncertainty over the perils that lie ahead—partly because of the inversion of the Baconian ideal, whereby power over nature becomes a threat to rather than a promise of human happiness (Jonas 1984: 141)—should act as a signal for a policy of caution. Far-sighted self-interest implies a policy of 'constructive prevention' (Jonas 1984: 183) rather than pursuing a risky utopianism. Jonas acknowledges that he might be accused of technological determinism and doom-mongering. Yet his argument can be seen as an extension of the logic expressed by Klein and O'Higgins in their well-founded concern about the perils of prediction in an 'age of uncertainty'.

To some extent, the concern of social policy strategists reflects a recognition of 'the limists to the rationality of "social democratic" or "labourist" state interventions derived from Keynesian policies' (Clegg, Dow and Boreham 1983: 2) and a questioning of the state's ability to bring about reforms. None the less, this recognition may be leading to a reformulation of assumptions about the 'functional rationality' of the state 'as an organisational apparatus'; and of its capacity to formulate and achieve goals in a 'technically legal-rational manner' (Clegg, Dow and Boreham 1983: 25). This tendency has been encouraged by the very nature of Thatcherite policies on the welfare state which, as we have shown, entail a restructuring rather than diminution of state intervention. As Jessop points out, the state ought to be seen as 'a complex institutional ensemble of forms of representation and intervention'; and its power as 'a form-determined reflection of the balance of political forces' (Jessop 1982: xiv).

Alternative strategists also have to face a number of other issues. Those who use new social movements as models for social change need to confront their critique of centralized progressivist ideology with a more careful assessment of demands they make for social welfare expenditure. Far-sighted planners may have to extend their perception of constraints on policy to include more than just their own or other Western nations. Jonas makes the not unrealistic prediction that nations will engage in far greater and more devastating struggles over scarce resources than they have until recently (Jonas 1984: 182). Some would argue, quite correctly, that even if we focus on Western nations alone, far-sightedness has to take far greater account of the real constraints on social policy (Gillion and Hemming 1985). Finally, far-sighted strategies need to win public consent. The Conservatives in Britain have been at pains to create the appropriate climate in which to undermine some of the foundations of the welfare state. As these attempts were modified in the face of institutional constraints and social pressures, rhetoric assumed an important role in papering over inconsistencies and contradictions. Yet the rhetoric has not been ineffective: in the area of social policy it has led to considerable debate over the private provision of public welfare. Alternative strategists have begun to adjust themselves to the long-term prospect of a low-growth economy and have, on this basis, drawn up a long list of remedies. What has not been done adequately is to assess the social and political context in which such strategies could be put into effect. The redirection of policy, as shown by recent attempts to privatize welfare services, can only be done through the political arena. There is an understandable tendency for those involved in debates over the relative merits of public and private welfare to pick out those colours in the political rainbow that best suit their taste. Other colours are either ignored or blended to match their own. What they may or may not realize is that this distorts all colours, *not least the one they picked out in the first place.*

Bibliography

Abrams , P. (1984) 'Realities of neighbourhood care: the interactions between statutory, voluntary and informal social care'. *Policy and Politics*, vol. 12, no. 4.

Alderston, S. (1962) *Britain in the Sixties: Housing*, Penguin, Harmondsworth.

Alt, J. (1979) *The Politics of Economic Decline*, Cambridge University Press, Cambridge.

Archbishop of Canterbury's Working Party on Deprived Urban Areas (1985) *Faith in the City*, Church House Publishing, London.

Arnot, M. (1986) 'State education policy and girls' educational experiences', In V. Beechey and E. Whitelegg (eds) *Women in Britain Today*, Open University Press, Milton Keynes.

Audit Commission (1986) *Making a Reality of Community Care*, London, HMSO.

Austerberry, H. and Watson, S. (1983) *Women on the Margins*, Housing Research Group, City University, London.

Avebury Report (1984) *Home Life: A Code of Practice for Residential Care*, Centre for Policy on Ageing, London.

Bacon, R. and Eltis, W. (1976) *Britain's Economic Problem: Too Few Producers*, Macmillan, London.

Balchin, P. (1981) *Housing Policy and Housing Needs*, Macmillan, London.

(1985) *Housing Policy: An Introduction*, Croom Helm, London.

Baldock, J. (1985) 'Doing more for less: social workers in search of the holy grail', in M. Brenton and C. Ungerson (eds) *Year Book of Social Policy—1985*, Routledge & Kegan Paul, London.

Ball, M. (1983) *Housing Policy and Economic Power: The Political Economy of Owner Occupation*, Methuen, London.

Barrett, M. (1980) *The Idea of Welfare*, Heinemann, London.

Bassett, K. and Short, J. (1980) *Housing and Residential Structure: Alternative Approaches*, Routledge & Kegan Paul, London.

Bean, P., Ferris, J. and Whynes, D. (eds) (1985) *In Defence of Welfare*, Tavistock, London.

Beechey, V. (1977) 'Some notes on female wage labour in the capitalist mode of production', in *Capital and Class*, no. 3.

Beechey, V. and Whitelegg, E. (eds) (1986) *Women in Britain Today*, Open University Press, Milton Keynes.

Bennett, F. (1983) 'The state, welfare and women's dependence', in L. Segal (ed.) *What Is to Be Done About the Family?* Penguin, Harmondsworth.

Beresford, R. and Croft, S. (1986) *Whose Welfare?* Lewis Cohen Urban Studies Centre, University of Sussex, Brighton.

Berry, F. (1974) *Housing: the Great British failure*, Charles Knight, London.

Berthoud, R. (ed.) (1985) *Challenges to Social Policy*, Gower, Aldershot.

Beveridge, W. (1942) *Social Insurance and Allied Services*, Cmnd 6404, HMSO.

Birmingham Centre for Contemporary Cultural Studies (1981) *Unpopular Education*, Hutchinson, London.

Blaug, M. (1984) 'Education vouchers—It all depends on what you mean', in J. Le Grand and R. Robinson (eds) *Privatisation and the Welfare State*, Allen & Unwin, London.

Board of Inland Revenue (1981) *Inland Revenue Statistics 1981*, HMSO, London.

(1983) *Inland Revenue Statistics 1983*, HMSO, London.

Boddy, M. (1980) *The Building Societies*, Macmillan, London.

Bosanquet, N. (1983) *After the New Right*, Heinemann, London.

(1984) 'Is privatisation inevitable?' in J. Le Grand and R. Robinson (eds) *Privatisation and the Welfare State*, Allen & Unwin, London.

Boyd, D. (1973) *Elites and Their Education*, NFER, Slough.

Brittan, S. (1975) 'The economic contradictions of democracy', *British Journal of Political Science*, vol. 5, no. 1.

Britten, N. and Heath, A. (1983) 'Women, men and social class', in E. Gamarnikov, D. Morgan, J. Purvis and E. Taylorson (eds), *Gender, Class and Work*, Hutchinson, London.

Brown, G. and Harris, T. (1978) *The Social Origins of Depression*, Tavistock, London.

Building Societies Association (1986a) *Housing in Britain*, Building Societies Association, London.

(1986b) *Fact Book*, Building Societies Association, London.

Bulmer, M. (1986a) 'Can caring come together?' *New Society*, 4 July.

(1986b) *Neighbours: The Work of Philip Abrams*, Cambridge University Press, Cambridge.

BUPA (1983) *Provident Scheme Statistics, 1982–83*, British United Provident Association, London.

Burke, G. (1981) *Housing and Social Justice*, Longman, London.

Burnet, F. (ed.) (1986) *The Public and Preparatory Schools Year Book, 1985*, Adam & Charles Black, London.

Butler, R. (1973) 'The politics of the 1944 Education Act', in V. Morris and J. Ozga (eds), *Decision-Making in British Education*, Heinemann, London.

Cameron, D. (1985) 'Public expenditure and economic performance in international perspective', in R. Klein and M. O'Higgins, (eds), *The Future of Welfare*, Blackwell, Oxford.

Cawson, A. (1982) *Corporatism and the Welfare State*, Heinemann, London.

Central Statistical Office (CSO) (1972) *Social Trends No. 3*, HMSO, London.

(1979) *Social Trends No. 9*, HMSO, London.

(1985a) *Regional Trends*, HMSO, London.

(1985b) *Social Trends No. 15*, HMSO, London.

(1986) *Social Trends No. 16*, HMSO, London.

(1987) *Social Trends No. 17*, HMSO, London.

Charvet, J. (1982) *Feminism*, Dent, London.

CIPFA, (1985) *Local Government Comparative Statistics*, 1985, Chartered Institute of Public Finance and Accountancy, London.

Clegg, S., Dow, G. and Boreham, P. (1983) 'Politics and crisis: the state of the recession', in S. Clegg, G. Dow and P. Boreham (eds) *The State, Class and the Recession*, Croom Helm, London.

Cockburn, C. (1986) *Machinery of Dominance: Women, Men and Technical Know-How*, Pluto Press, London.

Cohen, D. and Farrar, E. (1977) 'Power to the parents: the story of education vouchers', *The Public Interest*, no. 48.

Cohen, G. (1982) *Education Vouchers: Home Thoughts from California*, Civil Service College Working Paper No. 32.

COHSE (1986) *Notes on Private Cleaning Contractors*, mimeo, Confederation of Health Service Employees, London.

Congdon, T. (1986) 'Will the house buying boom save Thatcher?' *Times*, 17 June.

Conservative Party (1979) *General Election Manifesto*, Conservative Central Office, London.

(1987) *The Next Moves Foward* (1987 Election Manifesto), Conservative Central Office, London.

Cooper, M. and Culyer, A. (1968) *The Price of Blood*, Hobart Paper No. 41, Institute of Economic Affairs, London.

Corbett, A. (1978) *Much Ado about Education*, Macmillan, London.

Couper, M. and Brindley, T. (1975) 'Housing classes and housing values', *Sociological Review*, August, vol. 23, no. 3.

Creedy, J. (1982) *State Pensions in Britain*, Cambridge University Press, Cambridge.

Crompton, R. and Mann, M. (eds) (1986) *Gender and Stratification*, Macmillan, London.

Crouch, C. (1983) 'New thinking on pluralism', *Political Quarterly*, vol. 54, no. 4.

   (1985a) 'The scope for socialism: a pessimistic view', mimeo, London School of Economics.

   (1985b) 'Exit and voice in the future of the welfare state, *Government and Opposition*, vol. 20, no. 3.

Cullingworth, J. (1979) *Essays on Housing Policy*, Allen & Unwin, London.

Dale, A., Gilbert, N. and Arber, S. (1985) 'Integrating women into class theory', *Sociology*, vol. 19, no. 3.

Dale, J. and Foster, P. (1986) *Feminists and State Welfare*, Routledge & Kegan Paul, London.

David, M. (1980) *The State, the Family and Education*, Routledge & Kegan Paul, London.

Davies, B. and Challis, D. (1985) 'Long-term care for the elderly: the community care scheme', Discussion Paper No. 386, *Personal Social Services Research Unit*, University of Kent, Canterbury.

Davies, G. and Piachaud, D. (1983) 'Social policy and the economy', in H. Glennerster (ed.) *The Future of the Welfare State*, Heinemann, London.

Day, P. (1985) 'Regulating the private sector of welfare', *Political Quarterly*, vol. 56, no. 3.

Deacon, A. and Bradshaw, J. (1983) *Reserved for the Poor*, Martin Robertson, Oxford.

Deacon, R. (1985) 'Strategies for welfare: east and west', *Critical Social Policy*, vol. 6, no. 2.

Delamont, S. (1984) 'Debs. dollies, swots and weeds', in G. Walford (ed.) *British Public Schools Policy and Practice*, Falmer, Lewes.

Dennison, S. R. (1984) *Choice in Education*, Hobart Paper No. 19, Institute of Economic Affairs, London.

Department of Education and Science (DES) (1975) *Statistics of Education, 1975*, HMSO, London.

   (1983) *Statistics of Education, 1983*, HMSO, London.

   (1985) *Education Statistics for the UK*, HMSO, London.

Department of Employment (1986) *Family Expenditure Survey, 1985*, HMSO, London.

Department of the Environment (DoE) (1977) *Housing Policy, Technical Volume, Part I*, HMSO, London.

   (1979) *English House Conditions Survey, 1976, Part 2: Report of*

the Social Survey, HMSO, London.
(1980) *Housing and Construction Statistics, 1969–1979*, HMSO, London.
(1985) *Housing and Construction Statistics, 1974–84*, HMSO, London.
(1986) *Housing and Construction Statistics, 1986, Part 2*, HMSO, London.
Department of Health and Social Security (DHSS) (1981) *Growing Older*, Cmnd 8173, HMSO, London.
(1983) *NHS Management Inquiry Report (Griffiths Report)*, HMSO, London.
(1984a) *Greater Security for the Rights and Expectations of Members of Occupational Pension Schemes*, February, HMSO, London.
(1984b) *Consultative Document on Improved Transferability for Early Leavers from Occupational Pension Schemes*, May, HMSO, London.
(1984c) *Personal Pensions: A Consultative Document*, July, HMSO, London.
(1984d) *Population, Pension Costs and Pensioners' Incomes: A Background Paper for the Inquiry into Provision for Retirement*, HMSO, London.
(1985a) *The Reform of Social Security*, vol. 1, Cmnd 9517, vol. 2, Cmnd 9518, HMSO, London.
(1985b) *The Health Service in England: Helping More Patients Today—Planning for the Patients of Tomorrow*, HMSO, London.
(1986) *The Reform of Social Security: Programme for Action*, Cmnd 9691, HMSO, London.
Diamond Report (1976) *The Report of the Royal Commission on the Distribution of Incomes and Wealth*, Report No. 4, Cmnd 6626, HMSO, London.
Disney, R. (1982) 'Theorising the welfare state', *Journal of Social Policy*, vol. 11, no. 1.
(1985) 'Should we afford SERPS?' *New Society*, 12 July.
Donnison, D. (1967) *The Government of Housing*, Pelican, Harmondsworth.
(1979) 'Social welfare after Titmuss', *Journal of Social Policy*, vol. 8, no. 2.
(1984) 'The progressive potential of privatisation', in J. Le Grand and R. Robinson (eds) *Privatisation and the Welfare State*, Allen & Unwin, London.
Donzelot, J. (1980) *The Policing of Families*, Hutchinson, London.
Douglas, J. (1976). 'The over-loaded crown', *British Journal of*

Political Science, vol. 6, no. 4.

Doyal, L. (1983) 'Women, health and the sexual division of labour', *Critical Social Policy*, no. 7.

Doyal, L. and Elston, M. (1986) 'Women, health and medicine', in V. Beechey and E. Whitelegg (eds) *Women in Britain Today*, Open University Press, Milton Keynes.

Dryzek, J. and Goodin, R. (1986) 'Risk-sharing and social justice: the motivational foundations of the post-war welfare state', *British Journal of Political Science*, vol. 16, part 1.

Duclaud-Williams, R. (1978) *The Politics of Housing in Britain and France*, Heinemann, London.

Duke, V. and Edgell, S. (1984) 'Public expenditure cuts in Britain', *International Journal of Urban and Regional Studies*, vol. 8, no. 2.

Dunleavy, P. (1979a) 'The urban bases of political alignment', *British Journal of Political Science*, vol. 9.

(1979b) 'The political implications of sectoral cleavages and the growth of state employment—parts I and II,' *Political Studies*, vol. 28, nos 3 and 4.

(1980) *Urban Political Analysis*, Macmillan, London.

Dunleavy, P. and Husbands, C. (1985) *British Democracy at the Crossroads*, Allen & Unwin, London.

Economist (1985) 'A handsome package, but what is inside?', 8 June.

(1986) 'Contracted in', 18 January.

Eisenstadt, S. and Ahimeir, O. (eds) (1985) *The Welfare State in Crisis*, Croom Helm, London.

Equal Opportunities Commission (1980) *The Experience of Caring for Elderly and Handicapped Dependents*, EOC, Manchester.

Fair Deal for Housing (1971) Cmnd. 4728, London.

Ferris, J. (1985) 'Citizenship and the crisis of the welfare state', in P. Bean, J. Ferris and D. Whynes (eds) *In Defence of Welfare*, Tavistock, London.

Field, F. (1981) *Inequality in Britain*, Fontana, London.

Finch, J. (1984) *Education as Social Policy*, Longman, London.

Finch, J. and Groves, D. (1980) 'Community care and the family: a case for equal opportunities?' *Journal of Social Policy*, vol. 9, no. 4.

(eds) (1983) *A Labour of Love: Women, Work and Caring*, Routledge & Kegan Paul, London.

Fine, B. and Harris, L. (1979) *Rereading Capital*, Macmillan, London.

Flora, P. and Heidenheimer, A.J. (eds) (1981) *The Development of Welfare States in Europe and America*, Transaction Books, New Brunswick.

Forsyth, G. (1982) 'The semantics of health care policy and the inevitability of regulation', in G. McLachlan and A. Maynard (eds) *The Public/Private Mix for Health*, Nuffield Provincial Hospitals Trust, London.

Fox, I. (1984) 'The demand for a public school education', in G. Walford (ed.) *British Public Schools: Policy and Practice*, Falmer, Lewes.

Franklin, M. (1985) *The Decline of Class Voting in Britain*, Clarendon Press, Oxford.

Franklin, M. and Page, E. (1984) 'A critique of the consumption cleavage approach in British voting studies', *Political Studies*, vol. 32, no. 3.

Franks Commission (1966) *Report of a Commission of Inquiry*, Clarendon Press, Oxford.

Friedman, M. (1962) *Capitalism and Freedom*, Chicago University Press, Chicago.

Friedman, M. and Friedman, R. (1981) *Free to Choose*, Penguin, Harmondsworth.

Froland, C. (1980) 'Formal and informal care: discontinuities on a continuum', *Social Service Review*, vol. 54, no. 4.

Gallup Report (1984) *The Demand for Portable Pensions*, Gallup, London.

George, V. and Wilding, P. (1976) *Ideology and Social Welfare*, 1st edn, Routledge & Kegan Paul, London.

(1984) *The Impact of Welfare*, Routledge & Kegan Paul, London.

Gershuny, J. (1983) 'Technical change and social limits, in A. Ellis, and K. Kumar, (eds) *Dilemmas of Liberal Democracies*, Tavistock, London.

Giddens, A. (1985) *The Nation-State and Violence*, Polity Press, Cambridge.

Gilkes, A. (1957) *Independent Education*, Gollancz, London.

Gillion, C. and Hemming, R. (1985) 'Social expenditure: 1960–1990: a reply', *Journal of Public Policy*, vol. 5, part 2.

Ginsburg, N. (1979) *Class, Capital and Social Policy*, Macmillan, London.

Glennerster, H. (ed.) (1983) *The Future of the Welfare State*, Heinemann, London.

(1985) *Paying for Welfare*, Blackwell, Oxford.

Glennerster, H. and Wilson, G. (1970) *Paying for Private Schools*, Allen Lane, London.

Goldthorpe, J., Lockwood, E., Bechhofer, E. and Platt, J. (1969) *The Affluent Worker in the Class Structure*, Cambridge University Press, Cambridge.

Goodin, R. (1985) *Protecting the Vulnerable*, University of Chicago

Press, Chicago.

Goodin, R. and Le Grand, J. (1986) 'The middle-class infiltration of the welfare state: some evidence from Australia' Discussion Paper No. 10, *The Welfare State Programme*, London School of Economics.

Gough, I. (1979) *The Political Economy of the Welfare State*, Macmillan, London.

Government Actuary (1958) *Occupational Pension Schemes*, a survey by the Government Actuary, HMSO, London.

(1968) *Occupational Pension Schemes*, third survey by the Government Actuary, HMSO, London.

(1972) *Occupational Pension Schemes*, fourth survey by the Government Actuary, HMSO, London.

(1981) *Occupational Pensions Schemes*, sixth Survey by the Government Actuary, HMSO, London.

Graham, H. (1983) 'Caring: a labour of love', in J. Finch and D. Groves (eds) *A Labour of Love: Women, Work and Caring*, Routledge & Kegan Paul, London.

Grigsby, W. (1963) *Housing Markets and Public Policy*, University of Pennsylvania Press, Philadelphia.

Habermas, J. (1975) *Legitimation Crisis*, Heinemann, London.

(1976) 'Legitimation problems in late capitalism', in P. Connerton (ed.) *Critical Sociology*, Penguin, Harmondsworth.

Hadley, R. and Hatch, S. (1981) *Social Welfare and the Failure of the State*, Allen & Unwin, London.

Hague, D. (1980) 'The central problem of government expenditure', *Manchester Business School Review*, Autumn.

Halsey, A. (1987) 'Social trends since World War II', in Central Statistical Office, *Social Trends No. 17*, HMSO, London.

Halsey, A., Heath, A. and Ridge, J. (1980) *Origins and Destinations*, Clarendon Press, Oxford.

(1984) 'The political arithmetic of public schools', in G. Walford (ed.) *British Public Schools Policy and Practice*, Falmer, Lewes.

Handler, J. (1973) *The Coercive Social Worker*, Rand McNally, Chicago.

Harloe, C. (1979) *Private Rented Housing in England and the USA*, Centre for Environmental Studies, Heinemann, London.

Harris, R. and Seldon, A. (1979) *Over-ruled on Welfare*, Institute of Economic Affairs, London.

Harrison, A. and Gretton, J. (eds) (1984) *Health Care UK 1984*, Chartered Institute of Public Finance and Accountancy, London.

Hart, N. (1986) 'How the government buried its dead reckoning', *Guardian*, 30 July.

Hartmann, H. (1979) 'The unhappy marriage of marxism and feminism', *Capital and Class*, no. 8.

Harvey, D. (1973) *Social Justice and the City*, Edward Arnold, London.

Hayek, F. (1979) *Law, Legislation and Liberty, Vol. iii: The Mirage of Social Justice*, Routledge & Kegan Paul, London.

Heald, D. (1983) *Public Expenditure*, Martin Robertson, Oxford.

Heath, A., Jowell, R. and Curtice, J. (1985) *How Britain Votes*, Pergamon, Oxford.

Heclo, H. (1981) 'Toward a new welfare state?' in P. Flora and A.J. Heidenheimer (eds) *The Development of Welfare States in Europe and America*, Transaction Books, New Brunswick.

Henderson, J. and Cohen, D. (1984) 'No strategy for prevention', in A. Harrison and J. Gretton (eds) *Health Care UK 1984*, Chartered Institute of Public Finance and Accountancy, London.

Henwood, M. and Wicks, M. (1985) 'Community care, family trends and social change', *Quarterly Journal of Social Affairs*, vol. 1, no. 4.

Her Majesty's Inspectorate (1981) *Report on the Effects on the Education Service in England of Local Authority Expenditure Policies—1980–1*, Department of Education and Science, London.

Higgins, J. (1981) *States of Welfare*, Martin Robertson, Oxford.

Hill, M. (1986) 'The Future of Welfare', *Policy and Politics*, vol. 14, no. 3.

Hindess, B. (1987) *Freedom, Equality and the Market*, Tavistock, London.

Hirsch, F. (1976) *Social Limits to Growth*, Harvard University Press, Cambridge, Mass.

Hirschman, A.O. (1982) *Shifting Involvements: Private Interest and Public Action*, Martin Robertson, Oxford.

Holmes, M. (1985) *The First Thatcher Government, 1979–83*, Harvester Press, Brighton.

House of Commons (1981) *The Second Report of the Environmental Committee*, session 1980/81, HMSO, London.

Housing Programme, The, 1965–70 (1965) Cmnd. 2838, HMSO, London.

Illich, I. (1971) *Medical Nemesis*, Calder and Boyars, London.

Independent Schools Information Service (ISIS) (1983) *Annual Census*, ISIS, London.

(1986a) *Annual Census*, ISIS, London.

(1986b) *Independent Schools: The Facts*, ISIS, London.

(1986c) *School Fees; Some Ways of Planning Ahead to Reduce*

Fees, ISIS, London.

Inland Revenue (1983) 'The cost of tax relief for pension schemes', mimeo, Somerset House.

Jencks, C. (1970) *Education Vouchers*, Center for the Study of Social Policy, Cambridge, Mass.

Jessop, B. (1982) *The Capitalist State: Marxist Theories and Methods*, Martin Robertson, Oxford.

Jenkins, J. (1986) 'Health off the shelf', *New Statesman*, 19 September.

Johnson, R. (1976) 'Notes on the schooling of the English working class 1780–1951', in R. Dale, G. Esland and M. MacDonald (eds), *Schooling and Capitalism*, Routledge & Kegan Paul, London.

Jonas, H. (1972) 'Technology and responsibility: reflections on the new task of ethics', *Social Research*, vol. 40.

(1984) *The Imperative of Responsibility*, University of Chicago Press, Chicago.

Jones, C. (1985) *Patterns of Social Policy*, Tavistock, London.

Jones, M. (1982) 'Where charity began', *Guardian*, 24 August.

Jones, C. and Stevenson, J. (eds) (1982) *The Year Book of Social Policy in Britain, 1980–81*, Routledge & Kegan Paul, London.

Judge, K. (1981) 'State pensions and the growth of social welfare expenditure', *Journal of Social Policy*, vol. 10, no. 4.

Judge, K. and Knapp, M. (1985) 'Efficiency in the production of welfare', in R. Klein and M. O'Higgins (eds) *The Future of Welfare*, Blackwell, Oxford.

Judge, K., Smith, J. and Taylor-Gooby, P. (1983) 'Public opinion and the privatisation of welfare', *Journal of Social Policy*, vol. 12, no. 4.

Kemeny, J. (1981) *The Myth of Home-Ownership*, Routledge & Kegan Paul, London.

Kent County Council (1978) *Education Vouchers in Kent*, KCC, Maidstone.

Kent Social Services Department (1986) *Planning for the Future*, mimeo, KSSD, Maidstone.

Kilroy, B. (1979) 'Labour housing dilemma', *New Statesman*, 28 September.

(1980) *The Financial Implications of Government Policies on Home Ownership*, Shelter Housing Action Centre, London.

Kincaid, J. (1978) 'The politics of pensions' *New Society*, 16 February.

Kirwan, R. (1984) 'The demise of public housing', in J. Le Grand and R. Robinson (eds) *Privatisation and the Welfare State*, Allen & Unwin, London.

Klein, R. (1983) *The Politics of the National Health Service*, Longman, London.

(1984) 'Privatization and the welfare state', *Lloyds Bank Review*, no. 151.

Klein, R. and O'Higgins, M. (eds) (1985a) *The Future of Welfare*, Blackwell, Oxford.

(1985b) 'Social policy after incrementalism', in R. Klein and M. O'Higgins (eds) *The Future of Welfare*, Blackwell, Oxford.

Labour Party (1980) *Private Schools*.

(1986) *Freedom and Fairness*, Labour Party, London.

Lait, D. (1986) 'Privatization and voluntarization', *Quarterly Journal of Social Affairs*, vol. 2, no. 3.

Lansley, S. (1979) *Housing and Public Policy*, Croom Helm, London.

Laurence, J. (1987) 'Cosmetic surgery for the NHS', *New Society*, 6 March.

Lawton, D. (1980) *The Politics of the School Curriculum*, Routledge & Kegan Paul, London.

Lees, D. (1964) *Monopoly on Choice in Health Services*, Occasional Paper No. 3, Institute of Economic Affairs, London.

Le Grand, J. (1982) *The Strategy of Equality*, Allen & Unwin, London.

(1985) 'Comment on inequality, redistribution and recession', *Journal of Social Policy*, vol. 14, no. 3.

Le Grand, J. and Robinson, R. (eds) (1984) *Privatisation and the Welfare State*, Allen and Unwin, London.

Liberal Party (1986) *These Are Liberal Policies*, Liberal Party, London.

London Edinburgh Weekend Return Group (LEWRG) (1982) *In and Against the state*, mimeo, LEWRG, London.

Loney, M. (1986) 'Public spending—private profit', in *Community Care*, August.

Loney, M., Boswell, D. and Clarke, J. (eds) (1983) *Social Policy and Social Welfare*, Open University Press, Milton Keynes.

McLachlan, G. and Maynard, A. (eds) (1982) *The Public/Private Mix for Health*, Nuffield Provincial Hospitals Trust.

McLure, J.S. (ed.) (1974) *Education Documents*, Methuen, London.

Marshall, G., Rose, D., Vogler, C. and Newby, H. (1985) 'Class, citizenship and distributional conflict in modern Britain', *The British Journal of Sociology*, vol. 36, no. 2.

Marshall, T. (1963) 'Citizenship and social class', in T. Marshall *Sociology at the Crossroads*, Heinemann, London.

Martin, J. and Roberts, C. (1984) *Women and Employment: A Lifetime Perspective*, Department of the Environment/Office of

Population Censuses and Surveys, HMSO, London.

Maxwell, R. (1984) 'International comparisons: what can we learn?' in A. Harrison and J. Gretton (eds) *Health Care UK 1984*, Chartered Institute of Public Finance and Accountancy, London.

Maynard, A. (1982) 'The private health care sector in Britain', in G. McLachlan and A. Maynard (eds) *The Public/Private Mix for Health*, Nuffield Provincial Hospitals Trust, London.

(1983) 'Privatising the National Health Service', *Lloyds Bank Review*, no. 148, April 1983.

(1984) 'Privatisation and the National Health Service', in J. Le Grand and R. Robinson (eds) *Privatisation and the Welfare State*, Allen & Unwin, London.

Mencher, S. (1967) *Private Practice in Britain*, Bell & Sons, London.

Miliband, R. (1973) *The State in a Capitalist Society*, Quartet Books, London.

Milner Holland Report, The (1965) Report of the Committee on Housing in Greater London, Cmnd 2605, HMSO, London, March.

Minford, P. (1984) 'State expenditure: a study in waste', *Economic Affairs Supplement*, April–June.

Mishra, R. (1981) *Society and Social Policy,* Macmillan, London.

(1984) *The Welfare State in Crisis*, Harvester Press, Brighton.

Mohan, J. (1986) 'Private medical care and the British Conservative Government', *Journal of Social Policy*, vol. 15, no. 3.

Mohan, J. and Woods, K. (1985) 'Restructuring health care: the social geography of public and private health care under the British Conservative government', *International Journal of Health Services*, vol. 15, no. 2.

Murie, A. (1983) *Housing Inequality and Deprivation*, Heinemann, London.

Musgrave, P. (1968) *Society and Education in England since 1800*, Methuen, London.

National Association of Health Authorities (1985) *Registration and Inspection of Nursing Homes: A Handbook for Health Authorities*, NAHA, London.

National Audit Office (1986) *NHS: Level of Changes for Private Resident Patients*, HMSO, London.

Nevitt, A.A. (1966) *Housing, Taxation and Subsidies*, Nelson, London.

Newby, H., Marshall, G., Rose, D. and Vogler, C. (1986) 'From class structure to class action', in R. Finnegan *et al.* (eds) *New Approaches to Economic Life*, Manchester University Press, Manchester.

Newcastle Report, The (1861) *Report on the State of Popular Education in England*, Eyre and Spottiswoode for HMSO, London.

Newsom (1968) *The Public Schools Commission: First Report*, HMSO, London.

Norwood (1943) *Report on the Committee of the Secondary Schools Examination Council*, Board of Education, London.

Nove, A. (1983) *The Economics of Feasible Socialism*, Allen & Unwin, London.

O'Connor, J. (1973) *The Fiscal Crisis of the State*, St James' Press, New York.

OECD (1978) *Public Expenditure: Health*, OECD, Paris.

Offe, C. (1974) 'Structural problems of the capitalist state', in K. von Beyme (ed.) *German Political Studies*, Vol. I, Sage, New York.

—— (1984) *Contradictions of the Welfare State*, Hutchinson, London.

Office of Health Economics (1987) *Compendium of Health Statistics, 1987*, OHE, London.

Office of Population Census and Surveys (OPCS) (1978) *Occupational Mortality 1970–2; 1980–1 to 82–3*, HMSO, London.

—— (1982) *General Household Survey, 1980*, HMSO, London.

—— (1984) *General Household Survey, 1982*, HMSO, London.

—— (1985) *General Household Survey, 1983*, HMSO, London.

—— (1978, 1986) *Occupational Mortality, Decennial Supplements, 1970–2; 1980–1 to 82–3*, HMSO, London.

O'Higgins, M. (1983) 'Issues of redistribution in state welfare spending', in M. Loney, D. Boswell and J. Clarke (eds) *Social Policy and Social Welfare*, Open University Press, Milton Keynes.

—— (1984) 'Privatisation and social security', *Political Quarterly*, vol. 55, no. 2.

—— (1985) 'Welfare, redistribution and inequality', in P. Bean, J. Ferris and D. Whynes (eds) *In Defence of Welfare*, Tavistock, London.

—— (1986) 'Public spending: the pressure is off', *New Society*, 21 November.

O'Higgins, M. and Patterson, A. (1985) 'The prospects for public expenditure', in R. Klein and M. O'Higgins (eds) *The Future of Welfare*, Blackwell, Oxford.

Olson, N. (1965) *The Logic of Collective Action: Public Goods and the Theory of Groups*, Harvard University Press, Cambridge, Mass.

Opp, K.-D. (1986) 'Soft incentives and collective action', *British Journal of Political Science*, vol. 16, no. 1.

Owen, D. and Steel, D. (1987) *The Time Has Come*, Weidenfeld &

Nicolson, London.

Pahl, R. (1984) *Divisions of Labour*, Blackwell, Oxford.

Pahl, R. and Wallace, C. (1986) 'Neither angels in marble nor rebels in red', in D. Rose (ed.) *Social Stratification and Economic Decline*, Hutchinson, London.

Papadakis, E. (1984) *The Green Movement in West Germany*, Croom Helm, London.

(1986) 'The Green Alternative: Interpretations of Social Protest and Political Action', *Australian Journal of Politics and History*, vol. 32, no. 3.

Papadakis, E. and Taylor-Gooby, P. (1987) 'Consumer attitudes and participation in state welfare', *Political Studies*, vol. 35, no. 2.

Parry, R. (1985) 'Britain: stable aggregates, changing composition', in R. Rose (ed.) *Public Employment in Western Nations*, Cambridge University Press, Cambridge.

Pascall, G. (1986) *Social Policy: A Feminist Analysis*, Tavistock, London.

Piachaud, D. (1985) 'Can we afford SERPS?' *New Society*, 14 June.

Pilch, M. and Wood, V. (1960) *Pension Schemes*, Hutchinson, London.

Pinker, R. (1971) *Social Theory and Social Policy*, Heinemann, London.

(1979) *The Idea of Welfare*, Heinemann, London.

Plant, R. (1985) 'The very idea of a welfare state', in P. Bean, J. Ferris and D. Whynes (eds) *In Defence of Welfare*, Tavistock, London.

Pliatsky, L. (1985) *Paying and Choosing*, Blackwell, Oxford.

Plowden Report (1967) *Children and Their Primary Schools*, HMSO, London.

Radical Statistics Group (1986) 'Unsafe in their hands: health service statistics in England', *International Journal of Health Services*, vol. 16, no. 2.

Rae, J. (1981) *The Public School Revolution*, Faber & Faber, London.

Reddin, M. (1982) 'Occupation, welfare and social division', in C. Jones and J. Stevenson (eds) *The Year Book of Social Policy in Britain, 1980–81*, Routledge & Kegan Paul, London.

Reddin, M. and Hodges, S. (1982) 'Critique', in M. Fogarty (ed.) *Retirement Policy: The Next Fifty Years*, Heinemann, London.

Reid, I. (1979) *Social Class Differences in Britain*, Open Books, London.

Rex, J. and Moore, R. (1967) *Race, Community and Conflict*, Oxford Uiversity Press, Oxford.

Ridley Report, The (1945) Report of the Interdepartmental

Committee on Rent Control, Cmnd. 6621, HMSO, London.

Rimmer, L. (1983) 'The economics of work and caring', in J. Finch and D. Groves (eds) *A Labour of Love: Women, Work and Caring*, Routledge & Kegan Paul, London.

Rimmer, L. and Wicks, M. (1983) 'The challenge of change: demographic trends, the family and social policy', in H. Glennerster (ed.) *The Future of the Welfare State*, Heinemann, London.

Ritchie, J. and Barrowclough, R. (1983) *Paying for Equalisation: A Survey of Pension Age Preferences and Their Costs*, Equal Opportunities Commission and Social and Community Planning and Research, London.

Robbins Report (1983) *Higher Education*, Cmnd 2154, HMSO, London.

Roberts, B., Finnegann, R. and Gallie, D. (1985) *New Approaches to Economic Life*, Manchester University Press, Manchester.

Robinson, R. (1986) 'Restructuring the welfare state', *Journal of Social Policy*, vol. 15, no. 1.

Rogers, R. (1980) 'The myth of the "Independent" schools', *New Statesman*, 4 January.

Room, G. (1979) *The Sociology of Welfare*, Blackwell, Oxford.

Rose, D., Vogler, C., Marshall, G. and Newby, H. (1984) 'Economic restructuring: the British experience', *Annals of the American Academy of Political and Social Science*, no. 475.

Rose, H. (1981) 'Rereading Titmuss: the sexual division of welfare', *Journal of Social Policy*, vol. 10, no. 4.

Rose, H. and Rose, R. (1982) 'Moving right out of welfare', *Critical Social Policy*, vol. 2, no. 1.

Rose, R. (1980) *Class Does Not Equal Party*, Centre for the Study of Public Policy, University of Strathclyde.

(1985) *The State's Contribution to the Welfare Mix*, Centre for the Study of Public Policies, University of Strathclyde, Studies in Public Policy, No. 140.

Rose, R. and McAllister, I. (1986) *Voters Begin to Choose*, Sage, London.

Rowbotham S., Segal, L. and Wainwright, H. (1979) *Beyond the Fragments*, Merlin Press, London.

Rubinstein, D. (1979) *Education and Equality*, Penguin, Harmondsworth.

Rutter, M., Maughan, B., Mortimore, P. and Oustan, J. (1980) *Fifteen Thousand Hours*, Open Books, London.

Salter, B. and Tapper, E. (1984) 'Images of independent schooling', in G. Walford (ed.) *British Public Schools Policy and Practice*, Falmer, Lewes.

Sampson, A. (1983) *The New Anatomy of Britain*, Claremont, London.

Sarlvik, R. and Crewe, I. (1983) *Decade of Dealignment*, Cambridge University Press, Cambridge.

Saunders, P. (1979) *Urban Politics*, Hutchinson, London.

Seabrook, J. (1984) *The Idea of Neighbourhood*, Pluto Press, London.

Seldon, A. (1981) *The Emerging Consensus*? Institute of Economic Affairs, London.

(1986) *The Riddle of the Voucher*, Institute of Economic Affairs, London.

Siltanen, J. and Stanworth, M. (eds) (1984) *Women and the Public Sphere*, Hutchinson, London.

Silver, H. (1980) *Education and the Social Condition*, Methuen, London.

Silverman, D. (1984) 'Going private: ceremonial forms in a private oncology clinic', *Sociology*, vol. 18, no. 2.

Simon, B. and Bradley, I. (eds) (1975) *The Victorian Public School*, Gill & Macmillan, Dublin.

Sinfield, A. (1978) 'Analyses in the social division of welfare', *Journal of Social Policy*, vol. 7, no. 2.

Social Services Select Committee (1983) *Public Expenditure on the Social Services: Minutes of Evidence*, HCP 321, HMSO, London.

(1985) *Public Expenditure on the Social Services: Minutes of Evidence*, HCP 339, HMSO, London.

Spens, H. (1938) *Report of the Consultative Committee of the Board of Education on Secondary Education*, Board of Education, London.

Steel, D. and Heald, D. (1984) *Privatizing Public Enterprises*, Royal Institute of Public Administration, London.

Stillwell, J. (1984) 'Diagnostic procedures in the NHS', in A. Harrison and J. Gretton (eds) *Health Care UK 1984*, Chartered Institute of Public Finance and Accountancy, London.

Stone, M. (1981) *The Education of the Black Child in Britain*, Fontana, London.

Stow Report (1979) *Mortgage Finance in the 1980s*, Building Societies Association, London.

Stretton, H. (1974) *Housing and Government*, 1974 Boyer Lectures, Australian Broadcasting Commission, Syndey.

Sutcliffe, A. (ed.) (1974) *Multi-Storey Living: The British Working Class Experience*, Croom Helm, London.

Taylor-Gooby, P. (1985) *Public Opinion, Ideology and State Welfare*, Routledge & Kegan Paul, London.

(1986) 'Privatisation, power and the welfare state', *Sociology*, vol. 20, no. 2.

(1987) 'Welfare attitudes: cleavage, consensus and citizenship', *Quarterly Journal of Social Affairs*, vol. 3, no. 2.

Taylor-Gooby, P. and Dale, J. (1981) *Social Theory and Social Welfare*, Edward Arnold, London.

Taylor-Gooby, P. and Papadakis, E. (1985) 'Who wants the welfare state?' *New Society*, 19 July.

(1985b) *Attitudes to Welfare—Final Report to ESRC*, mimeo, University of Kent, Canterbury.

(1986) 'Positional satisfaction and state welfare', *Sociological Review*, vol. 34, no. 4.

Thane, P. (1977) '*The Working Class and the Welfare State*', mimeo, British Sociological Association Conference, University of Sheffield.

(1982) *Foundations of the Welfare State*, Longman, London.

Times Educational Supplement (1986) 'Boom continues for independents', 2 May.

Times (1984) *Times Guide to the House of Commons*, Times Newspapers, London.

Titmuss, R. (1955) 'The social division of welfare', in *Essays on the Welfare State*, Allen & Unwin, London.

(1967) *Choice and the Welfare State*, Fabian Tract No. 370, Fabian Society, London.

(1970) *The Gift Relationship*, Allen & Unwin, London.

Townsend, P. (1986) 'Why are the many poor?' *International Journal of Health Services*, vol. 16, no. 1.

Townsend, P. and Davidson, N. (eds) (1982) *Inequalities in Health: The Black Report*, Penguin, Harmondsworth.

Treasury (1979) *The Government's Expenditure Plans, 1980–1*, Cm 7746, HMSO, London.

(1984) *The Next Ten Years: Public Expenditure and Taxation into the 1990s*, Cm 9189, HMSO, London.

(1985) *The Government's Expenditure Plans, 1985–86 to 1987–88*, Cm 9428, HMSO, London.

(1986) *The Government's Expenditure Plans, 1986–7 to 1988–9*, Cm 9702, vol. II, HMSO, London.

(1987) *The Government's Expenditure Plans, 1987–8 to 1989–90*, Cm 56, vols, I and II, HMSO, London.

Ungerson, C. (1987) *Policy Is Personal: Sex Gender and Informal Care*, Tavistock, London.

Venning, P. (1973) 'Survival of the public schools' in R. Bell, G. Fowler and K. Little (eds) *Education in Great Britain and Ireland*, Routledge & Kegan Paul, London.

Walford, G. (ed.) (1984a) *British Public Schools Policy and Practice*, Falmer.

   (1984b) 'The changing professionalism of public school teachers', in G. Walford (ed.) *British Public Schools Policy and Practice*, Falmer, Lewes.

   (1986) *Life in Public Schools*, Methuen, London.

Walker, A. (ed.) (1982a) *Community Care: The Family, the State and Social Policy*, Blackwell and Robertson, Oxford.

   (1982b) 'The meaning and social division of community care', in A. Walker (ed.) *Community Care: The Family, the State and Social Policy*, Blackwell and Robertson, Oxford.

   (1984a) *Social Planning*, Blackwell, Oxford.

   (1984b) 'The political economy of privatisation', in J. Le Grand and R. Robinson (eds) *Privatisation and the Welfare State*, Allen & Unwin, London.

Walker, A. and Walker, C. (1987) *The Growing Divide*, Child Poverty Action Group, London.

Weale, A. (1983) *Political Theory and Social Policy*, Macmillan, London.

   (1985a) 'Mr Fowler's Psychology', *Political Quarterly*, vol. 56, no. 4.

   (1985b) 'The welfare state and two conflicting ideals of equality', *Government and Opposition*, vol. 20, no. 3.

   (1985c) 'Why are we waiting? The problem of unresponsiveness in the public social services', in R. Klein and M. O'Higgins (eds) *The Future of Welfare*, Blackwell, Oxford.

Webster, B. (1985) 'The impact of local authority cuts', *Local Government Studies*, vol. 11, no. 2.

West, P. (1984) 'Private health insurance', in J. Le Grand and R. Robinson (eds) *Privatisation and the Welfare State*, Allen & Unwin, London.

Whitehead, C. (1977) 'Where have all the dwellings gone?' *Centre for Environmental Studies Review*, vol. 1, no. 1.

   (1984) 'Privatisation and housing', in J. Le Grand and R. Robinson (eds) *Privatisation and the Welfare State*, Allen & Unwin, London.

Whitehead, M. (1987) *The Health Divide*, Health Education Council, London.

Whiteley, P. and Winyard, S. (1987) *Pressure for the Poor*, Methuen, London.

Whitty, G. and Edwards (1984) 'Evaluating policy change', in G. Walford (ed.), *British Public Schools Policy and Practice*, Falmer, Lewes.

Whitty, G., Fitz, J. and Edwards, T. (1986) 'Assisting whom?

Benefits and costs of the assisted places scheme' paper presented to the British Educational Research Association Conference, University of Bristol, 4 September.

Whyte, J. (1986) *Girls into Science and Technology*, Routledge & Kegan Paul, London.

Wilding, P. (1981) *Professional Power and the Welfare State*, Routledge & Kegan Paul, London.

Wilkinson, M. (1986) 'Tax expenditure and public expenditure in the UK', *Journal of Social Policy*, vol. 15, no. 1.

Williams, S. (1985) 'Welfare politics in Western democracies', in S. Eisenstadt and O. Ahimeir (eds) *The Welfare State in Crisis*, Croom Helm, London.

Willis, P. (1977) *Learning to Labour*, Saxon House, London.

Wilson Committee, The (1980) Report of the Committee to Review the Functioning of Financial Institutions, Cmnd. 7937, HMSO, London.

Wilson, A. and Mackay, G. (1941) *Old Age Pensions*, Oxford University Press, Oxford.

Wilson, E. (1983) 'Feminism and social policy', in M. Loney, D. Boswell and J. Clarke (eds) *Social Policy and Social Welfare*, Open University Press, Milton Keynes.

Winyard, S. (1985) 'Low pay', in D. Bell (ed.) *The Conservative Governments 1979–84: An Interim Report*, Croom Helm, London.

Wiseman, J. (1965) 'Occupational pension schemes', in G. Reid and D. Robertson (eds) *Fringe Benefits, Labour Costs and Social Security*, Allen & Unwin, London.

Witherspoon, S. (1986) *British Social Attitudes 1986 Survey: Technical Report*, Social and Community Planning Research, London.

Yeo, S. (1979) 'Working-class association, private capital, welfare and the state', in N. Parry, M. Rustin and C. Satyarmurti (eds) *Social Work and the State*', Edward Arnold, London.

Name Index

Subject Index

221